SCIENCE VISUAL RESOURCES

ENVIRONMENT

An Illustrated Guide to Science

The Diagram Group

CHELSEA HOUSE
PUBLISHERS
An imprint of Infobase Publishing

Environment: An Illustrated Guide to Science

Author:	Stephen Rudd
Editors:	Gordon Lee, Jamie Stokes
Design:	Anthony Atherton, bounford.com, Richard Hummerstone, Lee Lawrence, Phil Richardson
Illustration:	Peter Wilkinson
Picture research:	Neil McKenna
Indexer:	Martin Hargreaves

Chelsea House
An imprint of Infobase Publishing
132 West 31st Street
New York NY 10001

For Library of Congress Cataloging-in-Publication data, please contact the publisher.

ISBN 0-8160-6165-3

Chelsea House books are available at special discounts when purchased in bulk quantities for businesses, associations, institutions, or sales promotions. Please call our Special Sales Department in New York at 212/967-8800 or 800/322-8755.

You can find Chelsea House on the World Wide Web at
http://www.chelseahouse.com

Printed in China

CP Diagram 10 9 8 7 6 5 4 3 2

This book is printed on acid-free paper.

Introduction

Environment is one of eight volumes in the **Science Visual Resources** set. It contains seven sections, a comprehensive glossary, a Web site guide, and an index.

Environment is a learning tool for students and teachers. Full-color diagrams, graphs, charts, and maps on every page illustrate the essential elements of the subject, while parallel text provides key definitions and step-by-step explanations.

The human factor provides an overview of the impact of the human species on the environment. It examines the ways in which humanity has transformed the planet through the exploitation of its natural resources, the growth of the human population, and the general disposition of human societies around the globe.

Food and water examines the state of the humanity's agriculture and the security of its supply of safe fresh water. Issues such as pesticide resistance, sustainable development, and fertilizer use are outlined in this section.

Land and habitat is concerned with the processes that are threatening the continued existence of some of Earth's most valuable habitats. These processes include deforestation, desertification, wind and water erosion, and soil degradation.

Land and sea pollution describes the forms of pollution that threaten the terrestrial and marine biospheres. It looks in detail at the problems of industrial and domestic waste disposal, sewage, and the accumulation of toxic substances in food chains.

Air pollution describes the types of air pollution, their sources, and their influence on the environment. This section covers acid rain and greenhouse gases—two of the most significant threats to the environment.

Nature under threat looks at the growing threat to biodiversity posed by human activities. This section lists the most endangered plant and animal species, estimates the number of species that have become extinct due to human activity, and details biosphere reserves and other protected areas.

Environmental disasters describes events such as the nuclear disaster at Chernobyl, the chemical release at Bhopal, and their lasting impact on humanity and the planet.

Contents

1 THE HUMAN FACTOR

2 FOOD AND WATER

3 LAND AND HABITAT

4 LAND AND SEA POLLUTION

5 AIR POLLUTION

6 NATURE UNDER THREAT

7 ENVIRONMENTAL DISASTERS

APPENDIXES

Key words

biosphere
Gaia theory
organism

What is the environment?

- The environment is everything around us, both physical and organic, that creates the conditions in the *biosphere* in which we live.
- The forests, the air, the people, the land, and the sea all make up Earth's environment.
- The natural environment is the part of the environment that humanity does not directly control. It is, nonetheless, impacted by human activity.

Human impact

- All over the world, experts are concerned that the natural environment is being damaged by human activities and that Earth's ability to sustain life is being undermined.
- Habitat destruction, loss of species, and other environmental disasters are all consequences of the human impact on the environment.
- Humanity is changing habitats and natural processes as never before, and as a consequence will alter the global environment forever.

Uncertain future

- The *Gaia theory* suggests that Earth's environment acts as a self-sustaining, self-regulating *organism*.
- However, the planet as we know it faces an uncertain future because the environment is now being changed faster than it is able to regulate itself.

The environment

Environmental issues

sustainability

urbanization

car ownership

energy consumption

population growth

intensive farming

resource shortages

food consumption

land clearance

marine pollution

freshwater shortages

land degradation

topsoil erosion

forest clearance

water consumption

air pollution

overfishing

The human problem

Key words

pollution
urbanization

Social factors

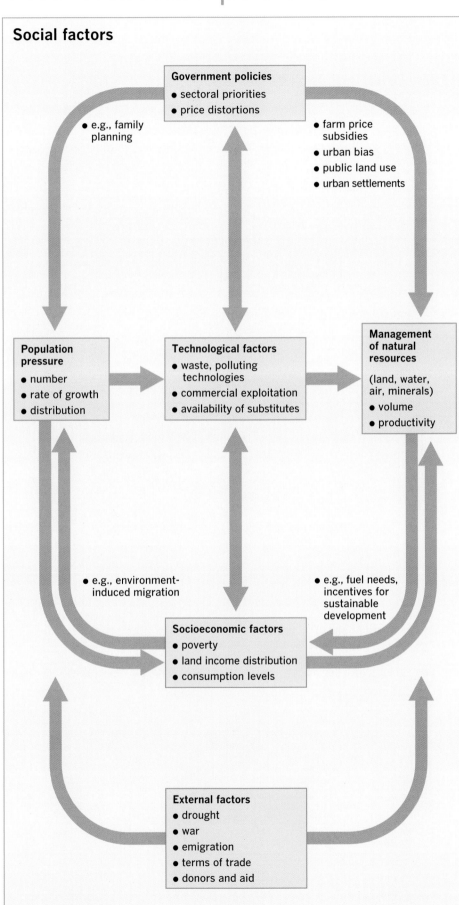

Government policies
- sectoral priorities
- price distortions

- e.g., family planning

- farm price subsidies
- urban bias
- public land use
- urban settlements

Population pressure
- number
- rate of growth
- distribution

Technological factors
- waste, polluting technologies
- commercial exploitation
- availability of substitutes

Management of natural resources
(land, water, air, minerals)
- volume
- productivity

- e.g., environment-induced migration

- e.g., fuel needs, incentives for sustainable development

Socioeconomic factors
- poverty
- land income distribution
- consumption levels

External factors
- drought
- war
- emigration
- terms of trade
- donors and aid

The human problem
- The world's population is increasing rapidly: by mid-2004 it had almost reached 6.4 billion.

Energy
- The demand for energy around the world continues to grow, especially in the *developed nations*.
- The United States contains about five percent of the global population but accounts for 25 percent of global energy consumption.
- China and India look likely to increase world energy consumption greatly in the coming years.

Food and water
- The increasing demand for food and water forces farmers and fishermen to overexploit soil, water resources, and fishing grounds, diminishing productivity.
- One in five people in the world do not have access to safe drinking water.

Habitat destruction
- Uncontrolled population growth has led to the overuse of *unsustainable* land clearance techniques and destructive coastal developments.

Urbanization and pollution
- Rural decline is prompting millions to migrate to cities to find work, food, and shelter. This *urbanization* will cause further increases in global *pollution*.

People and resources
- The connections between human population growth, human society, and the maintenance of Earth's resources are many and varied.
- Government policies, technological developments, religion, and external events such as wars and trade agreements all have complex interactions.

Key words	
arable land	fossil fuel
climate change	pesticide
ecosystem	
fertilizer	
food chain	

Human transformation

- Humans have been altering their environment for thousands of years.
- The most significant technological innovations in the last 10,000 years have arguably been the use of timber for building and the spread of crop cultivation.
- In the past 150 years these practices have accelerated, during which time the rising population has doubled the area of *arable land* in use.

Burning of fossil fuels

- The burning of *fossil fuels* has for many years caused high levels of air pollution and more recently has been linked to global *climate change*.
- Climate change is expected to alter many parts of the planet that have so far escaped deliberate transformation.

Environmental poisoning

- During the last 40 years the overuse of *fertilizers* and *pesticides* has saturated many *ecosystems* and *food chains* and has emerged as a new global-scale threat.

Link to population density

- The extent of ecosystem loss and alteration is closely related to population density, which is very uneven across the planet.
- Today 50 percent of the human population lives on less than ten percent of Earth's land.
- Europe and parts of Asia are the most heavily populated regions of the planet and also the most ecologically disturbed.

Influences on the environment

Human transformation of the land

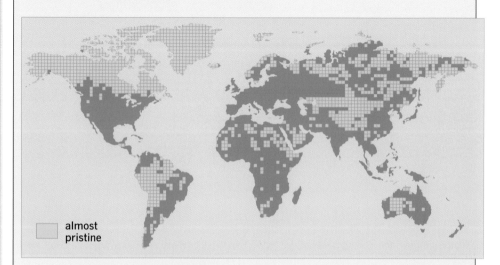

almost pristine

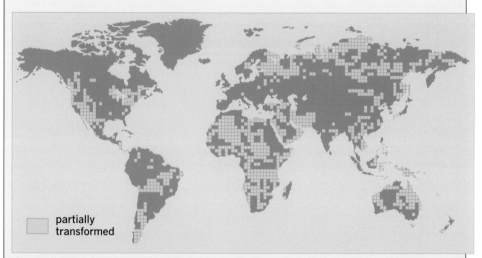

partially transformed

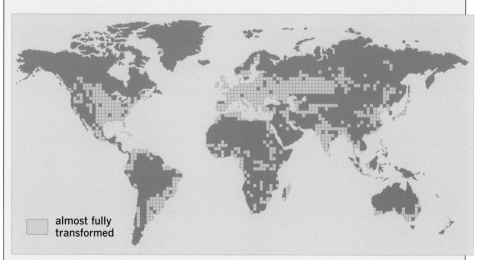

almost fully transformed

While the maps show a considerable proportion of the world's land as "almost pristine," in reality very little land has completely escaped human activity.

Demands on the environment

Key words

ecosystem
Food and
  Agriculture
  Organization
  (FAO)

Human exploitation of natural resources

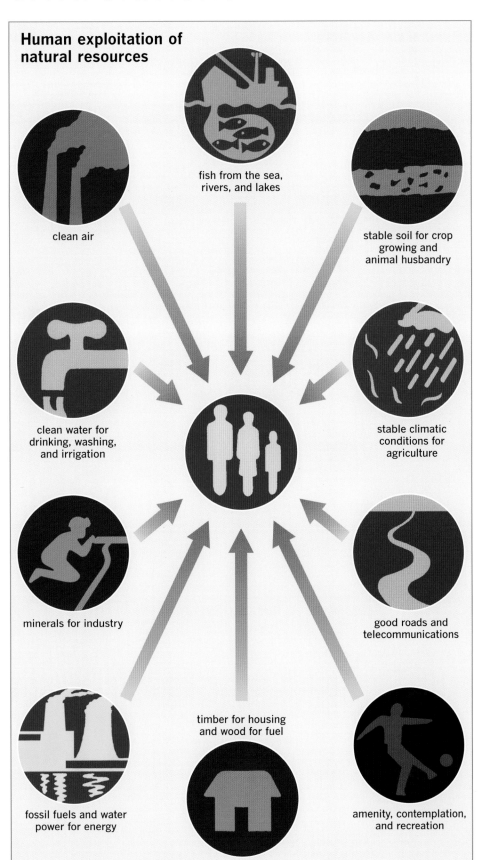

fish from the sea, rivers, and lakes

clean air

stable soil for crop growing and animal husbandry

clean water for drinking, washing, and irrigation

stable climatic conditions for agriculture

minerals for industry

good roads and telecommunications

fossil fuels and water power for energy

timber for housing and wood for fuel

amenity, contemplation, and recreation

Modern lifestyles

● The wealthiest populations generally expect their quality of life to improve by constantly rising *standards of living*.
● Such improvements are only possible, however, by exploiting an increasing proportion of the world's resources.
● As a result, the health of marine, freshwater, and forest ecosystems has suffered a considerable decline in recent years.

Growing demands

● Since 1950, the richest 20 percent of humanity has doubled its consumption of energy, meat, timber, steel, and copper, and quadrupled its car ownership.

Freshwater

● Global freshwater consumption rose sixfold during the twentieth century—more than twice the rate of population growth.

Overfishing

● In 2004 the UN's *Food and Agriculture Organization (FAO)* reported that 28 percent of global fish stocks were either significantly depleted or overexploited.
● A further 47 percent was reported as being either fully exploited or currently meeting maximum sustainable yield.
● As some fish species become scarcer, their market price increases, making them more desirable to fishermen.

Need for timber

● Timber is used around the world for building and fuel. However, it is rarely used sustainably.
● Almost half the forests that originally covered Earth have been cleared or fragmented for timber use.

© Diagram Visual Information Ltd.

Key words

industrialized
   nation

Population increase

- The world's population doubled from one billion to two billion between 1800 and 1927.
- Since then it has increased to almost 6.4 billion.
- Even though the world population has doubled over the last 40 years, it is thought that numbers will stabilize at approximately ten billion in the middle of this century.
- However, events such as wars or social changes such as those arising from technological or medical advances could alter this prediction dramatically.

Declines in rate of increase

- The global population growth rate began to decline about 30 years ago.
- Annual additions to the human population are still close to their highest ever level, however.
- Around 77 million are added every year, or more than 200,000 people every day.

Difference between countries

- The populations of some countries are growing much faster than others.
- At current growth rates, countries such as Pakistan and Nigeria will triple their populations by the middle of this century.
- By contrast, the population growth rates of most European countries are slowing to a halt.
- The United States is one of the few major *industrialized nations* to have a significant population growth rate.

World population growth: rate

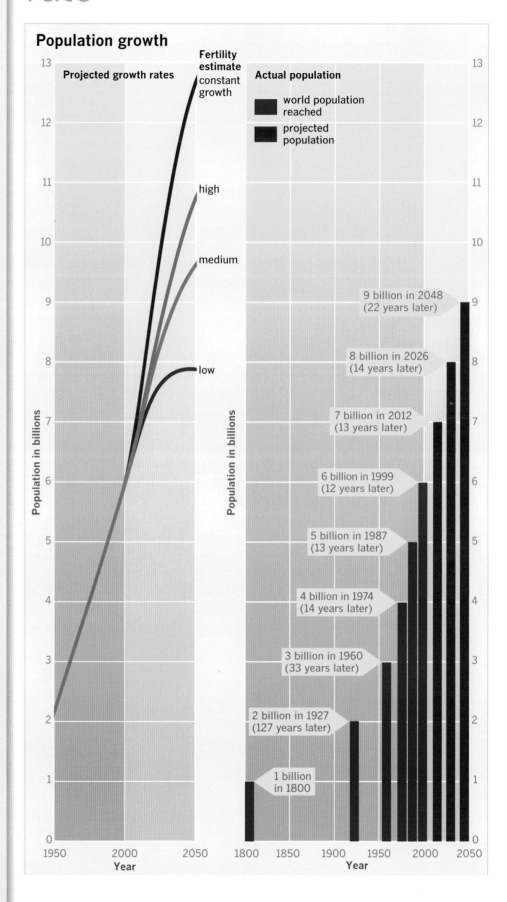

Population growth

Projected growth rates

Actual population

Fertility estimate
- constant growth
- high
- medium
- low

- world population reached
- projected population

9 billion in 2048 (22 years later)

8 billion in 2026 (14 years later)

7 billion in 2012 (13 years later)

6 billion in 1999 (12 years later)

5 billion in 1987 (13 years later)

4 billion in 1974 (14 years later)

3 billion in 1960 (33 years later)

2 billion in 1927 (127 years later)

1 billion in 1800

Population in billions

Year

World population growth: regions

Key words

AIDS
demography
epidemic
life expectancy

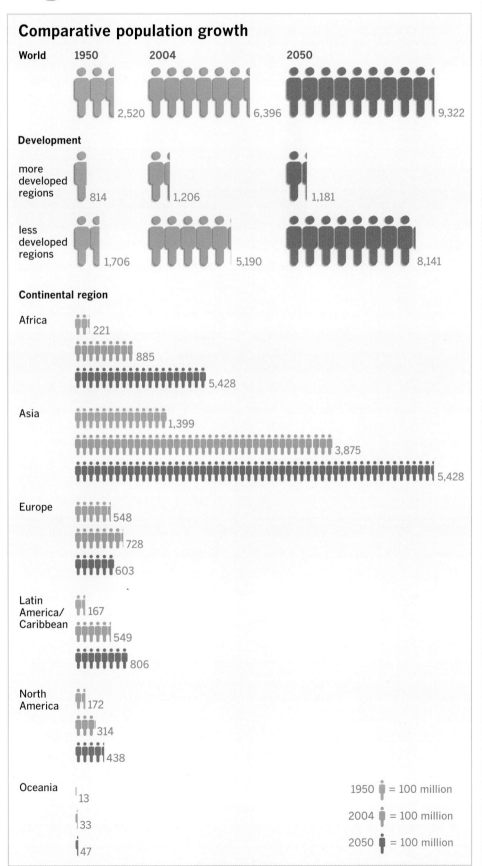

Comparative population growth

World

	1950	2004	2050
	2,520	6,396	9,322

Development

more developed regions: 814 / 1,206 / 1,181

less developed regions: 1,706 / 5,190 / 8,141

Continental region

Africa: 221 / 885 / 5,428

Asia: 1,399 / 3,875 / 5,428

Europe: 548 / 728 / 603

Latin America/ Caribbean: 167 / 549 / 806

North America: 172 / 314 / 438

Oceania: 13 / 33 / 47

1950 = 100 million
2004 = 100 million
2050 = 100 million

Changing demography

- *Demography* is the study of human populations. It deals with the size, density, distribution, and vital statistics of people.
- Different demographic growth rates are changing the distribution of the world's people.
- In 1950 Europe and North America accounted for 28.5 percent of the world's population; that share had fallen to 16.5 percent by 2004. It is expected to decline further to 11.2 percent by 2050.

Developing nations

- The population growth rates of *developing nations* are increasing much faster than more developed nations.
- It is thought that lower *life expectancy*, the economic advantages of having more children, and limited access to education and contraception are the main causes of this rapid increase.

Regions with fastest growth

- Africa's percentage share of world population rose from 8.8 percent in 1950 to 13.8 percent in 2004, and is projected as 21.5 percent by 2050.
- However, the effects of the current AIDS epidemic may not be fully integrated into this projection.
- In recent years Asia's population has increased faster than that of any other region.
- However, it is predicted that by 2050 this increase will become more stable with Asia containing approximately 58 percent of the world's population, down from its current 60.5 percent.

Recent population increases

- The rapid growth of the world population is a recent phenomenon.
- The population of the world 2,000 years ago was only about 300 million.
- It took a further 1,600 years for the population to double to 600 million.
- From the graph it can be seen that the percentage rate of global population increase peaked some 30 years ago.
- This type of growth is called "exponential:" populations increase with accelerating rapidity.

Slowing growth

- Even though the world growth rate has started to decline as a whole, there are still huge additions to the population each year.
- The continued high number of births in the face of declining *birthrates* is largely due to the increasing numbers of women entering reproductive age.
- This is the result of high fertility in previous years in the less developed countries.

Percentage growth

- From the maps, it can be seen that the highest population growth rates are found in the developing nations.
- However, some parts of North America are increasing at more than 3.5 percent per annum, which is unusual for a developed region.
- The majority of places on Earth where there is a growth rate greater than 3.5 percent lie in the developing world.
- Many parts of Africa, Asia, and South America are experiencing this level of growth.
- In these locations the population is doubling every 20 years or less.

World population growth: percentage

Population growth projections

Millions

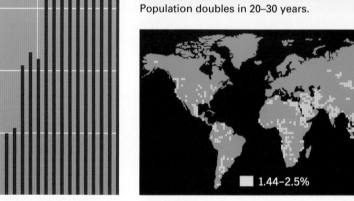

Annual additions

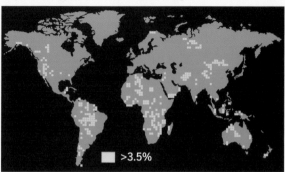

Population growth rates and doubling times

>3.5%

Population doubles in less than 20 years.

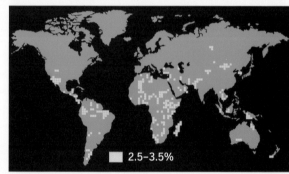

2.5–3.5%

Population doubles in 20–30 years.

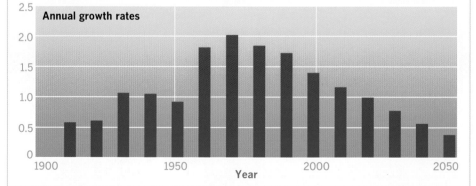

1.44–2.5%

Population doubles in 30–50 years.

Percentage

Annual growth rates

Demographic profiles: Africa

Demographic data for the countries and subregions of Africa

1	2	3	4	5	6	7	8
NORTH AFRICA	**191**	**26**	**7**	**2.0**	**3.4**	**67**	**70**
Algeria	32.3	20	4	1.5	2.5	73	37
Egypt	73.4	26	6	2.0	3.2	68	74
Libya	5.6	28	4	2.4	3.6	76	92
Morocco	30.6	21	6	1.5	2.5	70	47
Sudan	39.1	38	10	2.8	5.4	57	115
Tunisia	10.0	17	6	1.1	2.0	73	22
Western Sahara	0.3	29	8	2.1	4.1	62	103
WEST AFRICA	**263**	**42**	**15**	**2.8**	**5.8**	**51**	**141**
Benin	7.3	41	14	2.7	5.6	50	148
Burkina Faso	13.6	45	19	2.6	6.2	45	191
Cape Verde	0.5	29	7	2.3	4.0	69	74
Côte d'Ivoire	16.9	39	19	2.0	5.2	42	63
Gambia	1.5	41	13	2.9	5.6	54	169
Ghana	21.4	33	10	2.2	4.4	58	85
Guinea	9.2	43	16	2.7	6.0	49	231
Guinea-Bissau	1.5	50	20	3.0	7.1	45	207
Liberia	3.5	50	22	2.9	6.8	42	182
Mali	13.4	50	17	3.3	7.0	48	243
Mauritania	3.0	42	15	2.7	5.9	54	152
Niger	12.4	55	20	3.5	8.0	45	327
Nigeria	137.3	42	13	2.9	5.7	52	124
Senegal	10.9	37	11	2.6	5.1	56	126
Sierra Leone	5.2	50	29	2.1	6.5	35	100
Togo	5.6	38	11	2.7	5.5	54	74
EAST AFRICA	**270**	**41**	**18**	**2.3**	**5.7**	**46**	**134**
Burundi	6.2	40	17	2.2	6.2	43	147
Comoros	0.7	47	12	3.5	6.8	56	181
Djibouti	0.7	41	17	2.3	5.9	46	96
Eritrea	4.4	39	13	2.6	5.7	53	137
Ethiopia	72.4	41	18	2.4	5.9	52	139
Kenya	32.4	38	15	2.3	5.0	51	54
Madagascar	17.5	43	12	3.0	5.8	55	274
Malawi	11.9	51	21	3.1	6.6	44	296
Mauritius	1.2	16	7	1.0	1.9	72	22
Mayotte	0.2	41	9	3.2	5.6	60	219
Mozambique	19.2	40	23	1.7	5.5	40	63
Réunion	0.8	20	5	1.4	2.5	75	37
Rwanda	8.4	40	21	1.9	5.8	40	104
Seychelles	0.1	18	8	1.0	2.0	71	11
Somalia	8.3	47	18	2.9	7.1	47	207
Tanzania	36.1	40	17	2.3	5.3	45	105
Uganda	26.1	47	17	3.0	6.9	45	217
Zambia	10.9	42	24	1.8	5.6	35	70
Zimbabwe	12.7	32	20	1.2	4.0	41	15
CENTRAL AFRICA	**107**	**45**	**17**	**2.8**	**6.4**	**47**	**184**
Angola	13.3	49	24	2.6	6.8	40	206
Cameroon	16.1	37	15	2.2	4.9	42	65
Central African Republic	3.7	37	19	1.7	4.9	45	78
Chad	9.5	49	16	3.2	6.6	49	206
Congo	3.8	44	15	2.9	6.3	48	179
Congo, Democratic Republic	58.3	46	15	3.1	6.8	49	211
Equatorial Guinea	0.5	43	17	2.6	5.9	49	132
Gabon	1.4	33	12	2.1	4.3	57	84
São Tomé and Principe	0.2	34	6	2.8	4.3	69	112
SOUTHERN AFRICA	**53**	**25**	**14**	**1.0**	**2.9**	**52**	**-9**
Botswana	1.7	27	26	0.1	3.5	36	-43
Lesotho	1.8	33	22	1.1	4.4	38	23
Namibia	1.9	31	15	1.6	4.2	47	35
South Africa	46.9	24	13	1.0	2.8	53	-11
Swaziland	1.2	36	16	2.0	4.5	43	-2

1 country/region
2 population 2004 (millions)
3 births per 1,000 population
4 deaths per 1,000 population
5 rate of natural increase (percent)
6 total fertility rate (number of children per woman)
7 life expectancy at birth
8 projected population change 2004–2050 (percent)

Overview of Africa

- Africa mainly consists of poor nations with fast growing populations.
- An estimated 23 million Africans are living with *HIV/AIDS*, which is rapidly changing the demography of some countries.
- War and famine are common in many parts of Africa; this combined with a generally poor social and medical *infrastructure* means that *life expectancy* is on average lower than in other regions of the world.

Population and growth

- The most populous country in Africa is currently Nigeria with around 137 million people.
- Nigeria is expected to more than double its population by 2050 to more than 300 million, making it one of the fastest growing countries in the world.
- Many other large African countries will double their population by 2050, including Ethiopia and the Democratic Republic of Congo.

Births and deaths

- African countries have birthrates among the highest in the world.
- This is thought to be due to high *mortality rates*, especially in children.
- Other reasons include culture, the economic advantages of larger families, and the lack of available birth control.
- The highest birthrates in Africa and the world are in Niger with around 55 births per 1,000 people.
- In 2004 Sierra Leone had among the highest death rates in the world at 29 per 1,000 people per year.
- Many African countries have extremely low life expectancies.
- As recently as 2004, life expectancy at birth was just 35 years in Sierra Leone and Zambia.

Key words

demography
fertility
infrastructure
life expectancy

Overview of the Americas

- The Americas include two very different demographic regions:
- North America is composed of the United States and Canada, both developed nations with good infrastructure, healthcare, education, and relatively stable demographic profiles.
- The rest of the Americas consist of Latin America, Central America, and the Caribbean, which are on average less demographically stable, with higher numbers of births and deaths in the population.

Population and growth

- In 2004 the largest population in the Americas was that of the United States with 293.6 million.
- By 2050 this is expected to have increased by around 43 percent to almost 420 million.
- This is considered by experts to be a large increase in population for a developed nation, and many parts of the United States are growing at more than 3.5 percent per year.
- The total fertility rate for the United States was 2.0 in 2004, higher than any other developed nation.
- Countries within the Americas that are expected to grow the fastest are Guatemala with 115 percent growth by 2050 and Honduras with 109 percent.
- Canada is the country with the lowest total fertility rate at just 1.5 children per woman.

Deaths and life expectancy

- The highest death rate in 2004 was found on the Caribbean island of Haiti where on average, 14 people per 1,000 died per year.
- Life expectancy at birth was also low in Haiti, at just 51 years.
- This is almost certainly due to the poverty arising from ongoing war and political instability in the country.

Demographic profiles: the Americas

Demographic data for the countries and subregions of the Americas and the Caribbean

1	2	3	4	5	6	7	8
NORTH AMERICA	**326**	**14**	**8**	**0.5**	**2**	**78**	**40**
Canada	31.9	11	7	0.3	1.5	79	16
United States	293.6	14	8	0.6	2.0	77	43
LATIN AMERICA & THE CARIBBEAN	**549**	**22**	**6**	**1.6**	**2.6**	**72**	**42**
CENTRAL AMERICA	**146**	**26**	**5**	**2.1**	**3.0**	**74**	**54**
Belize	0.3	28	5	2.3	3.4	70	102
Costa Rica	4.2	18	4	1.4	2.1	79	49
El Salvador	6.7	26	6	2.0	3.0	70	48
Guatemala	12.7	34	7	2.8	4.4	66	115
Honduras	7.0	33	5	2.8	4.1	71	109
Mexico	106.2	25	5	2.1	2.8	75	41
Nicaragua	5.6	32	5	2.7	3.8	69	93
Panama	3.2	23	5	1.8	2.7	75	58
CARIBBEAN	**39**	**20**	**8**	**1.2**	**2.7**	**69**	**35**
Antigua and Barbuda	0.1	24	6	1.7	2.7	71	1
Bahamas	0.3	18	5	1.3	2.1	72	8
Barbados	0.3	15	8	0.6	1.7	72	-3
Cuba	11.3	11	7	0.5	1.6	76	-2
Dominica	0.1	17	7	1.0	1.9	74	19
Dominican Republic	8.8	25	6	1.9	3.0	69	52
Grenada	0.1	19	7	1.2	2.1	71	-3
Guadeloupe	0.4	17	7	1.0	2.2	78	19
Haiti	8.1	33	14	1.9	4.7	51	97
Jamaica	2.6	20	7	1.4	2.4	75	39
Martinique	0.4	14	8	0.7	2.0	79	5
Netherlands Antilles	0.2	15	7	0.8	2.1	76	11
Puerto Rico	3.9	14	7	0.7	1.8	77	-2
St. Kitts-Nevis	0.05	17	8	1.0	2.1	70	32
Saint Lucia	0.2	17	6	1.1	2.2	72	43
St. Vincent and the Grenadines	0.1	18	7	1.1	2.1	72	-21
Trinidad and Tobago	1.3	13	7	0.6	1.6	71	-7
SOUTH AMERICA	**365**	**21**	**6**	**1.5**	**2.5**	**71**	**38**
Argentina	37.9	19	8	1.1	2.4	74	40
Bolivia	8.8	28	9	1.9	3.8	63	75
Brazil	179.1	20	7	1.3	2.2	71	24
Chile	16.0	17	5	1.2	2.4	76	39
Colombia	45.3	23	6	1.7	2.6	72	48
Ecuador	13.4	25	4	2.1	3.0	71	54
French Guiana	0.2	31	4	2.6	3.9	75	95
Guyana	0.8	23	9	1.4	2.4	63	-34
Paraguay	6.0	30	5	2.5	3.8	71	101
Peru	27.5	23	6	1.7	2.8	69	55
Suriname	0.4	23	7	1.5	2.5	70	-19
Uruguay	3.4	16	9	0.6	2.2	75	24
Venezuela	26.2	24	5	1.9	2.8	73	59

1 country/region
2 population 2004 (millions)
3 births per 1,000 population
4 deaths per 1,000 population
5 rate of natural increase (percent)
6 total fertility rate (number of children per woman)
7 life expectancy at birth
8 projected population change 2004–2050 (percent)

Demographic profiles: Asia

Demographic data for the subregions and countries in Asia

1	2	3	4	5	6	7	8
ASIA	3,875	20	7	1.3	2.6	67	39
ASIA (excl. China)	2,575	24	8	1.6	3.0	65	53
WESTERN ASIA	209	27	6	2.0	3.7	68	89
Armenia	3.2	10	8	0.2	1.2	73	-24
Azerbaijan	8.3	14	6	0.8	1.8	72	40
Bahrain	0.7	20	3	1.7	2.7	74	76
Cyprus	0.9	12	7	0.5	1.6	78	14
Georgia	4.5	11	11	0.0	1.4	72	-32
Iraq	25.9	36	9	2.7	5.0	60	124
Israel	6.8	22	6	1.6	2.9	79	56
Jordan	5.6	29	5	2.4	3.7	77	80
Kuwait	2.5	18	2	1.7	4.0	78	182
Lebanon	4.5	23	7	1.7	3.2	73	53
Oman	2.7	26	4	2.2	4.1	74	93
Palestinian Territory	3.8	39	4	3.5	5.7	72	211
Qatar	0.7	20	4	1.6	4.0	72	67
Saudi Arabia	25.1	32	3	3.0	4.8	72	120
Syria	18.0	28	5	2.4	3.8	70	95
Turkey	71.3	22	7	1.4	2.5	69	37
United Arab Emirates	4.2	16	2	1.4	2.5	74	35
Yemen	20.0	43	10	3.3	7.0	60	255
SOUTH CENTRAL ASIA	1,587	26	8	1.8	3.3	62	60
Afghanistan	28.5	48	21	2.7	6.8	43	187
Bangladesh	141.3	30	9	2.1	3.3	60	98
Bhutan	1.0	34	9	2.5	4.7	66	113
India	1,086.6	25	8	1.7	3.1	62	50
Iran	67.4	18	6	1.2	2.5	69	43
Kazakhstan	15.0	17	11	0.6	2.0	64	-1
Kyrgyzstan	5.1	21	8	1.4	2.6	68	62
Maldives	0.3	18	4	1.4	3.7	73	69
Nepal	24.7	34	10	2.3	4.1	59	105
Pakistan	159.2	34	10	2.4	4.8	61	85
Sri Lanka	19.6	19	6	1.3	2.0	72	10
Tajikistan	6.6	25	6	1.9	3.1	68	52
Turkmenistan	5.7	25	9	1.6	2.9	67	53
Uzbekistan	26.4	24	8	1.6	2.9	70	84
SOUTHEAST ASIA	548	22	7	1.5	2.7	68	46
Brunei	0.4	22	3	1.9	2.3	76	85
Cambodia	13.1	32	10	2.2	4.5	57	104
East Timor	0.8	26	13	1.3	4.1	49	75
Indonesia	218.7	22	6	1.6	2.6	68	41
Laos	5.8	36	13	2.3	4.9	54	98
Malaysia	25.6	26	4	2.1	3.3	73	83
Myanmar	50.1	25	11	1.4	3.1	57	29
Philippines	83.7	26	6	2.0	3.5	70	76
Singapore	4.2	10	4	0.6	1.3	79	6
Thailand	63.8	14	7	0.8	1.7	71	15
Vietnam	81.5	18	6	1.2	2.1	72	41
EAST ASIA	1,531	12	7	0.6	1.6	72	7
China	1,300.1	12	6	0.6	1.7	71	11
China, Hong Kong	6.8	7	5	0.1	0.9	81	38
China, Macao	0.4	7	3	0.4	0.8	77	24
Japan	127.6	9	8	0.1	1.3	82	-21
Korea, North	22.8	17	11	0.7	2.0	63	10
Korea, South	48.2	10	5	0.5	1.2	77	-8
Mongolia	2.5	18	6	1.2	2.7	65	72
Taiwan	22.6	10	6	0.4	1.2	76	-3

1 country/region
2 population 2004 (millions)
3 births per 1,000 population

4 deaths per 1,000 population
5 rate of natural increase (percent)
6 total fertility rate (number of children per woman)

7 life expectancy at birth
8 projected population change 2004–2050 (percent)

Overview of Asia

- Asia incorporates a huge area of more than 50 countries with more than half of the world's population.
- Many of the countries within Asia are very poor and there is a high incidence of war and unrest.
- Consequently, many of the countries have lower than average life expectancies and high growth rates.

Population and growth

- Two of the world's most populous countries lie in Asia: India and China.
- China is currently the most populous country in the world, and in 2004 contained around 1.3 billion people.
- However, the population growth rate of China has slowed dramatically due to a government scheme allowing only one child per family.
- India with around 1.1 billion people is expected to grow by more than 50 percent over the next 50 years.
- It is due to take the lead from China as the most populous country in the world in the near future.

Births and deaths

- Countries experiencing war or unrest usually have the highest death rates.
- In 2004 Afghanistan had the highest death rate at about 21 people per 1,000.
- It also had one of the highest birthrates in Asia; about 48 per 1,000 people.

Life expectancy

- Japan, a developed nation, has one of the highest life expectancies in the world: in 2004 people were on average living to 82.

Key words

birthrate
demography
life expectancy

Overview of Europe

● Western, northern, and some of southern and eastern Europe is composed of developed nations with strong economies.

● Here people enjoy a relatively high standard of living and have a higher than world average life expectancy.

● Birthrates are low compared to other parts of the world, and many of the countries are experiencing negative population growth.

Population and growth

● Russia is by far the largest and the most populous country with around 144 million people in 2004.

● However, since the break-up of the USSR conditions have worsened there and life expectancy is comparatively low at 65 years (and only 58 for males).

● Other heavily populated countries in Europe include Germany with 82 million people, and France and the United Kingdom with about 60 million each.

Overview of Oceania

● Oceania comprises the islands of the southern, western, and central Pacific Ocean including Australia, New Zealand, and the Malay Archipelago.

● Many of these small island states can be classed as developing nations and have high birthrates and population growth, and lower than average life expectancies.

● Australia and New Zealand are the two developed nations in this region, and their demographic statistics can be compared to those of European countries.

Demographic profiles: Europe and Oceania

Demographic data for the subregions and countries in Europe and Oceania

1	2	3	4	5	6	7	8
EUROPE	**728**	**10**	**12**	**-0.2**	**1.4**	**74**	**-8**
NORTHERN EUROPE	**96**	**12**	**10**	**0.1**	**1.7**	**78**	**8**
Denmark	5.4	12	11	0.1	1.8	77	-3
Estonia	1.3	10	13	-0.4	1.4	71	-23
Finland	5.2	11	9	0.2	1.8	79	-8
Iceland	0.3	14	6	0.8	2.0	81	22
Ireland	4.1	16	7	0.8	2.0	77	16
Latvia	2.3	9	14	-0.5	1.3	72	-24
Lithuania	3.4	9	12	-0.3	1.3	72	-9
Norway	4.6	12	9	0.3	1.8	80	22
Sweden	9.0	11	10	0.1	1.7	80	18
United Kingdom	59.9	12	10	0.1	1.7	78	10
WESTERN EUROPE	**185**	**11**	**10**	**0.1**	**1.6**	**79**	**-1**
Austria	8.1	9	9	0.0	1.4	79	1
Belgium	10.4	11	10	0.1	1.6	79	5
France	60.0	13	9	0.4	1.9	79	7
Germany	82.6	9	10	-0.2	1.3	78	-9
Liechtenstein	0.03	12	6	0.5	1.5	80	18
Luxembourg	0.5	12	9	0.3	1.6	78	56
Monaco	0.03	23	16	0.6	—	—	27
Netherlands	16.3	12	9	0.4	1.8	79	8
Switzerland	7.4	10	9	0.1	1.4	80	-3
EASTERN EUROPE	**299**	**10**	**15**	**-0.5**	**1.3**	**68**	**-19**
Belarus	9.8	9	15	-0.6	1.2	69	-13
Bulgaria	7.8	9	14	-0.6	1.2	72	-38
Czech Republic	10.2	9	11	-0.2	1.2	75	-10
Hungary	10.1	9	13	-0.4	1.3	73	-25
Moldova	4.2	10	12	-0.1	1.2	68	-28
Poland	38.2	9	9	0.0	1.2	75	-15
Romania	21.7	10	12	-0.3	1.2	71	-27
Russia	144.1	10	17	-0.6	1.4	65	-0.6
Slovakia	5.4	10	10	0.0	1.2	74	-13
Ukraine	47.4	9	16	-0.8	1.2	68	-19
SOUTHERN EUROPE	**149**	**10**	**10**	**0.1**	**1.3**	**78**	**-7**
Albania	3.2	17	5	1.2	2.1	74	15
Andorra	0.1	11	3	0.8	1.3	—	-3
Bosnia-Herzegovina	3.9	10	8	0.1	1.2	74	-15
Croatia	4.4	9	11	-0.2	1.3	75	-14
Greece	11.0	9	9	0.0	1.3	78	-12
Italy	57.8	10	10	0.1	1.3	80	-10
Macedonia	2.0	14	9	0.5	1.7	73	3
Malta	0.4	10	8	0.2	1.5	78	-9
Portugal	10.5	11	10	0.0	1.4	77	-11
San Marino	0.03	10	7	0.3	1.2	80	17
Slovenia	2.0	9	10	-0.1	1.2	76	-15
Spain	42.5	10	9	0.1	1.3	79	-3
Yugoslavia	10.7	12	11	0.2	1.7	73	-4
OCEANIA	**33**	**17**	**7**	**1.0**	**2.1**	**75**	**43**
Australia	20.1	13	7	0.6	1.7	80	31
Fed. States of Micronesia	0.1	28	7	2.1	4.4	67	46
Fiji	0.8	25	6	1.9	3.3	67	18
French Polynesia	0.3	20	5	1.5	2.5	72	40
Guam	0.2	20	4	1.6	2.6	78	46
Kiribati	0.1	26	8	1.8	4.3	63	133
Marshall Islands	0.1	42	5	3.7	4.7	69	81
Nauru	0.01	23	5	1.8	4.4	61	92
New Caledonia	0.2	22	5	1.7	2.6	73	60
New Zealand	4.1	14	7	0.7	2.0	78	26
Palau	0.02	14	7	0.8	1.6	70	24
Papua-New Guinea	5.7	32	10	2.2	4.1	57	90
Solomon Islands	0.5	36	9	2.7	4.8	61	112
Tonga	0.1	25	7	1.8	3.4	71	20
Tuvalu	0.01	27	10	1.7	3.8	—	122
Vanuatu	0.2	28	6	2.2	4.8	67	124
Western Samoa	0.2	29	6	2.4	4.4	73	34

1 country/region
2 population 2004 (millions)
3 births per 1,000 population
4 deaths per 1,000 population
5 rate of natural increase (percent)
6 total fertility rate (number of children per woman)
7 life expectancy at birth
8 projected population change 2004–2050 (percent)

World fertility rates and trends

Key words

fertility

Births and deaths

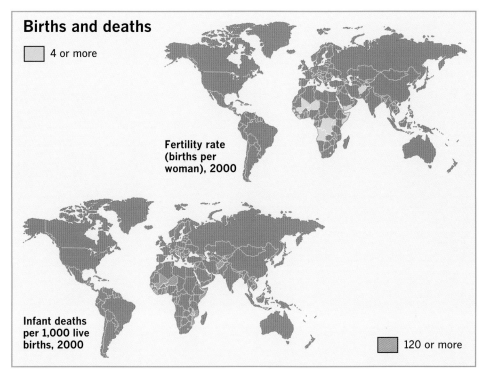

☐ 4 or more

**Fertility rate
(births per
woman), 2000**

**Infant deaths
per 1,000 live
births, 2000**

☐ 120 or more

Fertility trends
Actual and projected levels of childbearing

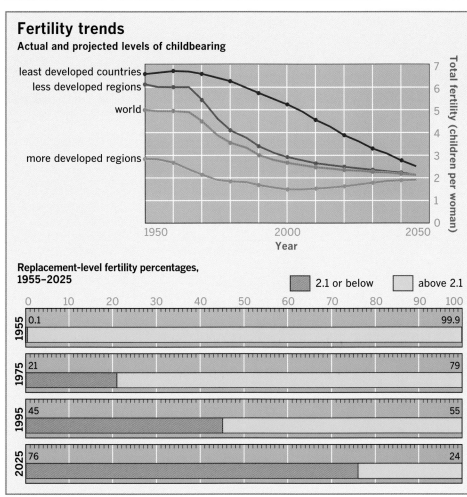

least developed countries
less developed regions
world
more developed regions

Total fertility (children per woman)

Year

**Replacement-level fertility percentages,
1955–2025**

☐ 2.1 or below ☐ above 2.1

1955	0.1	99.9
1975	21	79
1995	45	55
2025	76	24

Fertility
- *Total fertility* describes the average number of children women have.
- The total fertility of women varies greatly between countries.

Replacement level
- The level of fertility at which generations can be replaced is called the *replacement level*.
- If fertility is below this level, the overall population of a country might begin to decline.
- The replacement level is always higher than two because not all offspring reach child-bearing age.
- Most populations have a replacement level of 2.1 children per woman but this can rise in countries with higher mortality.

Developed nations
- In virtually all the developed nations, fertility is currently below replacement level and is expected to remain below that level.
- In 2004 the United States had a fertility rate of 2.0, higher than any other developed nation.

Developing nations
- In the less developed regions as a whole, fertility is still above replacement level with 3.1 children per woman.
- If China is removed from the calculation, total fertility in the less developed regions rises to 3.5.
- This is expected to fall to 2.17 children per woman by 2050.

Key words

family planning
habitat
pollution
migration

Family planning

● Experts believe that if the unmet need for family planning was satisfied in developing countries, population growth rates would begin to fall.

● However, in many countries infant mortality is so high that families often produce more children than they can support, knowing that not all of them will survive.

● In harsh economic environments it is also an asset to have more rather than fewer children.

Consequences of growth

● As populations become larger, more pressures are put on the environment from pollution and habitat loss.

● Resources become stretched and less money is spent on the environment.

● Parents are unable to afford schooling for children in large families, which increases crime and urban migration.

● Poverty causes slum and squatter areas to expand, further increasing the problem.

Africa

● In many African countries any benefit from economic growth is canceled out by population growth.

● Africa is the only continent where agricultural production per capita has been declining steadily while population and environmental degradation have increased.

● Policies are needed to reduce population growth rates by empowering women, through education and access to health advice and welfare.

Population growth: cause and effect

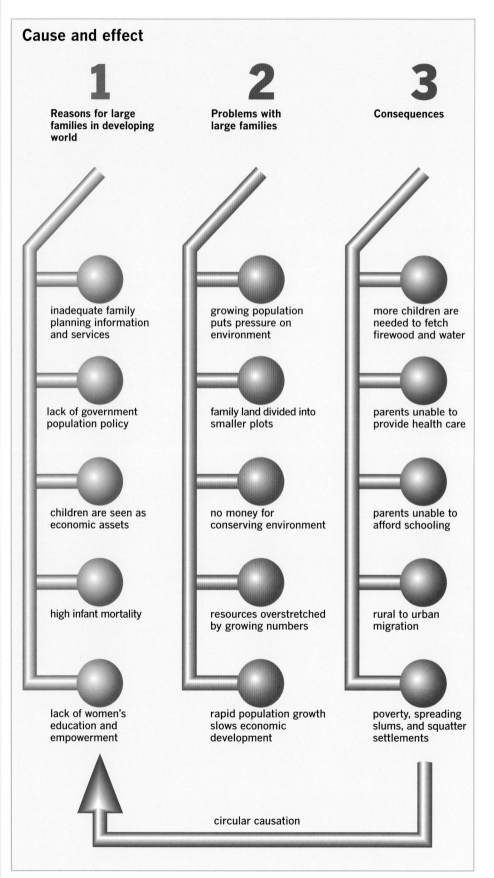

Cause and effect

1
Reasons for large families in developing world

- inadequate family planning information and services
- lack of government population policy
- children are seen as economic assets
- high infant mortality
- lack of women's education and empowerment

2
Problems with large families

- growing population puts pressure on environment
- family land divided into smaller plots
- no money for conserving environment
- resources overstretched by growing numbers
- rapid population growth slows economic development

3
Consequences

- more children are needed to fetch firewood and water
- parents unable to provide health care
- parents unable to afford schooling
- rural to urban migration
- poverty, spreading slums, and squatter settlements

circular causation

Contraceptive use

Key words

AIDS
contraception
family planning
HIV

Contraceptive use

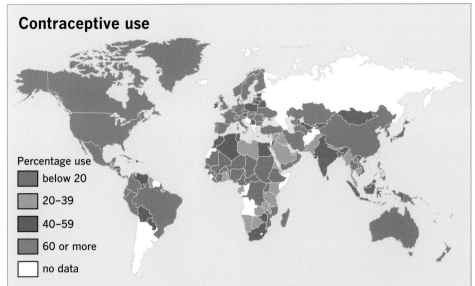

Percentage use
- below 20
- 20–39
- 40–59
- 60 or more
- no data

Types of contraception and proportions of people using them

- world
- more developed regions
- less developed regions

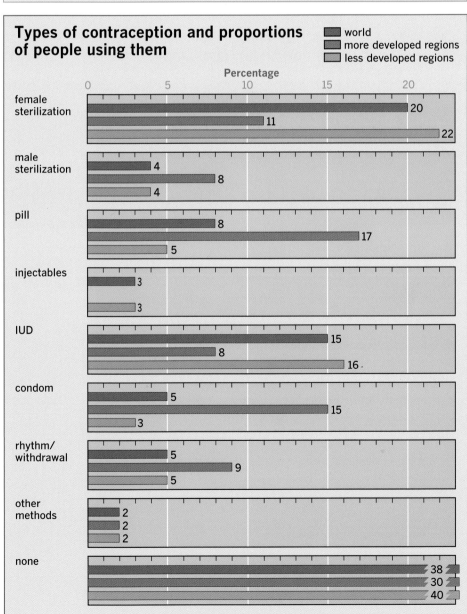

Percentage

Type	world	more developed regions	less developed regions
female sterilization	20	11	22
male sterilization	4	8	4
pill	8	17	5
injectables	3		3
IUD	15	8	16
condom	5	15	3
rhythm/withdrawal	5	9	5
other methods	2	2	2
none	38	30	40

Availability of contraception

- In many developing countries good quality family planning services and resources are still unavailable.
- Social traditions, religion, and other beliefs also hinder the widespread use of *contraception*.

High costs

- The costs involved in creating comprehensive contraception programs are often too great for the countries involved.
- Effective contraceptive programs need to provide not only contraception but also education and advice.
- Some parts of many countries are inaccessible, making these types of programs difficult.

Modern contraception

- Female sterilization is the most popular contraceptive method worldwide, followed by the intrauterine device (IUD).
- However, access to these modern methods is still very limited in Africa and in other regions.
- The condom remains the cheapest method of contraception and most effective means of protection against sexually transmitted diseases: not only is it reliable for family planning, it is also effective at controlling the spread of HIV/AIDS.

Africa and contraception

- Africa is one of the few regions in the world that is yet to decrease fertility effectively using contraception.
- From the map it can be seen that many African countries have a contraceptive use of less than 20 percent.

Key words

AIDS	HIV
carcinogen	malnutrition
communicable	noncommun-
disease	icable condition
healthcare	

Noncommunicable diseases

- In the developing regions, *noncommunicable conditions* or diseases are becoming as much a cause of disability and premature death as infectious or *communicable diseases*.
- The main killer is still HIV/AIDS, but noncommunicable diseases such as heart disease and respiratory conditions are close behind.
- These conditions may soon become more serious than infectious diseases and *malnutrition*.
- By 2020, noncommunicable diseases are expected to account for 70 percent of deaths in developing nations.
- In developed nations, the biggest killers are heart disease, stroke, and pulmonary problems—all noncommunicable conditions.

Healthcare dependence

- In 1990 the three leading causes of healthcare dependence in the world were: pneumonia, diarrheal diseases, and perinatal (birth-related) conditions.
- By 2020, heart disease, depression, and road traffic injuries are projected to have taken their place.

Main causes

- The main causes of death and disability worldwide can be linked to common risk factors.
- These are tobacco, alcohol use, diet, physical inactivity, and environmental *carcinogens*.
- By 2020 diseases related to tobacco use are expected to be more common than any other.

World causes of death and disability

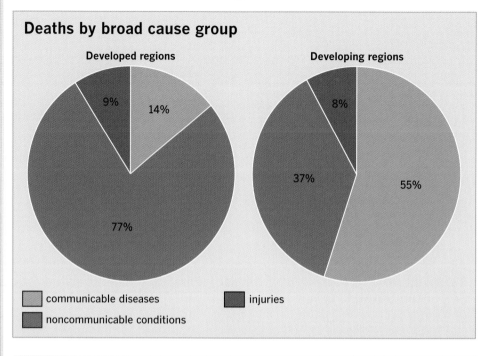

Deaths by broad cause group

Developed regions

Developing regions

- communicable diseases
- noncommunicable conditions
- injuries

Leading causes of death in 2001

	Developing nations	Number of deaths
1	HIV/AIDS	2,678,000
2	Lower respiratory infections	2,643,000
3	Ischemic heart disease	2,484,000
4	Diarrheal diseases	1,793,000
5	Cerebrovascular disease	1,381,000
6	Childhood diseases	1,217,000
7	Malaria	1,103,000
8	Tuberculosis	1,021,000
9	Chronic obstructive pulmonary disease	748,000
10	Measles	674,000
	Developed nations	**Number of deaths**
1	Ischemic heart disease	3,512,000
2	Cerebrovascular disease	3,346,000
3	Chronic obstructive pulmonary disease	1,829,000
4	Lower respiratory infections	1,180,000
5	Trachea/bronchus/lung cancers	938,000
6	Road traffic accidents	669,000
7	Stomach cancer	657,000
8	Hypertensive heart disease	635,000
9	Tuberculosis	571,000
10	Self-inflicted	499,000

source: *World Health Report*, WHO, 2002

The spread of AIDS

Estimated numbers of people living with HIV/AIDS, 2004

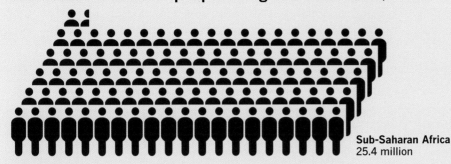

Sub-Saharan Africa
25.4 million

South and Southeast Asia
6.1 million

Latin America
1.7 million

Eastern Europe and Central Asia
1.4 million

East Asia and Pacific
1.1 million

North America
1 million

Western Europe
600,000

North Africa and Middle East
500,000

Caribbean
440,000

| **Australia and New Zealand**
13,600

 = 250,000

Key words

AIDS
HIV
sub-Saharan
  Africa

AIDS

- Acquired Immunodeficiency Syndrome (AIDS) was first identified in the early 1980s.
- Since then it has become one of the most devastating diseases to have affected humanity.

Mounting figures

- Worldwide in 2004, an estimated 38 million people were either infected with the HIV virus (were "HIV-positive"), or living with AIDS.
- It is estimated that in 2004 around 3.1 million people died from AIDS.
- This means that approximately 8,500 people die from the condition every day.
- Between 1981 and 2003 the total number of deaths from AIDS was around 20 million.

The spread of HIV/AIDS

- The spread of HIV and AIDS is accelerated in regions of conflict, poverty, heavy migration, and inequality between men and women.
- Worldwide, about 47 percent of all people infected with HIV are women.

Biggest killer in Africa

- AIDS is the leading cause of death in sub-Saharan Africa.
- In many of the worst-affected countries, the adult prevalence rates are still rising.
- Around 57 percent of the HIV-positive Africans are women.

Living with HIV/AIDS

- In 2003 young people aged 15–24 accounted for half the new worldwide infections.
- This is around 6,000 infections each day and most do not know they are carrying the disease.
- Many millions more know nothing or too little about HIV/AIDS to protect themselves against it.

© Diagram Visual Information Ltd.

Key words

AIDS
epidemic
GDP
HIV
per capita

The economic cost

- The HIV/AIDS epidemic is having and will continue to have a profound impact on growth, income, and poverty worldwide.
- By 2010, per capita gross domestic product (GDP) in some of the hardest hit countries may have dropped by eight percent.
- The most heavily hit countries could lose more than 20 percent of GDP by 2020.
- It is estimated that the annual per capita growth in half the countries of sub-Saharan Africa is falling by 0.5–1.2 percent as a direct result of AIDS.

Controlling HIV/AIDS

- In combating HIV/AIDS, young people must be a priority.
- Twenty-five years into the epidemic, millions of young people—the most sexually active part of the population—still know little about the disease.
- According to UNICEF, more than 50 percent of young people 15–24 in a dozen developing countries have never heard of HIV/AIDS, or have very inaccurate information about how it is transmitted.
- Providing young people with information and preventative advice is vital in halting the spread of HIV/AIDS.

Treatment of HIV/AIDS

- Huge amounts of money have been spent on developing treatment for HIV/AIDS.
- Although it is still incurable, the use of antiretroviral drugs in combination can mean an infected person may never develop the symptoms of full-blown AIDS.
- However, an estimated five million people in low and middle income countries do not have access to the drugs that could save their lives.

Living with AIDS

HIV-positive

Estimated number of adults infected with HIV, by WHO region, 1980–2003

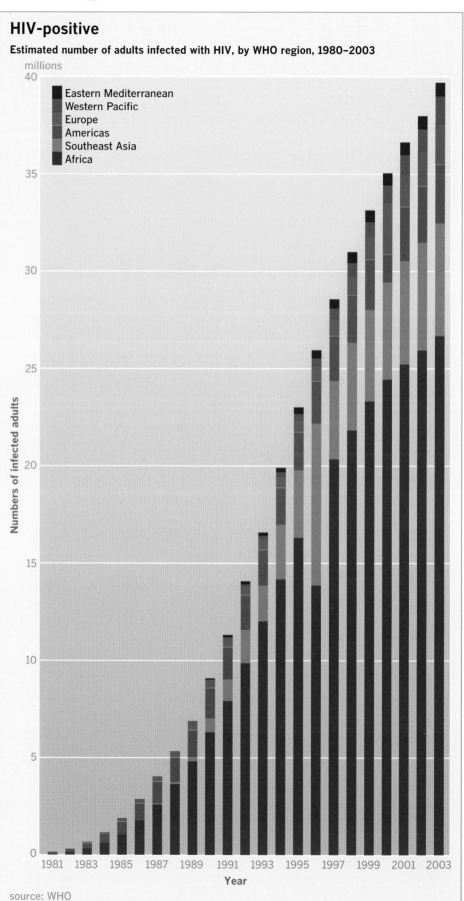

source: WHO

Malaria and climate change

Key words

climate change   irrigation
communicable
  disease
deforestation
food chain

Malaria

Farming

- Crop irrigation provides plentiful water in which mosquito larvae can develop and hatch.
- Livestock provide mosquitoes with the blood needed to maintain their high populations.

Settlement

- Growth in human populations has led to the construction of new roads and towns in areas where mosquitoes abound.
- This has allowed malaria to spread very rapidly within new communities.
- Dams also provide breeding grounds.

Transportation

- The growth of air travel has made "airport malaria" commonplace.

Anopheles mosquito

- The growth of populations of this insect means that the malaria parasite *Plasmodium* continues to thrive.

Logging and deforestation

- These activities also allow the malarial mosquito to spread, and provide stagnant water for breeding.

Climate change

- Global warming brings warmer and wetter conditions to some areas.
- This extends the range of the *Anopheles* mosquito.
- Many areas have experienced dramatic increases in the incidence of malaria during extreme weather events correlated to El Niño.

Control

- Considerable environmental damage has been done in attempts to eradicate malaria.
- Insecticides have poisoned the food chains of ecosystems, causing long-term environmental harm.

Most lethal parasite

- Malaria is by far the world's most lethal tropical parasitic disease.
- It continues to kill around 1.2 million people per year—more than any other communicable disease except tuberculosis.
- Worldwide prevalence of the disease is estimated to be 300–500 million clinical cases each year.
- In 2004, 1.136 million deaths from malaria, 90 percent of the worldwide total, were in Africa.

Spread by mosquito

- Malaria is a *vector-borne disease* caused by a parasite called *Plasmodium*, which is transmitted to humans by the *Anopheles* mosquito.
- These mosquitoes can breed readily in stagnant freshwater.

Disturbed areas

- Changes in land use are linked to an increased risk of the disease.
- Areas in the tropics with much road building, mining, logging, and agricultural and irrigation projects suffer a higher prevalence of malaria.

Climate change

- Changes in the global climate are also helping the spread of malaria.
- With global warming malaria may gradually expand out of the tropics to temperate regions.
- Other causes, such as collapsing health services, armed conflicts, El Niño, and the movement of refugees add to the spread of malaria.

Combating malaria

- Many attempts have been made to control the spread of malaria with insecticides.
- Better management of water resources reduces the transmission of malaria and other vector-borne diseases.

Key words

rural
urbanization

From the land to the cities

- The world is steadily becoming more urban as people move from the land to towns and cities in search of employment, education, and a higher standard of living.
- Huge numbers of people are leaving agricultural communities and land that can no longer support them, and accelerating the urbanization of the less developed countries.

Urban statistics

- The share of the global population living in urban areas increased from 33 percent in 1960 to 48 percent (three billion people) in 2003.
- This proportion is expected to increase to 60 percent by 2030: 5.0 billion people out of a projected global population of around 8.1 billion.
- Much of this growth will be due to natural fertility rather than migration.

Unequal growth

- The world's urban population is currently growing at four times the rate of the rural population.
- The number of urban dwellers now equals that of rural dwellers.

Rural growth slowing

- The growth of the world's rural population has been slowing markedly.
- In 1950, seven out of every 10 people on Earth lived in rural areas.
- Over the course of the next 50 years, rural population growth averaged 1.19 percent per year and the rural population nearly doubled.
- By 2030, rural population growth is expected to be minimal and the number of rural inhabitants will remain at around 3.2 billion.

Urban and rural population growth

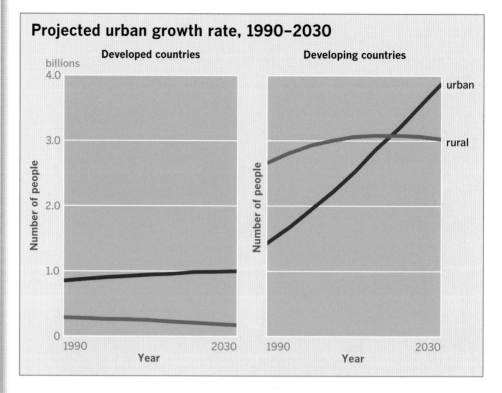

Projected urban growth rate, 1990–2030

Urban–rural distribution of global population, 1975–2015

World

Conurbation size	1975 population millions	1975 population percentage	2000 population millions	2000 population percentage	2015 population millions	2015 population percentage
5 million	195	4.8	418	6.9	623	8.7
1–5 million	327	8.0	704	11.6	1,006	14.1
Less than 1 million	1,022	25.1	1,723	28.5	2,189	30.6
Rural areas	2,531	62.1	3,210	53.0	3,337	46.6
Total population	4,075	100.0	6,055	100.0	7,154	100.0

More developed regions

Conurbation size	1975 population millions	1975 population percentage	2000 population millions	2000 population percentage	2015 population millions	2015 population percentage
5 million +	98	9.3	112	9.4	120	9.9
1–5 million	145	13.9	219	18.5	250	20.6
Less than 1 million	491	46.8	571	48.1	598	49.2
Rural areas	315	30.0	285	24.0	246	20.3
Total population	1,048	100.0	1,188	100.0	1,214	100.0

Less developed regions

Conurbation size	1975 population millions	1975 population percentage	2000 population millions	2000 population percentage	2015 population millions	2015 population percentage
5 million	97	3.2	305	6.3	503	8.5
1–5 million	182	6.0	485	10.0	756	12.7
Less than 1 million	531	17.6	1,152	23.7	1,591	26.8
Rural areas	2,217	73.2	2,925	60.0	3,091	52.0
Total population	3,026	100.0	4,867	100.0	5,940	100.0

Urbanization of the world population

Key words

GDP
pollution
urbanization

Urban–rural populations

urban rural

North America

total population: 326 million (258 million–68 million)

79%

21%

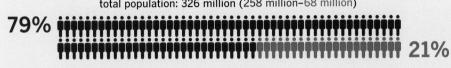

Latin America and Caribbean

total population: 549 million (412 million–137 million)

75%

25%

Europe

total population: 728 million (539 million–189 million)

74%

26%

Oceania

total population: 33 million (24 million–9 million)

72%

28%

Asia

total population: 3,875 million (1,511 million–2,364 million)

39%

61%

Africa

total population: 885 million (310 million–575 million)

35%

65%

Urbanization trends

- For the first time in history, more people will soon live in urban areas than rural areas.
- Cities occupy less than two percent of Earth's land surface, but house almost half the world's population and use 75 percent of the resources we take from the planet.
- Virtually all the population growth expected during 2000–2030 will be concentrated in the urban areas of the world.

Developing regions

- Between 2000 and 2030 the urban population of developing nations is predicted to grow by 2.3 percent per year.
- The urban populations of more developed nations are expected to increase very slowly, if at all.

Urbanization factors

- Cities are generally very productive.
- The World Bank estimates that urban areas in the developing world account for between 65 and 80 percent of national GDP.
- City dwellers tend to use more resources, but have fewer children and thus help to drive down national rates of population growth.
- On average, urban dwellers have higher incomes and live healthier lives than their rural counterparts.

Slums and pollution

- Between 26 and 50 percent of urban inhabitants in developing countries live in slums or squatter settlements.
- Worldwide, more than one billion people live in urban areas where air quality is poor enough to cause health concerns.

Key words

metropolitan
urbanization

Expanding towns and cities

- One result of increasing urbanization is the ever-expanding metropolitan area.
- These metropolitan areas, or "agglomerations," include a central city and neighboring communities linked to it by a continuous built-up area.
- Sometimes, these agglomerations have more than one central town or city.
- An urban agglomeration with ten million inhabitants or more is sometimes called a *megacity*.

Rapid growth

- In 1950 New York was the only megacity in the world.
- By 2006 there were 25 megacities, with 18 of these in the developing world.
- The growth rates of these large megacities are much higher than in developed countries.
- The number of megacities is expected to increase greatly in the coming years as more people move to urban areas to find work and a better standard of living.

Problems in urban areas

- The current pace and scale of change often strains the capacity of local and national governments to provide even the most basic services to urban residents.
- Many countries are developing new policies to address the demands created by the increasing number of people in cities.
- Governments are also keen to capitalize on the benefits of urbanization, such as economic growth.

The megacities

Megacities

Metropolitan areas with more than 15 million inhabitants, 2006

More than 15 million inhabitants	Population
Tokyo	34,200,000
Mexico City	22,800,000
Seoul	22,300,000
New York	21,900,000
São Paulo	20,200,000
Mumbai (Bombay)	19,850,000
Delhi	19,700,000
Shangai	18,150,000
Los Angeles	18,000,000
Osaka	16,800,000
Jakarta	16,550,000
Kolkata (Calcutta)	15,650,000
Cairo	15,600,000

Metropolitan areas with 10–15 million inhabitants, 2006

10–15 million inhabitants	Population
Manila	14,950,000
Karachi	14,300,000
Moscow	13,750,000
Buenos Aires	13,450,000
Dacca	13,250,000
Rio de Janeiro	12,150,000
Beijing	12,100,000
London	12,000,000
Tehran	11,850,000
Istanbul	11,500,000
Lagos	11,100,000
Shenzhen	10,700,000

Problems of the urban environment

Key words

epidemic
migration
sanitation

Urban issues

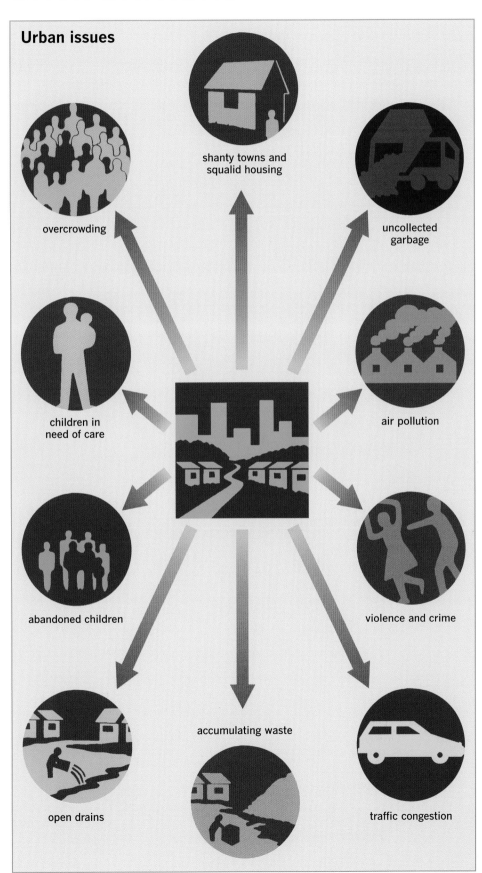

shanty towns and squalid housing

uncollected garbage

overcrowding

air pollution

children in need of care

violence and crime

abandoned children

open drains

accumulating waste

traffic congestion

Overcrowding

- An estimated 25–50 percent of urban inhabitants in developing nations live in impoverished and overcrowded slums and squatter settlements.
- These deprived areas generally have no access to adequate water supplies, sanitation, or refuse collection.
- Massive overcrowding is common because of land shortage and high rents.
- These living conditions promote epidemics of tuberculosis, diarrhea, and other communicable conditions.

Social problems

- Traditional family structures can break down, increasing the numbers of children in need of care.
- Violence and crime are generally much higher in deprived crowded areas.
- Poverty and lack of employment can mean many people turn to crime at an early age.
- These problems are especially severe in areas of new urban migration.

Pollution

- Worldwide, more than one billion people live in urban areas where air pollution exceeds acceptable levels.
- Traffic congestion adds greatly to air and noise pollution in these areas.

Positive aspect

- On the positive side, urban populations generally have greater access to education, health, and clean water and sanitation than their rural counterparts.

Key words

poverty

Measuring poverty

- Poverty is often measured using income or consumption levels.
- Someone is considered poor if their income falls below a minimum level necessary to meet basic needs.
- This minimum level is often referred to as the "poverty line."
- The World Bank assesses poverty by estimating the number of people living on $1–2 per day.
- Living on less than $2 per day is considered living in poverty, while living on less than $1 per day is referred to as "extreme poverty." An income greater than $2 per day is considered "non-poor."
- These definitions are disputed by some experts, who argue that poverty should be defined relatively.

Extreme poverty

- The number of people in developing nations suffering from extreme poverty declined only slowly during the 1990s.
- The share of the population of the developing world living on less than $1 per day fell from 28 percent in 1987 to 21 percent in 2001.

Trends in poverty

- The number of people living in extreme poverty has remained roughly constant, at nearly 1.3 billion, as the world population has increased.
- Trends in social indicators show that while there has been average progress with health and education, in all aspects of life the poor are systematically worse off than the non-poor.
- In 2004 it was estimated that roughly 2.8 billion people lived on less than $2 a day.

Poverty in the developing world

Extreme poverty by region

Population by regions living on less than $1 per day (in 1993 purchasing power parity terms), and regional proportions, in 1981, 1990, and 2001

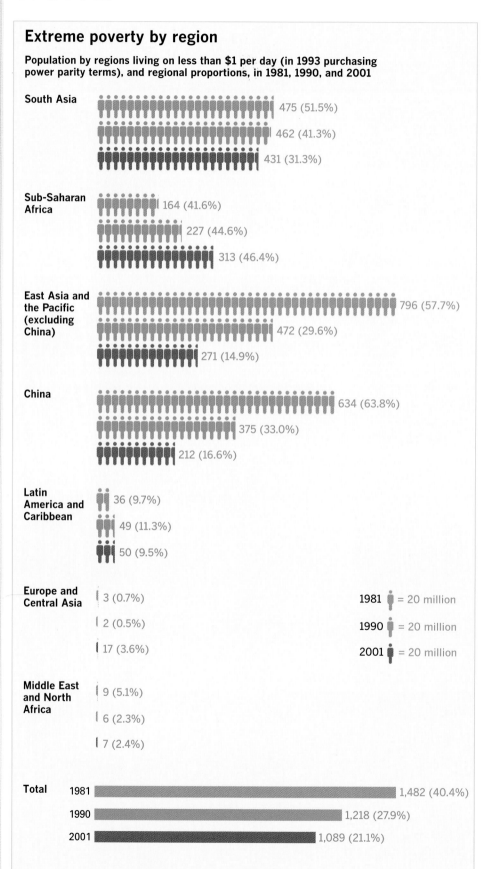

South Asia
475 (51.5%)
462 (41.3%)
431 (31.3%)

Sub-Saharan Africa
164 (41.6%)
227 (44.6%)
313 (46.4%)

East Asia and the Pacific (excluding China)
796 (57.7%)
472 (29.6%)
271 (14.9%)

China
634 (63.8%)
375 (33.0%)
212 (16.6%)

Latin America and Caribbean
36 (9.7%)
49 (11.3%)
50 (9.5%)

Europe and Central Asia
3 (0.7%)
2 (0.5%)
17 (3.6%)

Middle East and North Africa
9 (5.1%)
6 (2.3%)
7 (2.4%)

1981 = 20 million
1990 = 20 million
2001 = 20 million

Total
1981 1,482 (40.4%)
1990 1,218 (27.9%)
2001 1,089 (21.1%)

World distribution of wealth

Key words

development
  assistance
GNP
sanitation

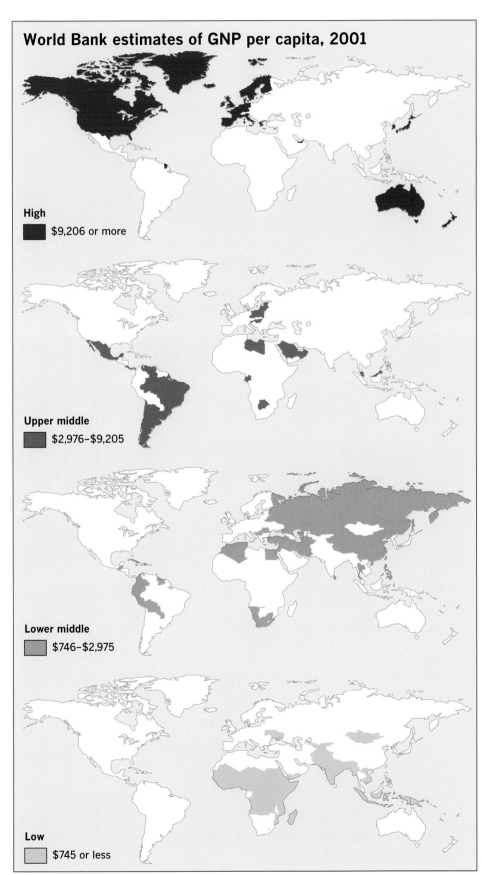

World Bank estimates of GNP per capita, 2001

High
$9,206 or more

Upper middle
$2,976–$9,205

Lower middle
$746–$2,975

Low
$745 or less

Unequal distribution

- The distribution of wealth around the world is very unequal.
- The relative gap between rich and poor in developing nations is at least as great as it is in the developed world.
- It is thought that one of the main challenges in today's global economy and society is "poverty in the midst of plenty."
- Many consider that fighting poverty is both a moral imperative and a necessity for a stable world.

Consequences

- More than 120 million primary school age children are out of school, more than half of them girls.
- Many people live without adequate food, shelter, clean water, or sanitation.
- While around 2.8 billion people in developing regions still live on less than $2 per day, those in more developed nations live in comparative luxury, though often in conditions regarded as very poor by the standards of their own countries.

Development and debt relief

- Two of the most important ways of reducing poverty on a global scale are development assistance and debt relief.
- Through the World Bank and the International Monetary Fund (IMF), the international community adopted development goals during the 1990s.
- Progress in meeting these goals has been slow and uneven across the world.
- Debt relief under the enhanced Heavily Indebted Poor Countries (HIPC) Initiative, is an important dimension of assistance to developing countries.

Key words

biomass	hydroelectric
Food and	particulate
Agriculture	pollution
Organization	sub-Saharan
(FAO)	Africa

Wood as fuel

- In 2003, 2.3 billion people still relied on *biomass*—organic matter—for their cooking and heating.
- In many countries of the world, wood is the only available source of biomass with which to cook food and provide warmth.
- Between 50 and 70 percent of all wood consumed on Earth is used for daily cooking purposes.
- Wood provides nearly all the energy needs of sub-Saharan African nations.
- Of all wood harvested, 92 percent in South Asia and 73 percent in Southeast Asia is used for fuel.

Wood shortages

- The UN Food and Agriculture Organization (FAO) estimated that by the year 2000, 2.4 billion people were either short of fuelwood or using it unsustainably.
- In 2000 the world fuelwood deficit had reached 1.255 billion cubic yards (1.0 billion m³ per year.

New cooking stoves

- Traditional wood-burning stoves and open fires usually operate at a low efficiency of around 6–8 percent.
- Improved fuelwood stoves are at least three times as efficient.
- The cost of five million fuel-saving stoves would be the same as the cost of one hydroelectric dam project in Africa.
- Using all these stoves combined would save five times the energy a typical hydroelectric dam could produce.
- New stoves would reduce pollution and particulates, both local and widespread; and reduce drudgery for women and children
- The firewood saved would help the conservation of forests.

The fuelwood crisis

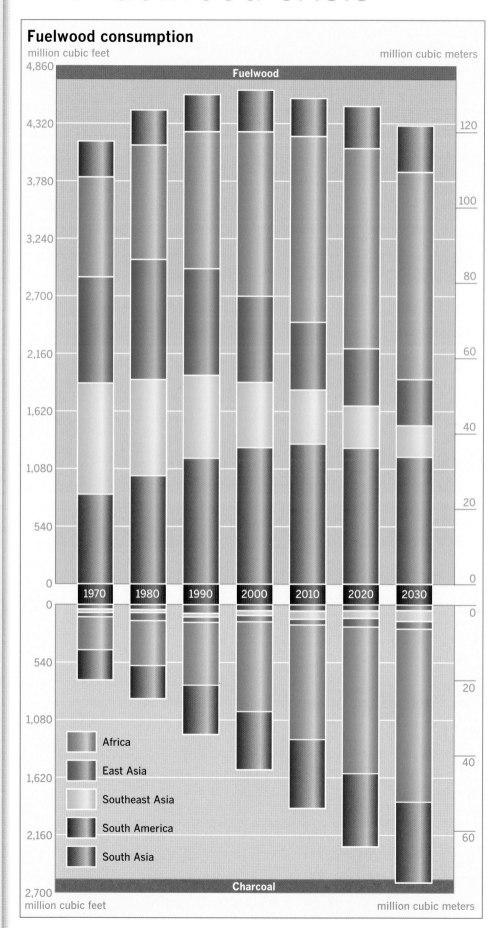

Fuelwood consumption

million cubic feet — million cubic meters

Fuelwood

1970 1980 1990 2000 2010 2020 2030

Charcoal

million cubic feet — million cubic meters

Legend:
- Africa
- East Asia
- Southeast Asia
- South America
- South Asia

The freshwater crisis

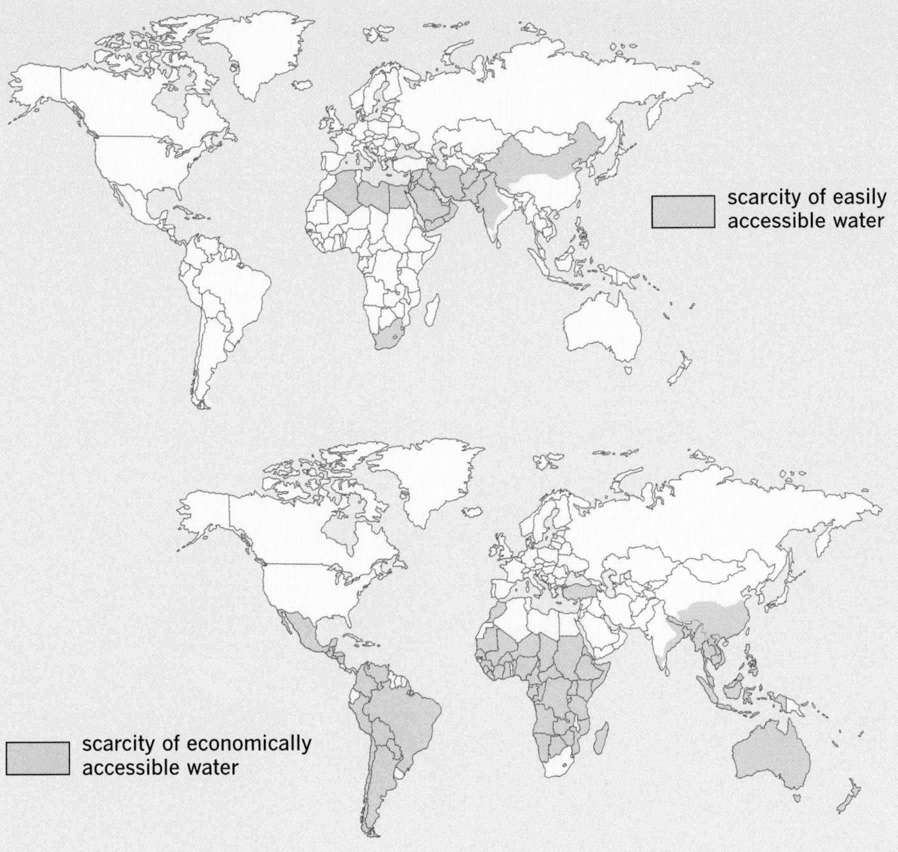

Key words

drought
per capita
sanitation
sub-Saharan
 Africa

Freshwater

Water proportions

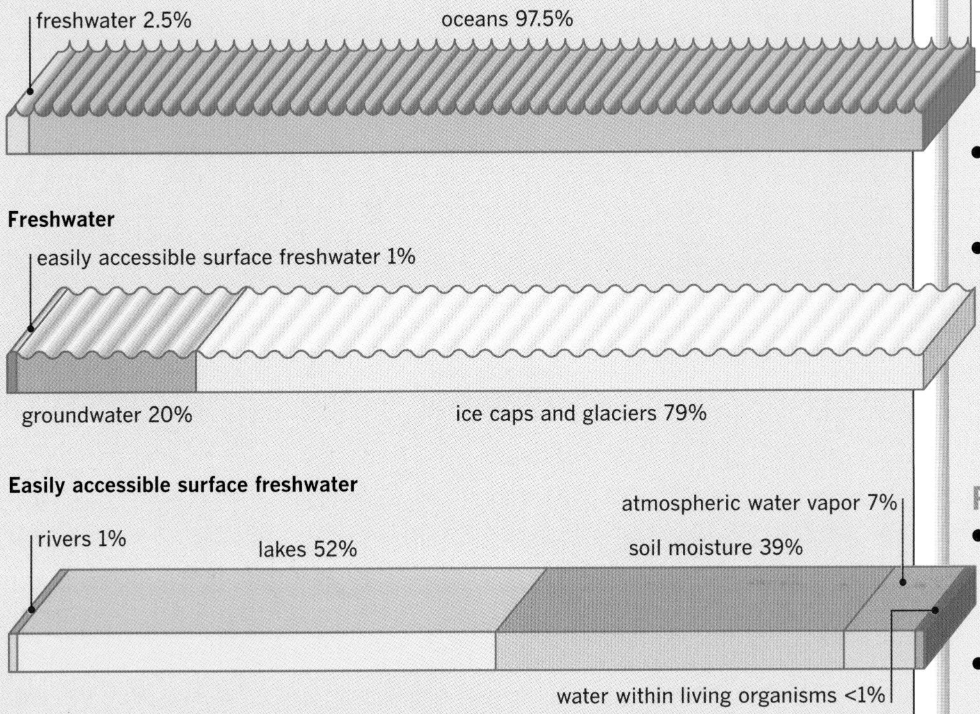

All water

freshwater 2.5%   oceans 97.5%

Freshwater

easily accessible surface freshwater 1%

groundwater 20%   ice caps and glaciers 79%

Easily accessible surface freshwater

rivers 1%   lakes 52%   atmospheric water vapor 7%

soil moisture 39%

water within living organisms <1%

Projected freshwater scarcity, 2025

scarcity of easily
accessible water

scarcity of economically
accessible water

Limited water supplies

● The supply of freshwater is limited, yet
 demand is rising rapidly as the world's
 population grows.
● Each year, between 432 and 486 billion
 cubic feet (12–14 billion m³) of water
 are available for human use.
  ● The UN recommends that people
   need a minimum of 13 gallons (50 l)
   of fresh water per day for drinking,
   washing, cooking, and sanitation.

Rising consumption

● Over the past 70 years the world
 population has tripled.
  ● Water use, however, has increased
   six-fold during this period.
● Per capita use of freshwater, especially
 in the more developed regions, is
 rising fast.
● This rise has been attributed to
 "modern living" in developed
 countries where more money is spent
 on luxury items, products, and
 services that consume water.

Water crisis in the future

● In 2004 it was estimated that a third of
 the world's population lived in
 water-stressed countries.
● This is expected to rise to two thirds
 by 2025.

Worst hit areas

● The areas most at risk from water
 shortages are the Middle East, North
 Africa, and sub-Saharan Africa.
● There are currently around 200 million
 sub-Saharan Africans living in drought
 regions.
● This figure will rise to 700 million
 by 2025.

© Diagram Visual Information Ltd.

Key words

Green Revolution
groundwater
irrigation

Rivers and groundwater

- Water use from rivers and underground reserves has grown by 2.5–3 percent annually since 1940—much faster than population growth.
- Little of the water in some of the world's major rivers now reaches the sea.
- The Nile and Colorado rivers are so heavily used that they no longer reach the sea for days at a time.

Yangtze River, China

- The Yangtze is China's longest river at 3,960 miles (6,380 km).
- Water use for industry and agriculture increased throughout the mid-twentieth century, and by the 1970s the Yangtze's water supply had begun to run out.
- Measures are now being taken to restore the water flow.

Irrigation of crops

- More than 60 percent of the water used in the world each year is diverted for crop irrigation.
- Egypt, which must irrigate all its crops, uses more than five times as much water per capita as Switzerland.
- Asia contains 66 percent of the world's irrigated land, and more than 85 percent of its water is used for irrigation.
- The *Green Revolution* in the late twentieth century made it possible to double the area under irrigation to more than one million acres (405,000 ha).

Possible wars and conflicts

- Experts believe that in the future water crises may become so acute that some countries will go to war over access to freshwater.

Freshwater scarcity

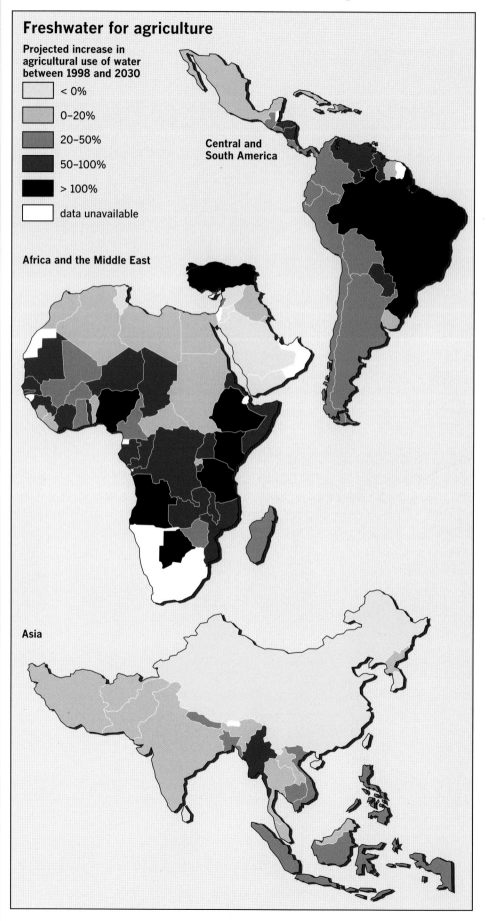

Freshwater for agriculture

Projected increase in agricultural use of water between 1998 and 2030

- < 0%
- 0–20%
- 20–50%
- 50–100%
- > 100%
- data unavailable

Central and South America

Africa and the Middle East

Asia

Living space

Living space per person

Percentage of population with floor area per person of

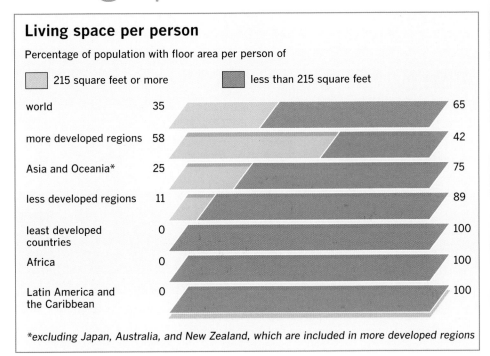

- [ ] 215 square feet or more
- [ ] less than 215 square feet

	215 sq ft or more	less than 215 sq ft
world	35	65
more developed regions	58	42
Asia and Oceania*	25	75
less developed regions	11	89
least developed countries	0	100
Africa	0	100
Latin America and the Caribbean	0	100

*excluding Japan, Australia, and New Zealand, which are included in more developed regions

Floor area per person in cities

in square feet

- [ ] 215 or more
- [ ] 160–204
- [ ] 100–150
- [ ] 54–97
- [ ] less than 97

percentage

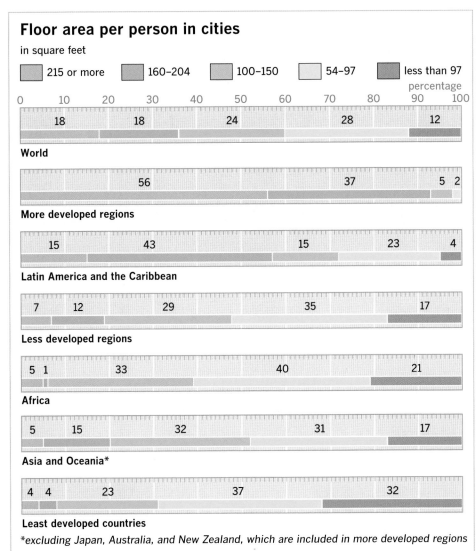

World 18 | 18 | 24 | 28 | 12

More developed regions 56 | 37 | 5 2

Latin America and the Caribbean 15 | 43 | 15 | 23 | 4

Less developed regions 7 | 12 | 29 | 35 | 17

Africa 5 1 | 33 | 40 | 21

Asia and Oceania* 5 | 15 | 32 | 31 | 17

Least developed countries 4 4 | 23 | 37 | 32

*excluding Japan, Australia, and New Zealand, which are included in more developed regions

Key words

industrialized
  country

Overcrowding

- As cities grow larger, there is usually less living space available, especially in developing nations.
- Overcrowding is common where there is inadequate provision for the expanding population.

Living conditions

- Living conditions in many parts of the world are deteriorating, mainly as a result of low levels of investment.
- Housing policies, such as large apartment blocks in urban areas, greatly affect the people's living conditions.
- Slums and squatter settlements are becoming more commonplace because lack of space has led to huge property and land price increases.

Floor space

- Around 60 percent of industrialized countries have a floor area per person of 215 square feet (20 m²) or more compared to only ten percent in developing nations.
- Floor space per person is less than 215 square feet (20 m²) for all African countries, and for 75 percent of Asian and Pacific countries.
- In less developed nations, only seven percent of cities have an average floor area of 215 square feet (20 m²) or more.
- More than half have an average floor area of less than 100 square feet (9 m²) per person.
- In nearly 60 percent of Latin American and Caribbean cities, the average floor area is at least 160 square feet (15 m²) per person.
- This is only the case in six percent of African cities and 20 percent of cities in Asia.

Key words

chlorofluoro-	infrastructure
carbons (CFCs)	ozone
climate change	ozone layer
ecosystem	particulate
greenhouse gas	pollution
habitat	

Global transportation

- The four main types of transportation used throughout the globe are road, rail, aviation, and maritime.
- All transportation has detrimental effects on the environment.

Pollution

- Much of the pollution produced by transportation damages human health, including: carbon monoxide (CO), ground level ozone (O_3), lead (Pb), nitrogen dioxide (NO_2), and particulate matter (PM).
- Many atmospheric toxins are known to cause serious diseases and health problems, including cancer and birth defects.

Greenhouse gases

- Pollution such as carbon dioxide, methane, and nitrous oxide are all greenhouse gases produced by transportation.
- They contribute to global climate change by trapping heat within the atmosphere.
- Chlorofluorocarbons are depleting the stratospheric ozone layer.

Habitat loss and damage

- The creation of new roads, railroads, airports, and docks has fragmented and destroyed habitats.
- Ecosystems can be irreversibly changed even by small disturbances.
- Hazardous materials can sometimes be released during transportation: for example, oil spillages from tankers can be devastating to marine life.

Environmental effects of transportation

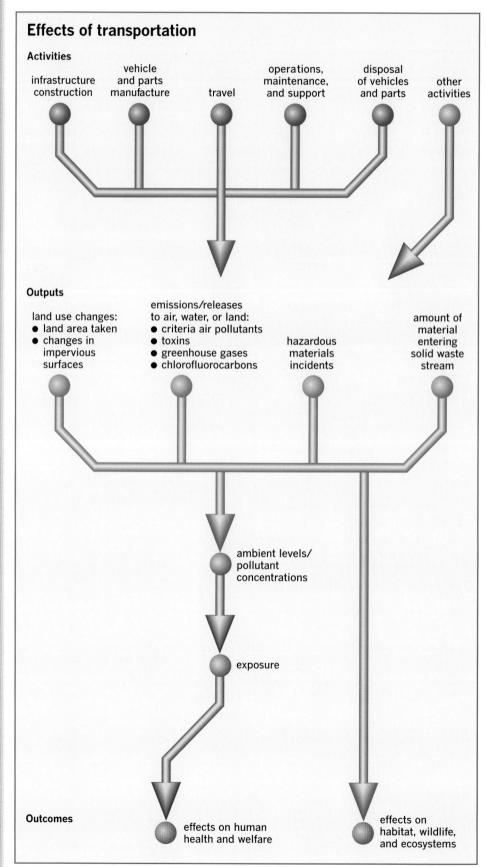

Effects of transportation

Activities

infrastructure construction · vehicle and parts manufacture · travel · operations, maintenance, and support · disposal of vehicles and parts · other activities

Outputs

land use changes:
- land area taken
- changes in impervious surfaces

emissions/releases to air, water, or land:
- criteria air pollutants
- toxins
- greenhouse gases
- chlorofluorocarbons

hazardous materials incidents

amount of material entering solid waste stream

ambient levels/pollutant concentrations

exposure

Outcomes

effects on human health and welfare

effects on habitat, wildlife, and ecosystems

Automobiles by country

Numbers of vehicles, 2002

= 1 million vehicles

P = passenger vehicle

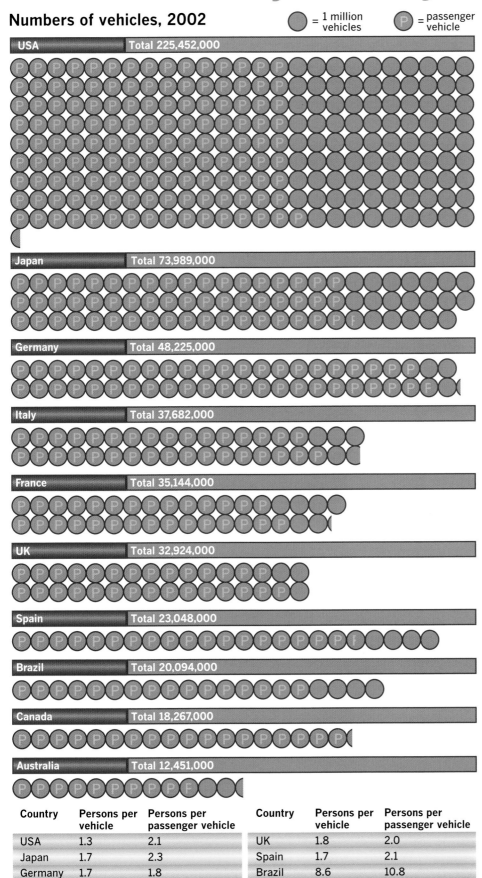

Country	Persons per vehicle	Persons per passenger vehicle	Country	Persons per vehicle	Persons per passenger vehicle
USA	1.3	2.1	UK	1.8	2.0
Japan	1.7	2.3	Spain	1.7	2.1
Germany	1.7	1.8	Brazil	8.6	10.8
Italy	1.5	1.7	Canada	1.6	1.9
France	1.7	2.0	Australia	1.6	1.9

Key words

greenhouse gas
pollution

Automobiles on the increase

- The number of motor vehicles in use around the world grew from only 8,000 in 1900 to 808 million by 2002.
- By 2025 there are likely to be more than one billion vehicles on the world's roads.
- It is estimated that there is currently one automobile for every 12 people in the world: ten times the figure 50 years ago.
- Two thirds of these vehicles are in Western Europe and North America.

Energy demands

- Transport accounts for one quarter of world energy use and roughly half the world's oil production.
- Motor vehicles currently use nearly 80 percent of all motor related energy.
- By using large amounts of energy, motor vehicles are a major contributor to greenhouse gas emissions and urban air pollution.

Urbanization

- As areas become more urbanized and cities expand, motorized transport becomes essential for commuting, shopping, and many other activities.
- In many countries, public transport is often of a poor standard and people aspire to own their own automobile.

Urban public transport

- Some developed nations can afford mass transit systems that are so efficient people prefer using them to driving automobiles in congested city streets.
- To cut congestion and pollution, some cities now restrict driving at peak times by charging or other means, as an incentive for people to use public transport instead.

© Diagram Visual Information Ltd.

Key words

greenhouse gas
per capita

Automobiles per person

- Per capita automobile ownership is high in the wealthy nations of North America, Europe, and Japan.
- It is still comparatively low in most developing countries, but is increasing fast.
- In 2002 the United States had 789 automobiles per 1,000 people, the highest density of automobile ownership in the world.

Increase in ownership

- Automobile ownership has risen steeply in China and India over recent years due to robust economies and decreasing ownership costs.
- The number of vehicles in China grew by 300 percent between 1980 and 1998.
- India's ownership figures expanded by nearly nine percent per year over the same period.
- India had only seven automobiles per 1,000 people in 1998 but is projected to have 382 by 2050.
- This would mean India may have 611 million automobiles by 2050, the highest number of automobiles owned in any country in the world.

The consequences

- The increased use of motor vehicles worldwide will have many consequences.
- In individual countries, there will be greater air pollution, more deaths on the road, and congestion will increase.
- On a worldwide scale, emissions of greenhouse gases will rise steeply.
- The increased demand for oil will mean prices will rise, putting pressure on the countries that rely on oil imports.

Automobile density

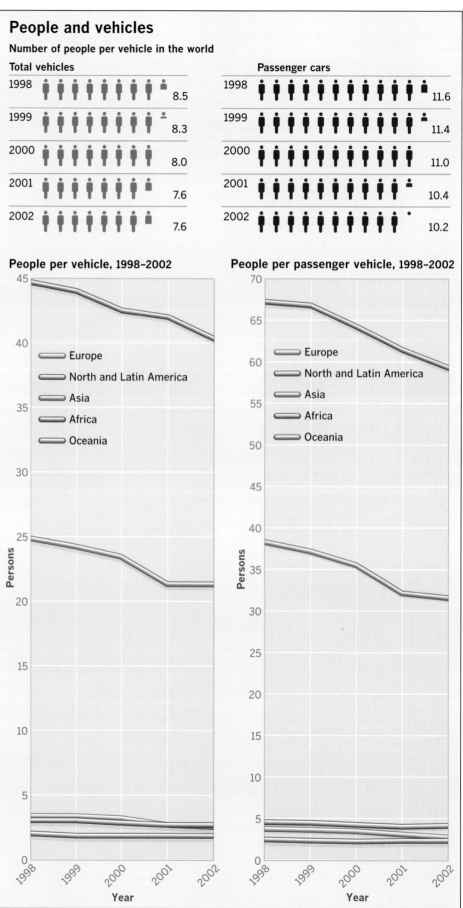

People and vehicles

Number of people per vehicle in the world

Total vehicles

1998	8.5
1999	8.3
2000	8.0
2001	7.6
2002	7.6

Passenger cars

1998	11.6
1999	11.4
2000	11.0
2001	10.4
2002	10.2

People per vehicle, 1998–2002

Europe
North and Latin America
Asia
Africa
Oceania

People per passenger vehicle, 1998–2002

Europe
North and Latin America
Asia
Africa
Oceania

Sanitation

Key words

infrastructure
sanitation

Global sanitation

Population using improved sanitation

less than 50%

50–75%

75–100%

Sanitation cover by region

	percent
North America	100
Europe and Russia	83
Western Asia	79
Latin America and Caribbean	75
North Africa	73
Southeast Asia	61
Oceania	55
East Asia	45
South Asia	37
Sub-Saharan Africa	36

Scale: 0 10 20 30 40 50 60 70 80 percent

Countries with lowest improved sanitation coverage

	percent
Ethiopia	6
Afghanistan	8
Chad	8
Congo	9
Eritrea	9
Burkina Faso	12
Niger	12
Guinea	13
Cambodia	16
Comoros	23

Scale: 0 5 10 15 20 25 percent

Access to sanitation

- Throughout the world, access to sanitation is even more limited than access to safe water.
- One quarter of the population of developing countries lacks access to safe water but more than half has no access to sanitation.
- 2.5 billion people in developing countries do not have proper sanitation compared to the 1.9 billion who do.
- More than half of African countries and more than one quarter of Asian countries lack access to proper sanitation.

Health issues

- The lack of sanitation in many countries has severe implications for health.
- Poor sanitation means that sewage and garbage remains near habitations and in urban areas.
- This encourages the spread of such diseases as cholera, typhoid, diarrhea, and intestinal parasites.
- Each year around 1.8 million people die from diarrheal diseases (including cholera); 90 percent are children under five years old.

Investment in sanitation

- Major investment is needed to provide effective sanitation for towns and cities by improving local infrastructure.
- A massive investment in facilities is required to achieve global access to sanitation, especially in the poorest countries.

Wellbeing of nations: 1

© Diagram Visual Information Ltd.

Key words

biodiversity
conservation
World
  Conservation
  Union (IUCN)

Wellbeing of nations

- A method of assessing quality of living, giving equal weight to people and the environment, was used in the Wellbeing of Nations Report, most recently published in 2001 by the World Conservation Union (IUCN).
- The survey ranked 180 countries by measuring human development and environmental conservation.
- Human development and the state of the environment were awarded points by looking at indicators such as wealth, education, freedom, and biodiversity.

The results

- The study found that most countries enjoying high standards of living are placing undue pressure on the environment.
- Four billion people live in countries with a poor level of human development.
- Fewer than one billion people live in countries with a fair or good standard of living.
- No country is sustainable or even close to sustainability.
- The leading countries (mostly in Europe and North America) have high standards of living but excessive impacts on the environment.
- About 27 countries (mostly in Africa) have low demands on the environment but are desperately poor.
- The report suggests that a high standard of living is possible without ruining the environment if countries change the way they pursue development.

The Wellbeing Index

Countries are ranked in order of the Wellbeing Index.
Small island nations and others with insufficient data are omitted.

a ranking (= joint) **b** country **c** wellbeing index points **d** human wellbeing index points **e** ecosystem wellbeing index points

a	b	c	d	e	a	b	c	d	e
1	Sweden	64.0	79	49	45	Mauritius	49.0	54	44
2	Finland	62.5	81	44	47	Benin	49.0	27	71
3	Norway	62.5	82	43	48	Costa Rica	48.5	56	41
4	Iceland	61.5	80	43	49	Sri Lanka	48.5	40	57
5	Austria	61.0	80	42	50	Bolivia	48.5	34	63
7=	Canada	60.5	78	43	51	Estonia	48.0	62	34
7=	Switzerland	60.5	78	43	52	Fiji	48.0	50	46
9	Belize	57.0	50	64	53	Belarus	48.0	46	50
10	Guyana	57.0	51	63	54	Poland	47.5	65	30
11	Uruguay	56.5	61	52	55	Argentina	47.5	55	40
12	Germany	56.5	77	36	56	Dominican Rep.	47.5	49	46
13	Denmark	56.0	81	31	58	Korea, South	47.0	67	27
14	New Zealand	55.5	73	38	59	Barbados	47.0	62	32
15	Suriname	55.0	52	58	60	Cape Verde	47.0	47	47
16	Latvia	54.0	62	46	61	Spain	46.5	73	20
17	Ireland	54.0	76	32	62	Samoa	46.5	43	50
18	Australia	53.5	79	28	63	Nepal	46.0	28	64
19	Peru	53.0	44	62	64	Croatia	45.0	57	33
20	Slovenia	53.0	71	35	65	Russian Federation	45.0	48	42
22	Lithuania	52.5	61	44	66	Gabon	45.0	28	62
23	Cyprus	52.5	67	38	67	Bulgaria	44.5	58	31
24	Japan	52.5	80	25	68	Jamaica	44.5	54	35
27	United States	52.0	73	31	69	Panama	44.5	52	37
28	Italy	52.0	74	30	71	Georgia	44.5	48	41
29	France	52.0	75	29	73	Venezuela	44.5	43	46
30=	Czech Republic	51.5	70	33	74	Macedonia, FYR	44.0	46	42
30=	Greece	51.5	70	33	75	Namibia	44.0	34	54
32	Portugal	51.5	72	31	76	Togo	43.5	21	66
33	United Kingdom	51.5	73	30	77	Congo, Republic	43.5	15	72
34	Belgium	51.5	80	23	79	Chile	42.5	55	30
35	Botswana	51.0	34	68	80	Trinidad & Tobago	42.5	53	32
36	Slovakia	50.5	61	40	81	Colombia	42.5	43	42
37	Luxembourg	50.5	77	24	82	Cuba	42.5	40	45
38=	Armenia	50.0	45	55	84	Malta	42.0	70	14
38=	Netherlands	50.0	78	22	85	Israel	42.0	59	25
41	Ecuador	49.5	43	56	86	Albania	42.0	38	46
42	Mongolia	49.5	39	60	87	Indonesia	42.0	36	48
43	Singapore	49.0	66	32	88	Malawi	42.0	22	62
44	Hungary	49.0	65	33	89	Egypt	41.0	39	43

Wellbeing of nations: 2

Key words

ecosystem

The Wellbeing Index (continued)

a ranking (= joint) **b** country **c** wellbeing index points **d** human wellbeing index points **e** ecosystem wellbeing index points

a	b	c	d	e	a	b	c	d	e
90	El Salvador	41.0	36	46	132	Tanzania	36.0	18	54
91	Central African Rep	41.0	16	66	133	Nigeria	36.0	16	56
92	Brazil	40.5	45	36	134	Chad	36.0	13	59
93	Paraguay	40.5	35	46	135	Congo, Dem. Rep.	36.0	7	65
94	Lesotho	40.5	24	57	136	South Africa	35.0	43	27
95	Guinea	40.5	15	66	137	Azerbaijan	35.0	42	28
96	Bhutan	40.5	14	67	138	Iran	35.0	38	32
97	Romania	40.0	50	30	139	Myanmar	35.0	21	49
98	Kyrgyzstan	40.0	38	42	140	Eritrea	35.0	10	60
99	Malaysia	39.5	46	33	143	Kenya	34.5	18	51
100	Yugoslavia	39.5	42	37	144	Rwanda	34.5	12	57
101	Cameroon	39.5	15	64	145	Sierra Leone	34.5	6	63
102	Guinea-Bissau	39.5	13	66	146	Morocco	34.0	36	32
103	Honduras	39.0	33	45	147	Tajikistan	33.5	28	39
104	Swaziland	39.0	24	54	148	Guatemala	33.5	23	44
105	Zimbabwe	39.0	23	55	149	Niger	33.5	11	56
106	Djibouti	39.0	18	60	150	Mexico	33.0	45	21
107	Gambia	39.0	16	62	151	Jordan	33.0	38	28
108	Laos	39.0	15	63	152	Uzbekistan	33.0	36	30
109	Lebanon	38.5	40	37	154	Yemen	33.0	15	51
110=	Nicaragua	38.5	28	49	155	Mozambique	33.0	11	55
110=	Vietnam	38.5	28	49	156	Burundi	33.0	6	60
112=	Cambodia	38.5	20	57	157	Mali	32.5	21	44
112=	Côte d'Ivoire	38.5	20	57	160	China	32.0	36	28
115	Ethiopia	38.5	13	64	164	Libya	31.0	38	24
116=	Philippines	38.0	44	32	165	Turkmenistan	31.0	32	30
116=	Tunisia	38.0	44	32	166	Haiti	31.0	19	43
118	Moldova	38.0	41	35	167	Pakistan	31.0	18	44
119	Kuwait	37.5	50	25	168	Ghana	30.0	22	38
120	Kazakhstan	37.5	43	32	169	Oman	29.5	31	28
121	Papua New Guinea	37.5	22	53	170	Zambia	29.5	16	43
122	Burkina Faso	37.5	17	58	171	Sudan	29.5	13	46
123	Angola	37.5	8	67	172	India	29.0	31	27
124	Madagascar	37.0	24	50	173	United Arab Emirates	28.5	41	16
125	Senegal	37.0	20	54	174	Mauritania	28.5	17	40
127	Thailand	36.5	50	23	176	Saudi Arabia	27.0	31	23
128	Ukraine	36.5	47	26	177	Uganda	27.0	10	44
129	Turkey	36.5	45	28	179	Syria	26.5	28	25
130	Algeria	36.5	29	44	180	Iraq	25.0	19	31
131	Bangladesh	36.5	27	46					

Highest scoring countries

- Sweden, Finland, and Norway are the top three countries on the comparison of national wellbeing table, each with scores above 60 points.
- One of the reasons for the high scoring of Sweden is its comprehensive welfare system that provides free schooling, childcare, healthcare, pensions, care for the elderly, and social services.
- This boosts the human wellbeing index score and gives a high overall result even though the ecosystem wellbeing score is below that of some other countries.
- Sweden's "cradle to the grave" approach to the welfare of its citizens is the key to its high ranking.

Developing nations

- Some developing nations, for example Belize and Guyana, appear high up on the comparison of national wellbeing table.
- These countries do not have a standard of living close to that of Sweden, Finland or Norway. They do however have high ecosystem wellbeing scores that compensate for the lower human wellbeing scores and increase their overall points.

Lowest scoring countries

- Some lower scoring countries on the table are India with 29, Uganda with 27, and Syria with 26.5 points.
- There are many reasons why some countries have very low wellbeing index scores, including war, poverty, political instability, and oppressive regimes.

Key words

GDP
per capita
recycling

Increasing municipal waste

- In 2004, the global total of municipal waste generated was two billion tons, an increase of seven percent on 2003.
- In general, more affluent societies generate more municipal waste than less affluent societies.
- A 40 percent increase since 1980 in the GDP of countries belonging to the Organisation for Economic Co-operation and Development (OECD) has been accompanied by a 40 percent increase in municipal waste.

Social trends

- Certain social trends, such as an increase in single-person households and aging populations, leads to higher per capita waste.
- Many people in developed nations, especially in cities, demand pre-packaged foods for convenience, further adding to the waste problem.

Recycling

- The level of recycling in industrialized countries is still very low and is not keeping pace with waste increases.
- The countries that recycle the most are Switzerland with 40 percent and Austria with 20 percent.
- Switzerland recycles more than 80 percent of its glass. The United States and Canada recycle only about 20 percent.

Global municipal waste

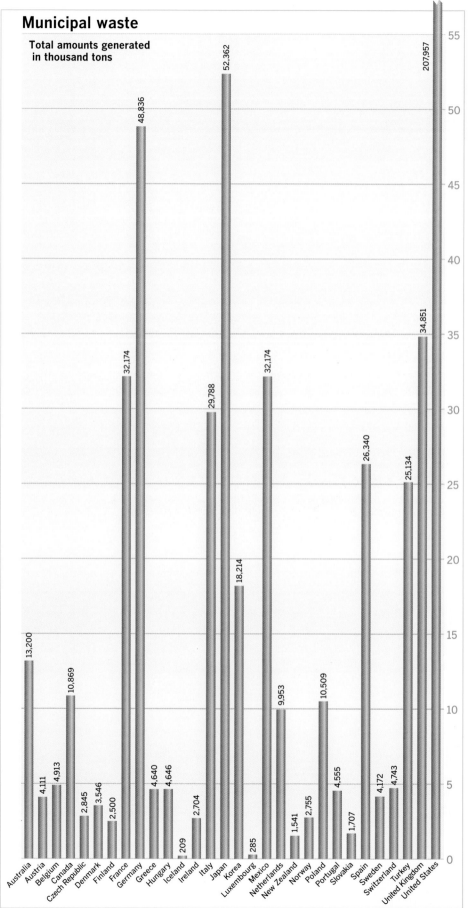

Municipal waste

Total amounts generated in thousand tons

Country	Thousand tons
Australia	13,200
Austria	4,111
Belgium	4,913
Canada	10,869
Czech Republic	2,845
Denmark	3,546
Finland	2,500
France	32,174
Germany	48,836
Greece	4,640
Hungary	4,646
Iceland	209
Ireland	2,704
Italy	29,788
Japan	52,362
Korea	18,214
Luxembourg	285
Mexico	32,174
Netherlands	9,953
New Zealand	1,541
Norway	2,755
Poland	10,509
Portugal	4,555
Slovakia	1,707
Spain	26,340
Sweden	4,172
Switzerland	4,743
Turkey	25,134
United Kingdom	34,851
United States	207,957

International aid

Key words

debt relief	Official
national debt	Development
non-governmental	Assistance
organization	(ODA)
(NGO)	

Major donor countries

ODA given = more than $1 billion in 2004

Canada	France	Italy	Netherlands	Spain	United Kingdom
Denmark	Germany	Japan	Norway	Sweden	United States

Major recipient countries

net ODA received = more than $100 million in 2003

Albania	Iran	Mongolia	Slovakia
Algeria	Iraq	Morocco	Somalia
Angola	Israel	Mozambique	South Africa
Armenia	Jordan	Myanmar	Sri Lanka
Azerbaijan	Kazakhstan	Namibia	Sudan
Bangladesh	Kenya	Nepal	Suriname
Barbados	Korea, North	Nicaragua	Syria
Belize	Kyrgyzstan	Niger	Tajikistan
Benin	Laos	Nigeria	Tanzania
Bolivia	Latvia	Pakistan	Tunisia
Bosnia-Herzegovina	Lebanon	Palestinian Territories	Turkey
Brazil	Liberia	Papua New Guinea	Uganda
Bulgaria	Lithuania	Peru	Ukraine
Burkina Faso	Macedonia, FYR	Philippines	Uzbekistan
Cambodia	Madagascar	Poland	Vietnam
Cameroon	Malawi	Romania	Yemen
Chad	Mali	Russia	Yugoslavia
China	Mauritania	Rwanda	Zambia
Colombia	Mexico	Senegal	Zimbabwe
Indonesia	Moldova	Sierra Leone	

Economic aid

- Many of the more affluent countries of the world now routinely give aid in the form of economic and humanitarian assistance to poorer countries. This is known as *Official Development Assistance* (ODA).
- This assistance is used to help relieve national debt, to assist with development, or to provide aid after a natural or man-made disaster.
- By relieving some of the financial burden on poverty-stricken countries, aid may allow these countries to invest more time and money in their environmental health, something of low national priority.

Use of resources

- The more developing nations stay in debt, the more they will be forced to use their environmental resources unsustainably.
- A country in debt is also less able to spend money on improving infrastructure: social, educational, health, environmental, and employment programs all suffer as a direct result of debt.

NGOs

- There are also many non-governmental organizations (NGOs) that provide international aid.
- NGOs such as CARE and Oxfam work toward providing aid to needy people in developing countries.
- Often, they concentrate their efforts in specific areas such as helping children, providing safe water, or helping to distribute food during famine or war.

Key words

*Official
Development
Assistance
(ODA)*

ODA donor countries

- Official Development Assistance (ODA) refers to aid from the governments of the wealthy nations, and does not include private contributions or investments.
- The main objective of ODA is to promote development in poor countries.
- It is seen by some as a measure of the priority that governments give to helping others.

Agenda 21

- In 1992 the world's governments met at the Earth Summit in Rio de Janeiro.
- A program called "Agenda 21" was adopted, to be directed by the United Nations.
- Within this program an ODA aid target of 0.7 percent *gross national income* (*GNI*) was set for rich nations.
- Even though 22 countries signed up to these targets and agendas, almost all of them have consistently failed to reach the agreed target.
- For many countries, the amount of aid has been around 0.2–0.4 percent (or around $100 billion) short of the pledge.
- In 2004 only five countries had given 0.7 percent GNI or more: Denmark, Luxembourg, Netherlands, Norway, and Sweden.

Percentage of GNI

- As a percentage of GNI, the United States has almost always given less than any other industrialized nation, although in actual amounts it is the biggest donor.
- For years Japan was the world leader in aid provision, though the amount it donates has dropped recently.

Official development assistance

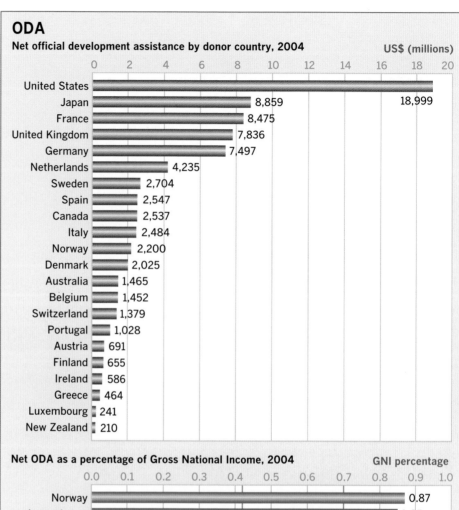

ODA

Net official development assistance by donor country, 2004　　US$ (millions)

Country	US$ (millions)
United States	18,999
Japan	8,859
France	8,475
United Kingdom	7,836
Germany	7,497
Netherlands	4,235
Sweden	2,704
Spain	2,547
Canada	2,537
Italy	2,484
Norway	2,200
Denmark	2,025
Australia	1,465
Belgium	1,452
Switzerland	1,379
Portugal	1,028
Austria	691
Finland	655
Ireland	586
Greece	464
Luxembourg	241
New Zealand	210

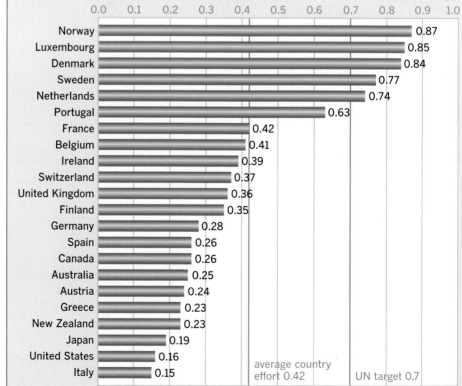

Net ODA as a percentage of Gross National Income, 2004　　GNI percentage

Country	GNI percentage
Norway	0.87
Luxembourg	0.85
Denmark	0.84
Sweden	0.77
Netherlands	0.74
Portugal	0.63
France	0.42
Belgium	0.41
Ireland	0.39
Switzerland	0.37
United Kingdom	0.36
Finland	0.35
Germany	0.28
Spain	0.26
Canada	0.26
Australia	0.25
Austria	0.24
Greece	0.23
New Zealand	0.23
Japan	0.19
United States	0.16
Italy	0.15

average country effort 0.42　　UN target 0.7

Third World debt

Key words

debt relief

Most heavily indebted countries

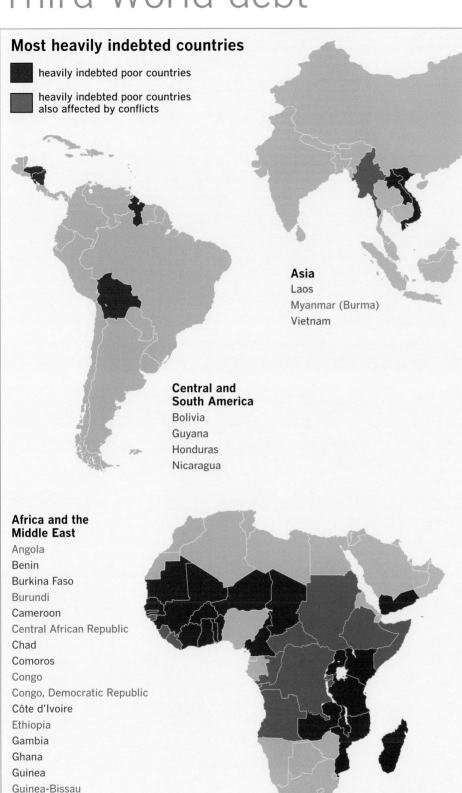

■ heavily indebted poor countries

■ heavily indebted poor countries also affected by conflicts

Asia
Laos
Myanmar (Burma)
Vietnam

Central and South America
Bolivia
Guyana
Honduras
Nicaragua

Africa and the Middle East
Angola
Benin
Burkina Faso
Burundi
Cameroon
Central African Republic
Chad
Comoros
Congo
Congo, Democratic Republic
Côte d'Ivoire
Ethiopia
Gambia
Ghana
Guinea
Guinea-Bissau
Kenya
Liberia
Madagascar
Malawi
Mali
Mauritania
Mozambique

Niger
Rwanda
Sierra Leone
São Tomé and Principe
Senegal
Somalia
Sudan

Tanzania
Togo
Uganda
Yemen
Zambia

Debt repayments

- Each year, the developing world gives Western countries nine times more in debt repayments than it receives in aid.
- Heavily indebted poor countries are caught in a downward spiral of debt service, which diverts resources away from economic development.
- Forced to meet the debt repayments, countries sacrifice health, education, and environmental programs.
- Africa spends four times as much on debt repayments as on healthcare.

Environmental pressures

- Countries with large debt burdens put more pressure on the environment as the need to generate money to pay debts increases.

Debt relief program

- The Heavily Indebted Poor Countries (HIPC) Initiative was launched in 1996 with the aim of ensuring that no poor country faces a debt burden it cannot manage.
- The World Bank and the International Monetary Fund (IMF) have identified 42 countries as having unsustainable debts.
- Of these countries, 13 are affected by conflicts.
- By 2004, debt relief packages were approved for 27 countries, 23 of them in Africa.
- To relieve the debt of the 20 worst affected countries would cost between $5.5 billion and $7.7 billion. This is less than the cost of development of a single Stealth Bomber.

© Diagram Visual Information Ltd.

Key words

hydroelectric
  power

Narmada Valley project

- The Narmada Valley Development Project started in the 1960s and is the single largest river development scheme in India.
- It is one of the largest hydroelectric projects in the world and involves the construction of more than 3,000 dams of various size.
- It is likely to displace a total of around 1.5 million people from three states (Gujarat, Maharashtra, and Madhya Pradesh).
- Environmentalists believe that the cost to the environment will be huge.

Sardar Sarovar

- The Sardar Sarovar dam is the largest single dam under construction with a proposed height of 360 feet (110 m).
- If completed, the dam will flood more than 91,400 acres (37,000 ha) of forest and agricultural land, displacing up to half a million people.

Displacement

- Many of those affected by the project are tribal people (Adivasis and Dalits).
- Most will not get compensation for resettlement and rehabilitation because the government views their occupation of the land as illegal.
- People who live downstream and whose lives are affected are not entitled to any compensation.

Controversial project

- The Narmada project continues to face increasing opposition both at home and abroad.
- The World Bank, which originally supported the project, withdrew its funding after an independent review.

Environmental refugees: Narmada Valley development, India

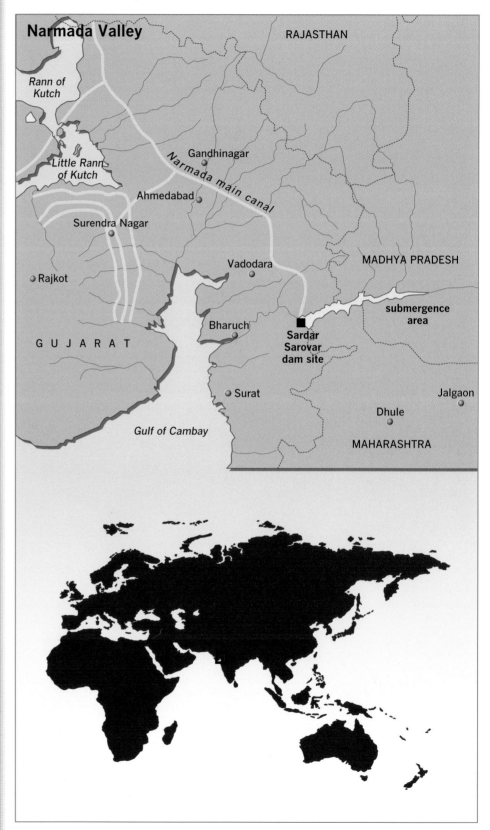

Environmental refugees: forced resettlement in Indonesia

Displaced persons throughout Indonesia

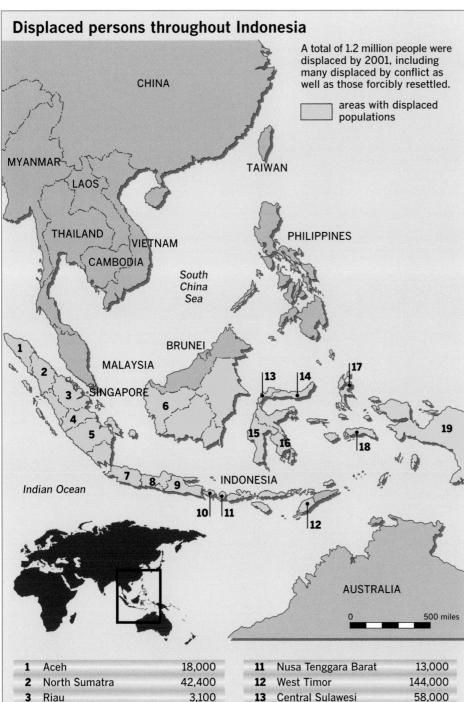

A total of 1.2 million people were displaced by 2001, including many displaced by conflict as well as those forcibly resettled.

☐ areas with displaced populations

1	Aceh	18,000
2	North Sumatra	42,400
3	Riau	3,100
4	Jambi	2,100
5	South Sumatra	1,700
6	West Kalimantan	69,000
7	West Java	9,300
8	Central Java	13,300
9	East Java	166,000
10	Bali	3,000
11	Nusa Tenggara Barat	13,000
12	West Timor	144,000
13	Central Sulawesi	58,000
14	North Sulawesi	40,000
15	South Sulawesi	36,100
16	Southeast Sulawesi	161,000
17	North Moluccas	166,300
18	Moluccas	300,000
19	Irian Jaya	17,000

Conflict

- Since 1999, serious conflicts and population displacement have occurred in the Moluccas, Kalimantan, Sulawesi, Aceh, Timor, and Irian Jaya.
- The problems have been exacerbated by Indonesia's political and economic crisis.
- The conflict in each of these regions has been fueled by resentments stemming from Indonesia's former policy of relocations, under which residents of Java and other heavily crowded islands were forcibly moved to less populated areas.

Relocation

- The relocation program forced indigenous people in areas receiving immigrants to cede social and economic rights such as traditional rights to land, water, and other natural resources in favor of the migrants.

The result

- In 2001, there were more than 1.2 million Internationally Displaced Persons (IDPs) throughout Indonesia.
- These included at least 460,000 IDPs in the Moluccas, more than 179,000 in Sulawesi; up to 18,000 in Aceh, and more than 42,000 Acehnese IDPs in other areas of North Sumatra.
- Instability in the region continued into 2005, and shows no signs of ending.

Tsunami

- The tsunami that devastated Aceh in December 2004 has further added to the problems there by making more people homeless.

Key words

UNHCR

Severe drought

- Several years of intermittent rains resulted in poor harvests and have produced a severe drought in the Horn of Africa.
- The drought, which by 2005 was in its sixth continuous year, has affected millions of people throughout the region.
- Worst hit is southern and eastern Ethiopia, southern Somalia, and northern Kenya.
- Other countries affected by the drought include Eritrea, Djibouti, and Sudan.

Consequences of drought

- The drought conditions have resulted in a serious deterioration of food security, the loss of livestock and agriculture, and decreased livestock prices.
- Migration and cross-border movements have further strained resources, as people search for additional pasture and external assistance.

Increased competition

- Decreased and limited resources have led to increased tensions and competition in many drought-affected areas.
- The drought-affected populations by country in 2001 were: ten million in Ethiopia; 2.2 million in Kenya; 750,000 in Somalia; 335,000 in Eritrea; and 150,000 in Djibouti.

Appeal for aid

- In 2004, the president of Kenya, Mwai Kibaki, declared a national disaster in parts of the country.
- He appealed for $118 million in emergency aid to help feed approximately 3.3 million Kenyans facing food shortages.

Environmental refugees: famine, Horn of Africa

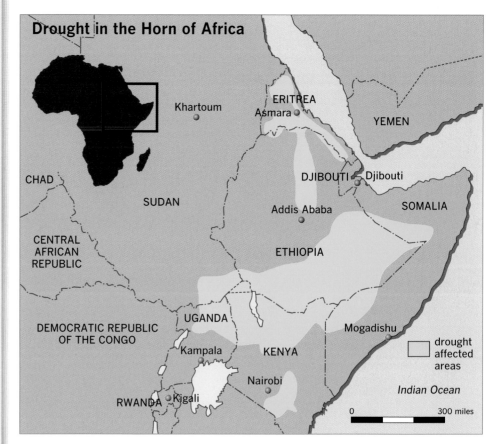

Drought in the Horn of Africa

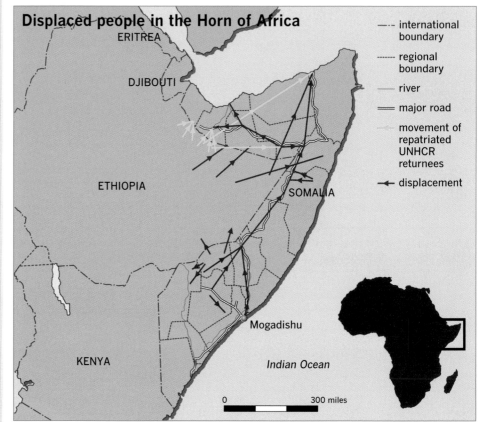

Displaced people in the Horn of Africa

Environmental refugees: Central Africa

Key words

genocide

Great lakes region and affected countries

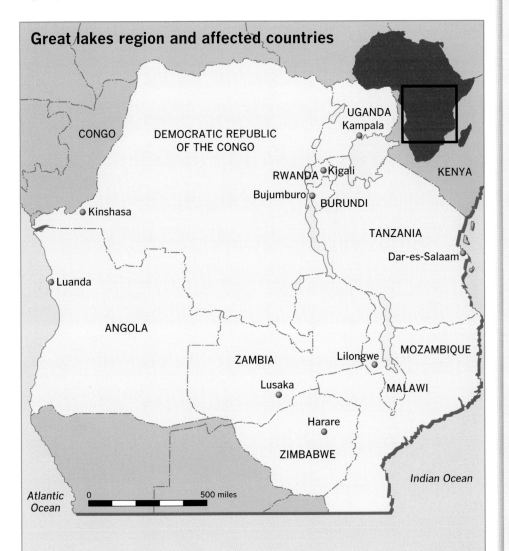

Host country	Refugee numbers and origin			IDP figures
Angola	11,830 DRC	74 *Rwanda*	6 *Burundi*	
Burundi	28,800			432,818
Congo, Democratic Republic	361,720			2,045,000
Malawi	1,817 DRC	2,706 *Rwanda*	824 *Burundi*	
Mozambique	1,444 DRC	266 *Rwanda*	652 *Burundi*	
Rwanda	33,934			
Tanzania	543,145			
Uganda	175,819			535,107
Zambia	52,071 DRC	5,223 *Rwanda*	2,008 *Burundi*	
Zimbabwe	4,092 DRC	2,729 *Rwanda*	824 *Burundi*	

Genocide in Rwanda

- The Rwandan genocide (1994) sparked massive population shifts in the country and across the Great Lakes Region (GLR).
- Millions of people became displaced and scattered in the wake of the mass murders and displacement caused by the conflict.
- The landscape of human settlement was consequently completely altered.

After the conflict

- Following the horrific events in Rwanda, the GLR is still affected by the ongoing wars in Burundi and the Democratic Republic of the Congo (DRC, formerly Zaire).
- Most of the 1.2 million Rwandans who left their country for Zaire or Tanzania at the time of the conflict have returned, though tens of thousands are still refugees.

Displaced people

- At the end of 2001, approximately one million people from the region were refugees, and a further three million were displaced within their own countries.
- Many people have been displaced as a result of the ongoing conflict in the DRC, as well as those who are refugees from ethnic persecution in Rwanda and Burundi.

Returnees

- Many of the refugees have managed to return home but have not received any land or help.
- Most of the returnees are the poorest in their communities, without access to shelter, healthcare, or education for their children.

© Diagram Visual Information Ltd.

Key words

*Food and
Agriculture
Organization
(FAO)*

Progress at the price

● There has been much progress in feeding the world in the last 30 years.
● However, the intensification of agriculture has had a profound impact on the environment.

Food shortages

● The UN Food and Agriculture Organization (FAO) estimates that total food production will grow at about 1.5 percent per annum over the next 30 years, ahead of the expected population growth of 1.3 percent per year.
● Despite this, about 800 million people still go hungry every day because food is not available where it is most needed.

Food imports

● Developing nations will become increasingly dependent on imports of certain foods.
● Net cereal imports are expected to rise from 107 million tons in 1995–97 to 270 million by 2030.

Overfishing

● Average world consumption of fish per person could grow from 35 pounds (16 kg) per year in 1997 to 41–44 pounds (19–20 kg) by 2030.
● This would raise the total food use of fish to 150 million tons per year.
● The sustainable yield of marine creatures is currently estimated at only 100 million tons.

Water

● Freshwater sources are dwindling or becoming contaminated throughout the world.
● There is currently 500 billion cubic feet (14 billion m³) of freshwater available for human use annually, but it is very unevenly distributed, with two thirds of the population receiving only one quarter of its rainfall.

Food and water supply

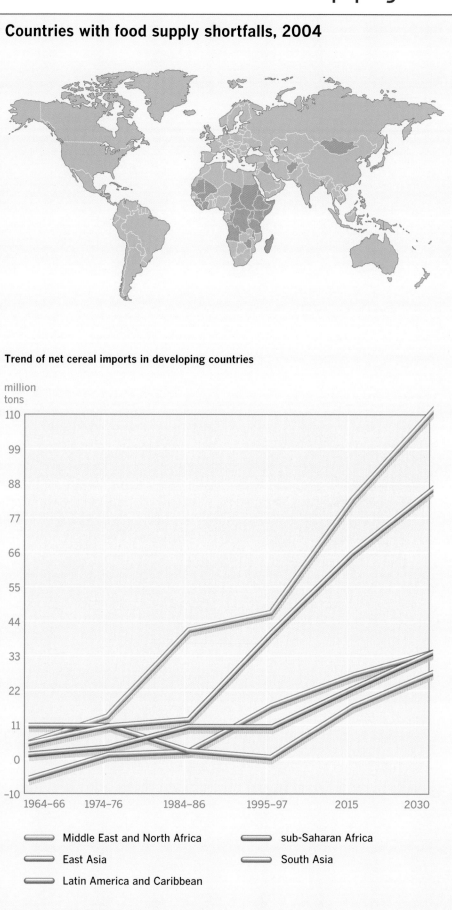

Countries with food supply shortfalls, 2004

Trend of net cereal imports in developing countries

million tons

Legend:
- Middle East and North Africa
- East Asia
- Latin America and Caribbean
- sub-Saharan Africa
- South Asia

Origins of agriculture

Key words

gene bank
genetic diversity
global warming

Geographic origins of agriculture

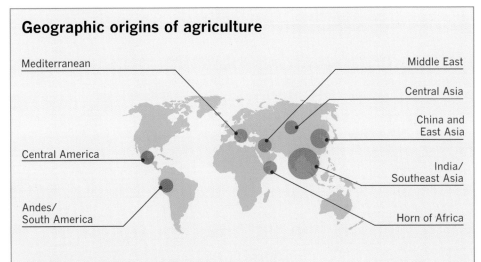

Mediterranean

Middle East

Central Asia

China and East Asia

Central America

India/ Southeast Asia

Andes/ South America

Horn of Africa

Origins of plants cultivated as crops

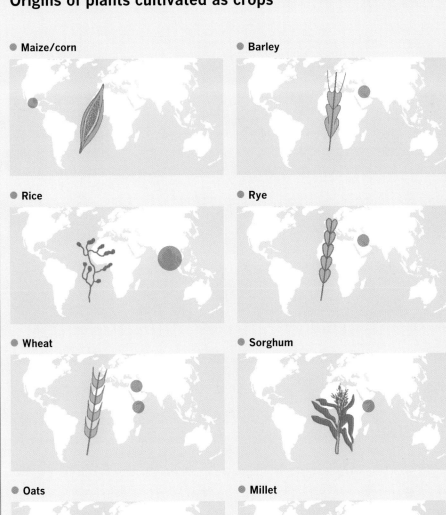

● Maize/corn

● Barley

● Rice

● Rye

● Wheat

● Sorghum

● Oats

● Millet

Domestication of food plants

● Of 270,000 plants known to exist, only 7,000 have ever been cultivated as food.

● Of those 7,000, only 120 are widely cultivated today.

● Of these 120, nine species provide 75 percent of human food and 21 species provide 20 percent.

Genetic diversity

● Crop genetic diversity is disappearing from fields at an estimated 1–2 percent per year.

● Many of the traditional plant varieties can now be found only in gene banks.

● The ability of different plant varieties to grow in different conditions depends on their genes.

● Some plants are better able to withstand drought, grow on poor soil, resist insects and disease, or prosper in local environments or under global warming.

● As the genetic diversity of food crops decreases, they become more susceptible to disease, attack from insects, or changes in environmental conditions.

Corn

● Corn probably originated in Central America or Mexico, where it has been cultivated for more than 5,600 years.

● The wild corn plant, from which present-day varieties have arisen, no longer exists.

Wheat

● Wheat probably originated in the Middle East, and is currently grown on more land area worldwide than any other crop.

● Primitive wheat relatives have been found that date from 9,000 years ago.

© Diagram Visual Information Ltd.

Key words

sub-Saharan
  Africa

Potato and potato blight

- Potatoes originated in the Andes mountains of Bolivia and Peru, and have been cultivated for at least 2,400 years.
- The potato was taken to Europe in the sixteenth century and was cultivated heavily in Ireland, quickly becoming the staple food.
- Potato blight in Ireland caused by a fungus spread through the crop, causing it to fail in successive harvests in 1845–49.
- This resulted in famine and mass emigration.

Cassava and the mealybug

- Cassava originated in Brazil and Paraguay and is grown for its enlarged starch-filled roots, which are eaten much like potatoes.
- Cassava cannot be eaten raw because of the toxic levels of cyanide it contains.
- Today it is the staple food in most of sub-Saharan Africa, providing up to half the daily calories of 200 million people.
- In the 1970s an insect called the cassava mealybug threatened to destroy much of the African crop.
- The mealybug was eventually controlled by a species of wasp that uses the mealybug as a host for laying its eggs.

Rice

- Rice probably originated in northern Thailand or southern China around 4000 BCE.
- It is by far the most important food in the world, and has fed more people over a longer period of time than any other crop in history.

Food crops

Origins of plants cultivated as crops (continued)

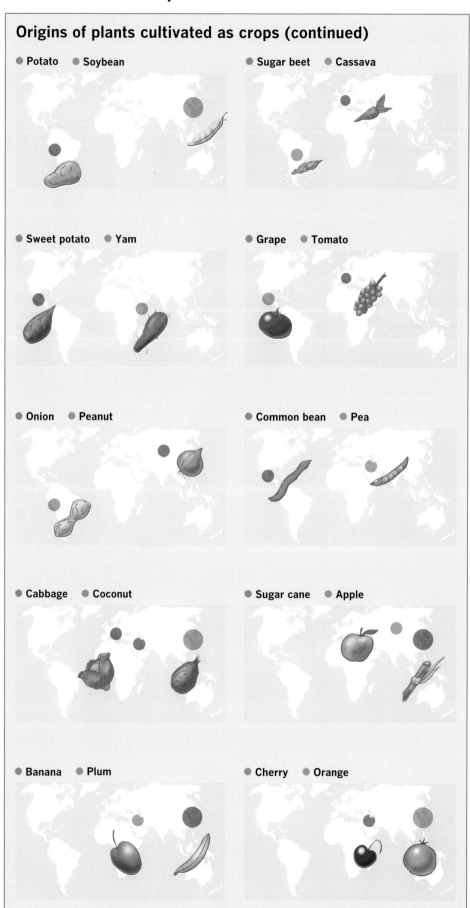

- Potato - Soybean
- Sugar beet - Cassava
- Sweet potato - Yam
- Grape - Tomato
- Onion - Peanut
- Common bean - Pea
- Cabbage - Coconut
- Sugar cane - Apple
- Banana - Plum
- Cherry - Orange

Origin of non-food crops

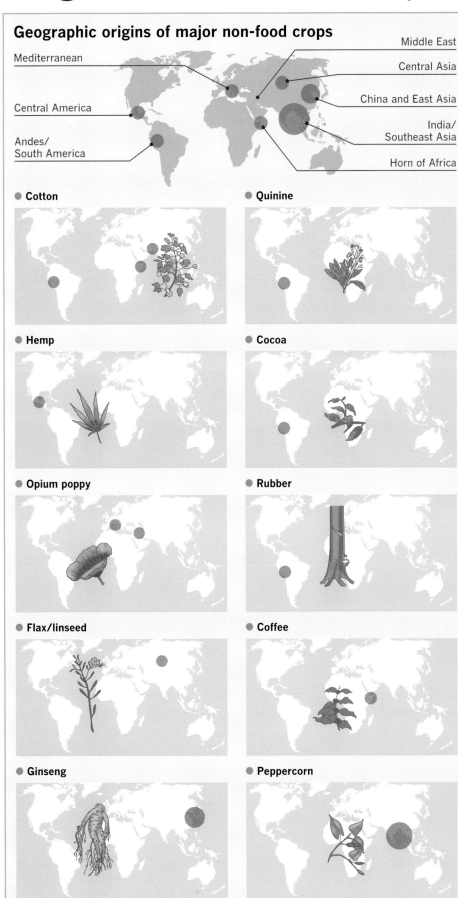

Geographic origins of major non-food crops

Mediterranean

Central America

Andes/
South America

Middle East

Central Asia

China and East Asia

India/
Southeast Asia

Horn of Africa

- Cotton
- Quinine
- Hemp
- Cocoa
- Opium poppy
- Rubber
- Flax/linseed
- Coffee
- Ginseng
- Peppercorn

Key words

cash crop
habitat

Coffee

- The coffee bean was discovered in eastern Africa about 1,000 years ago.
- As a drink, it quickly spread around the world as a luxury commodity and stimulant.
- Today, coffee is a global industry employing more than 20 million people.
- In many tropical countries, natural habitats are being destroyed to grow cash crops such as coffee.

Cotton

- Cotton can be traced back to East Africa, Western Asia, and South America circa 3200 BCE.
- It is the fruit of a shrubby plant called the cotton plant.
- Cotton production and trade are very important to many poorer countries.
- Of the 85 cotton-producing countries in the world in 2005, 80 were developing nations.

Pepper

- Pepper originated as a spice almost 3,000 years ago in India.
- It quickly became very valuable, and during the Middle Ages, was worth more than its weight in gold, and was sometimes used as currency.
- Today it is still one of the most widely traded spices in the world, making up around 25 percent of the spice trade.
- It is grown only in a few countries within 15 degrees of the equator.

Rubber

- Rubber is made from latex, which is the sap of various plants, most notably the rubber tree.
- It is thought that rubber originated with the Mayan people of South America who used the latex to make rubber balls and bindings for tools.
- Today, most rubber is synthetic, although the natural product is still produced in Southeast Asia.

© Diagram Visual Information Ltd.

Key words

extinction

Domestication of animals

- Humans have domesticated animals using selective breeding for thousands of years.
- Domesticated animals such as sheep, horses, chickens, and cattle are used for food or to help with production and transport.
- Domestication arises when humans interact sufficiently with an animal species to have a direct influence on how they breed and how they survive.
- Different animals have been domesticated at different times in history.

The sheep

- Present-day sheep breeds originated in Mesopotamia (now Iraq).
- They all have a common ancestor, the mouflon, which still lives in the wild in Europe.
- It is thought that sheep farming for wool, a renewable source of clothing and trade, is humanity's oldest industry.
- Sheep are also kept for their meat.

The horse

- The horse was domesticated around 6,000 years ago in Central Asia.
- Since then it has been used extensively all over the world for transport, warfare, and food.
- The Przewalski wild horse from Mongolia is the only true wild horse. All domesticated horses are descended from it.
- It became extinct in the wild in the 1960s, but was reintroduced in small numbers in the 1990s.

Origin of livestock

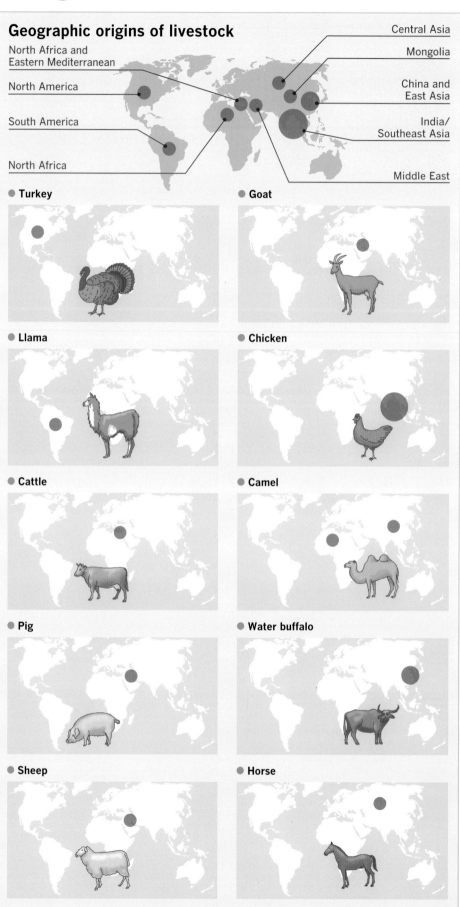

Geographic origins of livestock

North Africa and Eastern Mediterranean

North America

South America

North Africa

Central Asia

Mongolia

China and East Asia

India/ Southeast Asia

Middle East

- Turkey
- Llama
- Cattle
- Pig
- Sheep
- Goat
- Chicken
- Camel
- Water buffalo
- Horse

Vavilov Centers of crop diversity

Key words

gene bank
genetic diversity
in vitro

Vavilov Centers of high crop diversity

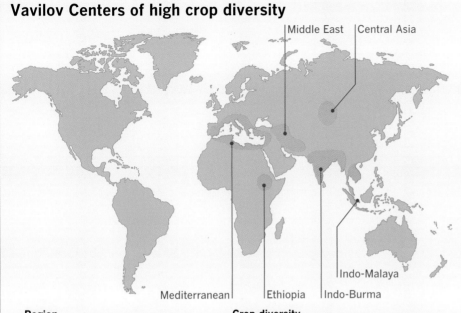

Region	Crop diversity
Ethiopia	barley, coffee, sorghum, wheat
Mediterranean	oats, olives, wheat
Middle East	barley, lentil, oats, wheat
Central Asia	apple, chickpea, lentil
Indo-Burma	eggplant, rice, yam
Indo-Malaya	banana, coconut, sugar cane

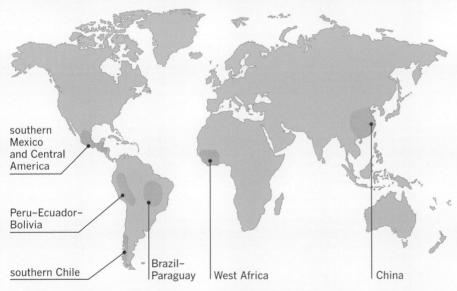

Region	Crop diversity
China	sorghum, millet, soybean
southern Mexico and Central America	bean, corn, tomato
Peru-Ecuador-Bolivia	bean, potato, squash
southern Chile	potato
Brazil-Paraguay	peanut
West Africa	millet, sorghum

Vavilov Centers

- Some areas of the world have been identified as prime locations for the preservation of the genetic diversity of crops.
- These regions are known as *Vavilov Centers of Diversity* after Nikolai Ivanovich Vavilov (1887–1943), the Russian botanist who first described the patterns.
- The Vavilov Centers are important because they contain different varieties of crops in the field.

Center characteristics

- The centers of crop diversity are characterized by a long agricultural history, ecological diversity, mountainous terrain, cultural diversity, and a lack of heavy forest cover.
- The crop centers are not necessarily located where the crop originated or was first domesticated, but where the crops are most diverse today.
- Wheat and barley were domesticated in southwest Asia, but a current center of their diversity is in Ethiopia.

Different crops

- The different Vavilov Centers were chosen to represent different crop types after numerous collecting expeditions to those locations.
- Ethiopia was explored by Vavilov in 1927 and was established as an important area and center of origin and variety for coffee, barley, sorghum, and millet.
- China was recorded as the earliest and largest independent center.
- It was credited with important millets, soya beans, and sorghum—with 136 species listed altogether.

Key words

drought   pesticide
fertilizer
Green Revolution
irrigation
per capita

Agriculture and livestock

● Of the world's agricultural land, only around a third is used to grow crops.

● The remaining two thirds are dedicated to livestock pasture.

● The world has doubled food production in the past 35 years— more than keeping pace with population growth.

Green Revolution

● The Green Revolution was a term coined by the Agency for International Development in 1968.

● It was a concentrated drive to eliminate hunger by increasing crop yields through new crop cultivars, irrigation, fertilizers, pesticides, and mechanization.

● However, the rate of increase of crop yields has slowed in the last ten years, and per capita productivity has declined in some regions.

● The modern methods used to increase yields with pesticides and fertilizers have caused many environmental problems and the overall cost of production has risen.

Poor quality land

● From the graphs it can be seen that land productivity in many developing countries falls well below that of North America and the other developed nations.

● The main problem facing many of the world's poorest people is that they live in areas with climatic and ecological conditions unsuitable for agriculture.

● These areas include arid uplands in the Middle East and large tracts of drought-afflicted areas of Africa and India.

Land productivity

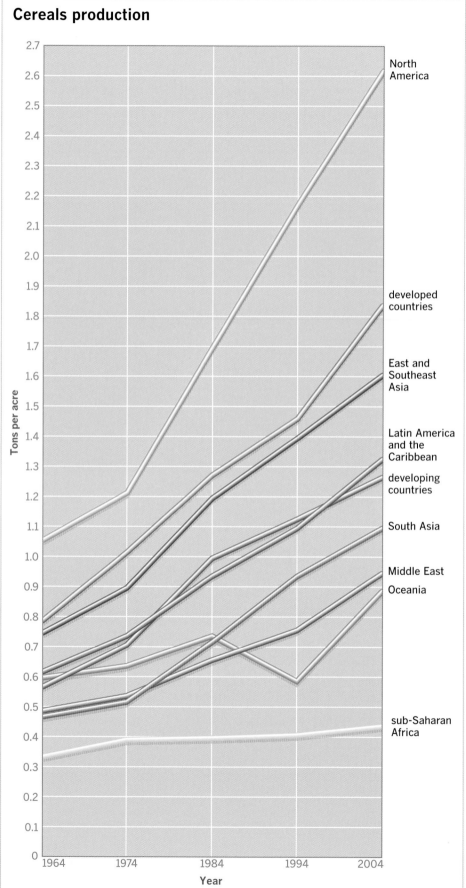

Cereals production

Land use and population

Key words

cash crop
ecosystem
irrigation
subsistence
urbanization

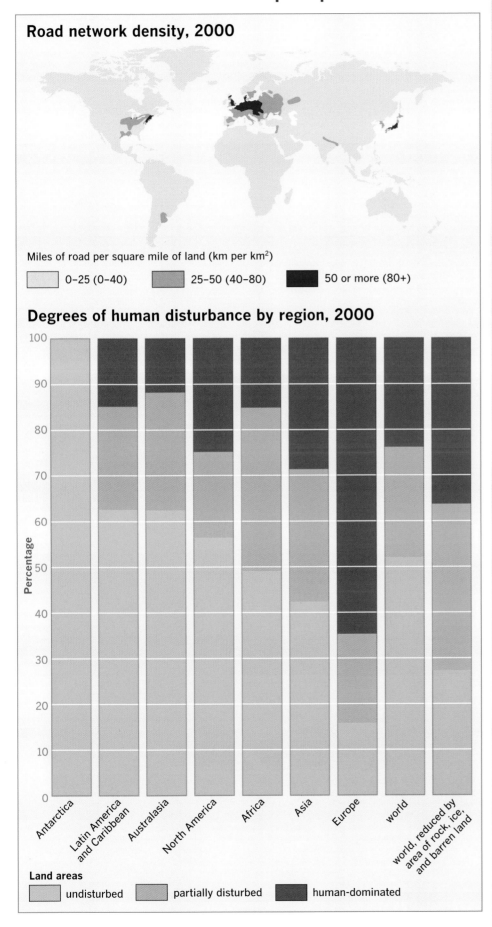

Road network density, 2000

Miles of road per square mile of land (km per km²)

☐ 0–25 (0–40)   ☐ 25–50 (40–80)   ■ 50 or more (80+)

Degrees of human disturbance by region, 2000

Percentage

Antarctica · Latin America and Caribbean · Australasia · North America · Africa · Asia · Europe · world · world, reduced by area of rock, ice, and barren land

Land areas

☐ undisturbed   ☐ partially disturbed   ■ human-dominated

Arable land change

- As the world population and the global economy grows, ever more land is cleared, drained, or irrigated for cash crops or livestock.
- The extension of arable land has been a response to fast-growing populations, with food production the main driving force.

Increasing cultivation

- The 60 years from 1860 to 1920 saw more than one billion acres (440 million ha) of land brought under cultivation, an area larger than India.
- Most of this took place in North America and the Soviet Union.
- A similar scale of transformation took place in the subsequent 60 years, from 1920 to 1980.
- By this time much of the potentially productive temperate lands of the Northern Hemisphere were occupied and the rate of population growth was slowing.
- The new "frontier lands," where population growth rates remained high, were in Africa, South Asia, and South America.

Urban land change

- The second half of the twentieth century saw an unprecedented covering of the landscape with concrete and macadam.
- This process continues to destroy and displace wildlife and causes major disruption to rivers and drainage by preventing natural seepage.
- Mining, industrial development, and urbanization have also contributed to the transformation of natural ecosystems into human landscapes.

Key words

chaco
deforestation
fertilizer

Converting land to farmland

- New land for arable farming is usually obtained through deforestation or the conversion of grazing pastures.
- In some areas of the world, huge tracts of land have been converted to farmlands.
- The largest areas of pastures converted to cropland have been in the Great Plains of the United States, the South African veldt, the Russian steppe, and the forests and pampas of Brazil and Argentina.
- With the potential for new colonization reduced in much of the world, farming has increasingly invested in intensification by an increased use of fertilizers, high-yield seeds, and machinery.

South American soybean

- Massive areas of land in South America are currently undergoing conversion to grow soybeans.
- Areas of natural forest, pampas grassland, and grazing pastures in Brazil, Argentina, Bolivia, Uruguay, and Paraguay have been converted and cleared to grow the crop, most of which is to be exported to China.
- It is thought that by 2020 South America could be the world's leading producer of soybean.
- Some of the land has been seized illegally and it is estimated that 15.5 million acres (6.3 million ha) of Argentine *chaco* could disappear over the next 15 years.
- Also, the soybean boom is responsible for the clearing of rainforest in parts of Brazil.
- Poor local farmers stand to gain little from soybean production, as it requires large tracts of continuous land to be grown efficiently.

Land use categories

Total world land use, 2000

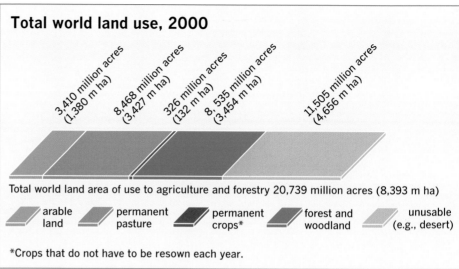

3,410 million acres
(1,380 m ha)

8,468 million acres
(3,427 m ha)

326 million acres
(132 m ha)

8, 535 million acres
(3,454 m ha)

11,505 million acres
(4,656 m ha)

Total world land area of use to agriculture and forestry 20,739 million acres (8,393 m ha)

- arable land
- permanent pasture
- permanent crops*
- forest and woodland
- unusable (e.g., desert)

*Crops that do not have to be resown each year.

Percentage regional land use, 2000

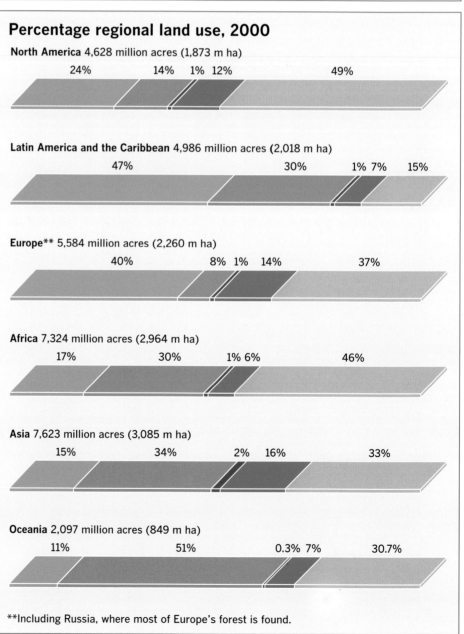

North America 4,628 million acres (1,873 m ha)

24%   14%   1%   12%   49%

Latin America and the Caribbean 4,986 million acres (2,018 m ha)

47%   30%   1%   7%   15%

Europe** 5,584 million acres (2,260 m ha)

40%   8%   1%   14%   37%

Africa 7,324 million acres (2,964 m ha)

17%   30%   1%   6%   46%

Asia 7,623 million acres (3,085 m ha)

15%   34%   2%   16%   33%

Oceania 2,097 million acres (849 m ha)

11%   51%   0.3%   7%   30.7%

**Including Russia, where most of Europe's forest is found.

Plant species used for food

Key words

gene bank
genetic diversity

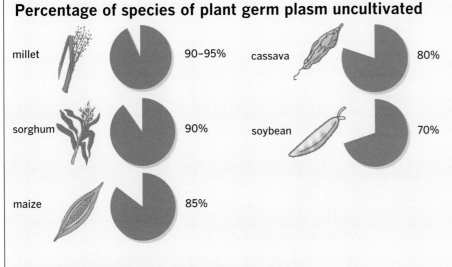

Percentage of species of plant germ plasm uncultivated

millet	90–95%
sorghum	90%
maize	85%
cassava	80%
soybean	70%

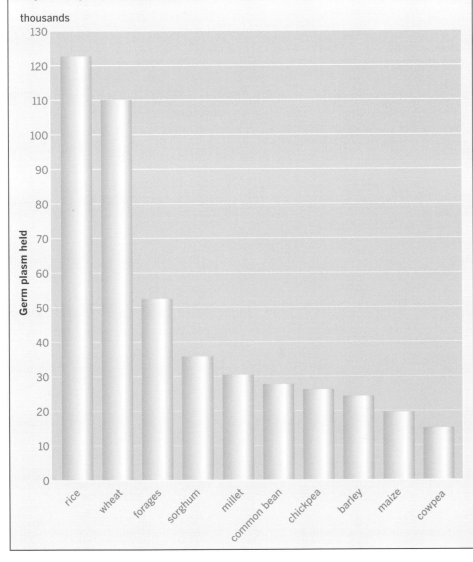

Germ plasm (reproductive tissue) of nutritionally important crops held by international centers

thousands

Y-axis: Germ plasm held (0–130)

X-axis: rice, wheat, forages, sorghum, millet, common bean, chickpea, barley, maize, cowpea

Important crops

- The world currently uses only a small fraction of the available plants for food.
- The most important food crops are rice, wheat, maize, sorghum, millet, potatoes, soybean, yams, and cassava.

Diversity of crops

- For thousands of years, farmers have bred new crop varieties and tailored their farming methods to maintain both a food supply and the fertility of their land.
- The result was a huge diversity of plant varieties and farming methods.
- Today, there are many considerations facing a producer who is choosing which crop variety to grow.
- The variety chosen depends on factors such as the location, year, time of seeding, disease pressure, soil conditions, temperature, weed control, precipitation, and fertility.

Lost diversity

- In the drive to standardize on a few high-yielding crop varieties, much diversity was lost from farms and genebanks, though this trend is now reversing.
- Around 70 percent of wild rice species and 90 percent of wild millet and sorghum species have yet to be collected and stored in genebanks.

Human diets

- The diets of human populations can be placed in three main dietary groups: grain eaters (the vast majority); root crop or plantain eaters; and meat and dairy produce eaters.
- With so much of the world's population relying heavily on grains and other crops, it is essential to maintain genetic crop diversity for successful future farming.

Key words

Green Revolution

Increasing food output
- Over the past four decades, the rate of worldwide food production has increased faster than the rate of world population growth.
- Gains in food availability have been greatest in the developing world, where the Green Revolution enabled a rise of 38 percent between 1961 and 1998 to 2,660 calories per person daily.

Cereal production
- Not all food output has increased: world cereal production per person has declined since 1984.
- This decline has been due to reductions in the area of cereal cropland under cultivation, particularly in the United States. The primary reason for this reduction has been the low world price of cereals in recent years.

Increasing demands
- By 2020, global demand for cereals is projected to increase by 41 percent and for meat by 63 percent.
- Much of the increase in demand is expected to occur in developing nations. However, in these nations food production is unlikely to keep pace with the increases in demand.

Unequal balance
- The developed world, with only a quarter of the world's population, still consumes around 49 percent of the world's agricultural products, partly because it converts more grain to meat.
- Even so, differences in food availability within the developing world are now greater than those between typical developed and developing nations.

World food output

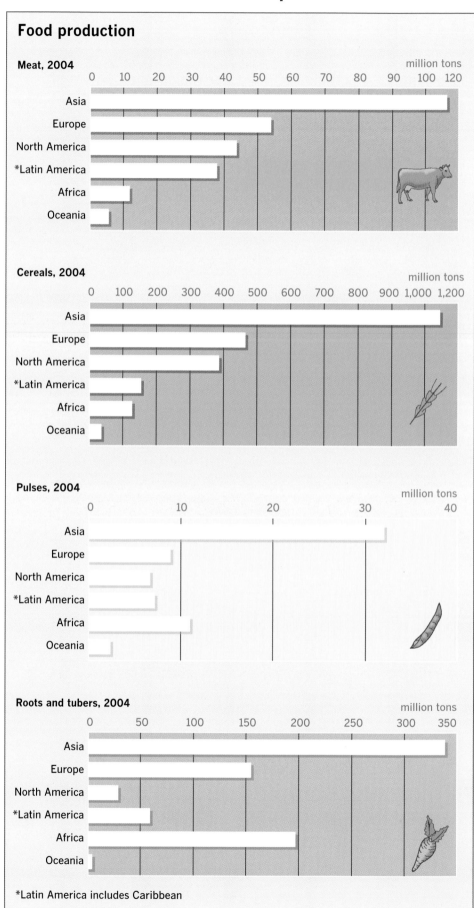

Food production

Meat, 2004

Cereals, 2004

Pulses, 2004

Roots and tubers, 2004

*Latin America includes Caribbean

The costs of modern agriculture

Key words

deforestation
genetic diversity
irrigation
pollution
soil erosion

Environmental impacts of intensive farming

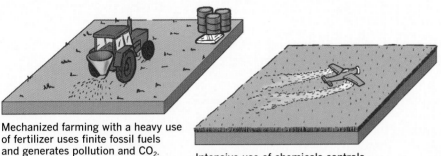

Mechanized farming with a heavy use of fertilizer uses finite fossil fuels and generates pollution and CO_2.

Intensive use of chemicals controls resistant pests.

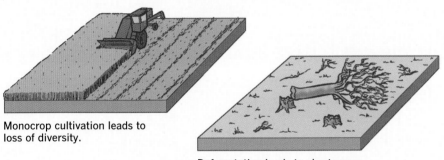

Monocrop cultivation leads to loss of diversity.

Deforestation leads to shortages of wood for fuel.

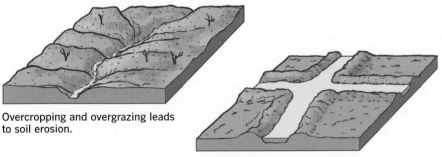

Overcropping and overgrazing leads to soil erosion.

Demands on water resources for irrigation destroys soil by salinization.

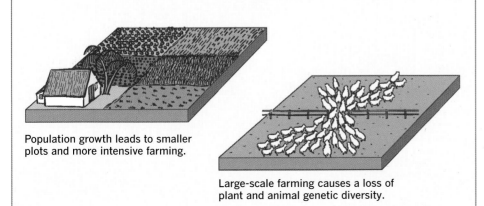

Population growth leads to smaller plots and more intensive farming.

Large-scale farming causes a loss of plant and animal genetic diversity.

Environmental impacts of intensive farming

- Modern agriculture causes massive environmental damage through soil erosion, deforestation, pollution, and loss of plant and animal genetic diversity.
- Supplies of land, water, and firewood are shrinking in many regions.
- It is estimated that by 2020, Southeast Asia will have less than 2.5 acres (1 ha) of arable land per person.
- Experts believe that in the near future, 300 million people, mainly in North Africa, will face water shortages due to agriculture.
- Already, an estimated 130 million Africans live in areas where fuelwood consumption outpaces the regenerative capacity of their forests.

Reducing the impact

- It is possible to increase food production while protecting the environment.
- This requires production systems that can increase productivity while reducing pollution and resource degradation.
- Many countries, mostly in the developed regions, now routinely use some ecologically sound techniques.
- These include biological control of pests, agroforestry, biogas digesters, and improved irrigation management.
- The sustainable use of natural resources must also be socially and economically viable.

Large losses of grain crops

- It is estimated that in developing nations, post-harvest losses of food grains from spoilage, pest infestation, and mishandling is about 25 percent.
- This means that one quarter of grain produced never reaches the consumer, and the money spent producing and harvesting it is wasted.

Modern harvesting methods

- In developed nations crops are harvested using modern machinery to maximize gains and minimize damage.
- Harvested crops can then be stored, transported, and distributed using the latest technology to avoid spoilage from disease or pests.
- Many developing nations do not have this technology or up-to-date information and consequently some estimates put losses of sweet potatoes, plantain, tomatoes, bananas, and citrus fruit as high as 50 percent.

Perishing crops

- Fruit, vegetables, and root crops perish quickly after harvesting.
- This process is accelerated if proper care is not taken during their harvesting, handling, and transport.
- Farmers in developing nations may not be able to sell their damaged produce easily, or they may be forced to sell at a reduced price.
- Reducing losses by following some basic rules helps to increase productivity: fruit and vegetable crops, for example, should be harvested in the morning.
- In the morning, when the dew has evaporated, there is less sunlight and the crop is firmer with fewer insect or disease pests.

Post-harvest losses

Post-harvest losses

Physiological deterioration
Physiological deterioration can be caused by extremes of temperature, atmospheric modification, or contamination. This may cause unpalatable flavors, failure to ripen, or other changes in the living processes of the produce, making it unfit for use.

Mechanical damage
Mechanical damage can result from the careless handling of fresh produce, causing internal bruising, splitting, or skin breaks, thus rapidly increasing water loss and the normal rate of physiological breakdown. Skin breaks also provide sites for infection by disease organisms and fungi, causing decay.

Diseases and pests
All living material is subject to attack by parasites. Grain is often eaten by rodents. Fresh produce can become infected before or after harvest by diseases widespread in the air, soil, and water. Some diseases are able to penetrate the unbroken skin of produce; others require an injury in order to cause infection. Damage so produced is probably the major cause of loss of fresh produce.

Transportation
Transportation can often speed deterioration through vibration and exposure to heat or cold.

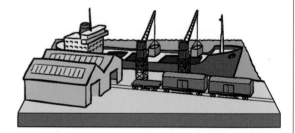

Treatment
Careless harvesting and handling can add to loss. Some crops need to be stored at a constant temperature to "cure" them, or sprayed with fungicide to prolong their shelf life.

Problems of overfishing

Key words

by-catch
overfishing

FAO fishing zone catches, 2003

million tons caught

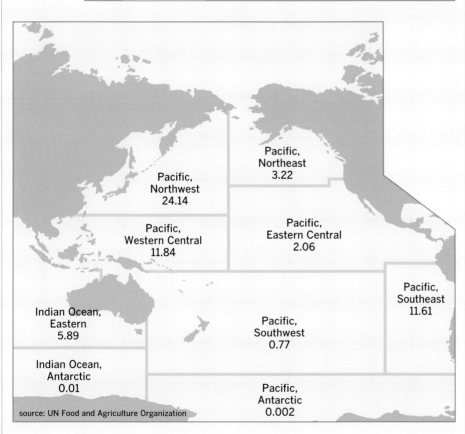

Atlantic, Northwest 2.56

Atlantic, Northeast 11.32

Mediterranean and Black Sea 1.62

Atlantic, Western Central 1.94

Atlantic, Eastern Central 3.63

Atlantic, Southwest 2.27

Atlantic, Southeast 1.92

Indian Ocean, Western 4.71

Indian Ocean, Antarctic 0.01

Atlantic, Antarctic 0.14

Pacific, Northeast 3.22

Pacific, Northwest 24.14

Pacific, Western Central 11.84

Pacific, Eastern Central 2.06

Indian Ocean, Eastern 5.89

Pacific, Southwest 0.77

Pacific, Southeast 11.61

Indian Ocean, Antarctic 0.01

Pacific, Antarctic 0.002

source: UN Food and Agriculture Organization

Scale of overfishing

- The world marine catch stands at about 100 million tons per year.
- One quarter of this is "cheap fish" such as pollock, jack mackerel, and pilchards, most of which ends up as animal feed.

By-catch

- About 27 million tons of the annual marine haul is *by-catch*—unwanted fish caught with the target species—due to the widespread use of unselective fishing equipment and techniques.
- In the Gulf of Mexico, nine pounds of dead fish are discarded for every pound of saleable shrimps caught.
- The by-catch death toll also includes whales, dolphins, turtles, sharks, and sea birds that die after becoming entangled in nets or lines.

Collapsing fisheries

- Many of the world's fisheries are being overfished and some have collapsed.
- The collapse of cod stocks off Newfoundland in 1992 forced the closure of the fishery. More than 40,000 people lost their jobs.

Linked to population

- More and more people around the world rely on fish as a food source.
- More than one billion people in Asia depend on ocean fish for protein, as do one in five Africans.

Government subsidies

- Government subsidies have allowed national fisheries to grow to the point where they are not sustainable.
- The World Wildlife Fund (World Wide Fund for Nature, WWF) estimates that Europe alone has 40 percent more boats than it needs.

Key words

by-catch
driftnet
purse seine net

Advanced technology

- Fishing techniques today use modern technologies.
- Fishing-radar, sonar, and global positioning systems (GPS) allow great efficiency in finding and then catching all the fish in a stock.
- Modern net designs scour the seabed of all living organisms.
- There are very high levels of by-catch of unwanted species, or juveniles that would be illegal to land.

Unsustainable methods

- Distant Water Fleets (DWF) use mechanized fishing methods that catch fish at a rate two and a half times that which would ensure that fish stocks are able to replenish themselves.
- Factory trawlers haul baglike bottom trawl nets the length of football fields across the ocean floor.
- They have heavy chains and rollers attached, which destroy habitats and scrape all life from the ocean floor.
- These nets can catch 400 tons of fish in one scoop and inflict enormous damage to non-target fish and deep ocean life.

Purse seine and driftnets

- Some fishing nets and practices are particularly damaging to the environment.
- Driftnets kill millions of marine creatures while targeting just one or two commercially valuable species.
- Purse seine nets frequently kill marine mammals such as whales and dolphins in large numbers.

Modern fishing techniques

Factory trawlers

Location technology

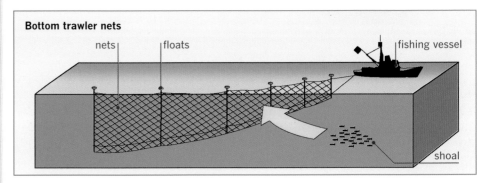

Bottom trawler nets

nets · floats · fishing vessel · shoal

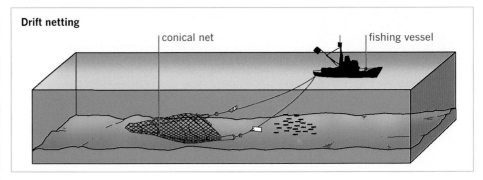

Drift netting

conical net · fishing vessel

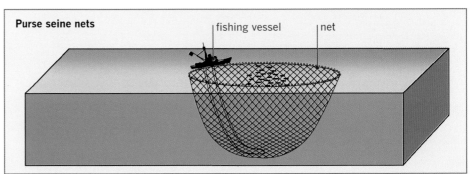

Purse seine nets

fishing vessel · net

World fish catch and target species

Key words

*Food and
  Agriculture
  Organization
  (FAO)
overfishing*

Fish species: million ton catches

More than a million tons of these species were caught in 2002 (FAO figures). Not all are destined for human consumption: the species with the highest tonnage, the anchoveta, is used for the production of fishmeal and fish oil.

million tons

Anchoveta	10.7
Alaska pollock	3.0
Skipjack tuna	2.2
Capelin	2.2
Atlantic herring	2.1
Japanese anchovy	2.1
Chilean jack mackerel	2.0
Blue whiting	1.8
Chub mackerel	1.7
Largehead hairtail	1.7

World fisheries production: inland and marine

million tons

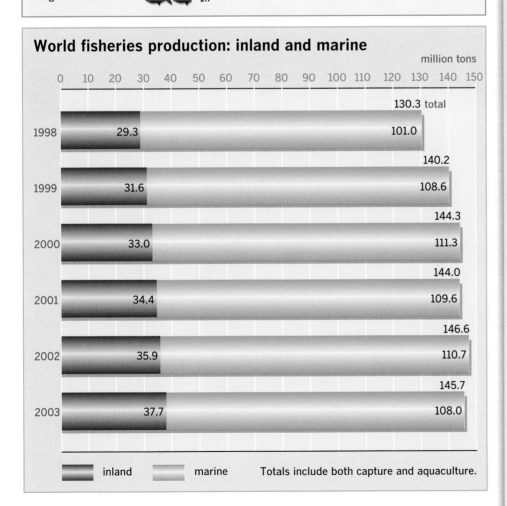

Year	inland	marine	total
1998	29.3	101.0	130.3
1999	31.6	108.6	140.2
2000	33.0	111.3	144.3
2001	34.4	109.6	144.0
2002	35.9	110.7	146.6
2003	37.7	108.0	145.7

■ inland ▢ marine **Totals include both capture and aquaculture.**

The importance of fish

- Worldwide, humanity obtains 16 percent of its animal protein from marine sources.
- About 35 million people gain their livelihoods from harvesting the oceans.

Catch levels plateau

- Of the 4.1 million fishing vessels known to be at sea worldwide, more than one million are decked vessels capable of sustained periods at sea.
- Despite increasing investment in ships, nets, and tracking equipment, the catch levels began to plateau in the 1990s.

Species disappear

- The impact of overfishing has resulted in the reduced catch of several major species, including the Atlantic cod, haddock, and Alaska pollock.
- In the North Atlantic, cod stocks are at half their former levels, while in the North Sea stocks are at just ten percent of their 1970 level.
- Asian fleets fished out the North Atlantic squid stocks in the 1980s.
- Atlantic mackerel, redfish, and herring catches are all less than half the size they were 30 years ago.

Total fish catch

- According to the UN's Food and Agriculture Organization (FAO), the total world catch (marine and inland waters) for 2002 was 147 million tons.
- Experts estimate that this will rise to about 200 million tons by 2015.

© Diagram Visual Information Ltd.

Key words

artisanal fishing
overfishing

Artisanal fishing

- Of the estimated 4.1 million fishing vessels worldwide, around 1.3 million are decked and 2.8 million undecked.
- Of the undecked vessels, 65 percent are not powered.
- These undecked vessels mainly constitute the artisanal fisheries of the world and are involved with small-scale, coastal, and inshore fishing.
- In developing nations the small-scale fishing sector produces far more economic and social benefits than the industrial sector.
- Small-scale fishing uses less fuel, produces less by-catch, causes less impact on the environment by using more selective fishing gear, and tends to provide fish for the domestic market rather than for export.
- Artisanal fishing also differs from industrial fishing in that it is almost impossible to lead to overfishing.
- The fisher is working close to nature with less investment, so if there are no more fish he can more readily change to another livelihood.

Large-scale industrial fishing

- A small percentage of the decked fishing vessels constitute around 50–60 percent of the total vessel capacity (measured by tonnage) of the world's fishing fleet.
- Industrial large-scale fishing employs only about 200,000 people worldwide, but is responsible for massive reductions in fish stocks.
- By contrast, around 200 million of the world's poorest people depend on fishing for their livelihood in smaller fisheries.

Industrial and artisanal fisheries

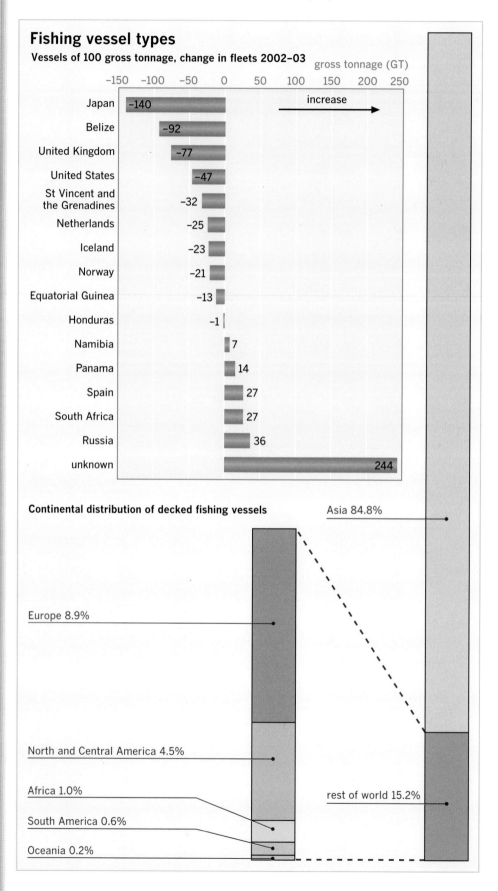

Fishing vessel types

Vessels of 100 gross tonnage, change in fleets 2002–03

gross tonnage (GT)

Country	Change
Japan	-140
Belize	-92
United Kingdom	-77
United States	-47
St Vincent and the Grenadines	-32
Netherlands	-25
Iceland	-23
Norway	-21
Equatorial Guinea	-13
Honduras	-1
Namibia	7
Panama	14
Spain	27
South Africa	27
Russia	36
unknown	244

increase →

Continental distribution of decked fishing vessels

- Asia 84.8%
- Europe 8.9%
- North and Central America 4.5%
- Africa 1.0%
- South America 0.6%
- Oceania 0.2%
- rest of world 15.2%

Daily food intake

Key words

*World Health
   Organization
   (WHO)*

Daily per capita food intake by region

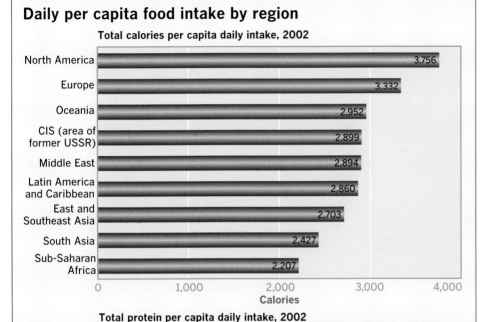

Total calories per capita daily intake, 2002

Region	Calories
North America	3,756
Europe	3,332
Oceania	2,952
CIS (area of former USSR)	2,899
Middle East	2,894
Latin America and Caribbean	2,860
East and Southeast Asia	2,703
South Asia	2,427
Sub-Saharan Africa	2,207

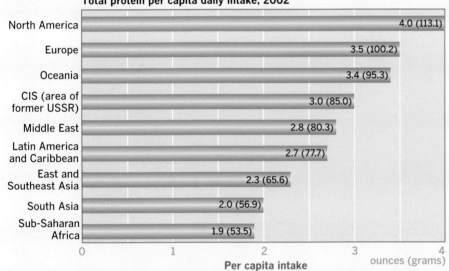

Total protein per capita daily intake, 2002

Region	Per capita intake ounces (grams)
North America	4.0 (113.1)
Europe	3.5 (100.2)
Oceania	3.4 (95.3)
CIS (area of former USSR)	3.0 (85.0)
Middle East	2.8 (80.3)
Latin America and Caribbean	2.7 (77.7)
East and Southeast Asia	2.3 (65.6)
South Asia	2.0 (56.9)
Sub-Saharan Africa	1.9 (53.5)

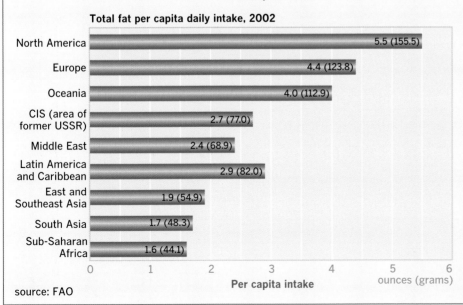

Total fat per capita daily intake, 2002

Region	Per capita intake ounces (grams)
North America	5.5 (155.5)
Europe	4.4 (123.8)
Oceania	4.0 (112.9)
CIS (area of former USSR)	2.7 (77.0)
Middle East	2.4 (68.9)
Latin America and Caribbean	2.9 (82.0)
East and Southeast Asia	1.9 (54.9)
South Asia	1.7 (48.3)
Sub-Saharan Africa	1.6 (44.1)

source: FAO

Average daily food intake

- The average total food intake per day worldwide is approximately 2,800 calories.
- The World Health Organization (WHO) recommended minimum daily per capita energy requirement is 2,100 calories and the average safe protein intake per person per day is 1.6 ounces (46 g) of a mixed-protein diet.
- These are average figures and a large subset of the population such as adolescents and pregnant and lactating women require considerably more protein.

Varying diets

- There is a wide divergence of food intake—in both quantity and variety—between the developing and industrialized worlds.
- This divergence is directly related to food availability, especially in the developing regions.
- Quite often in poorer countries there is a very limited choice of food and people usually eat only what they can grow.

Diet composition

- In many parts of Africa and Asia, local populations obtain their daily calorific intake from only one or two sources.
- The majority of the calorific intake in developing countries usually comes from carbohydrates such as rice or cassava.
- However, a proportion of the diet must be made up of proteins, and populations living on or near coasts usually make this up from fish.
- In some parts of the world protein is harder to find, especially if wild animals have been hunted to extinction.
- Some cultures have to supplement protein in their diet by eating insects and other invertebrates.

Key words

sub-Saharan
  Africa

Trends in food consumption

- The tables show how different regions of the world obtain their calories from different sources.
- The source foods from which the majority of calories are obtained generally reflect the health of a nation.

Fish and meat

- On average, people in North America obtain about 475.5 calories per day from fish and meat compared to just 35.6 in South Asia and 68.9 in sub-Saharan Africa.
- In the developing nations of the world, there tends to be much less reliance on fish and meat and much more on crop-based foods.

Cereals

- In all regions of the world, the importance of cereals in the diet as a provider of calories can be seen.
- Populations in the Middle East and those of East and Southeast Asia rely most heavily on cereals for calories.

Overconsumption

- These patterns of food consumption are directly related to food availability.
- In developed nations, people have more choice about what they eat and tend to pick more convenience and luxury foods.
- This has an adverse effect on the health of these regions: in developing nations there is less incidence of dietary conditions related to overindulgence, such as obesity and heart disease than there is in rich countries.

Daily food intake, by region and food type

Daily food intake by food type, 2002

Per capita — ☐ calories   ☐ protein   ☐ fat

	Sub-Saharan Africa	East & Southeast Asia	Europe	Latin America and Caribbean	Middle East	North America	Oceania	South Asia	CIS (area of former USSR)
Eggs and milk	51.3	32.3	209.6	170.5	112.0	239.2	170.2	85.2	251.4
	2.7	2.1	12.1	9.7	5.9	14.1	9.5	4.3	14.2
	3.0	2.1	12.3	9.4	7.2	13.7	9.5	5.3	14.2
Fish and Meat	68.9	182.6	382.5	304.7	115.9	475.5	452.9	35.6	226.1
	6.5	15.1	30.6	23.9	10.3	45.4	39.8	3.7	18.5
	4.5	13.0	27.9	22.3	8.0	31.1	31.2	2.2	16.3
Sugars (calories only)	105.6	204.7	380.0	478.4	250.2	662.4	373.4	222.0	325.5
Pulses	93.0	35.9	25.5	107.4	72.3	39.4	14.6	102.7	12.1
	6.1	2.3	1.7	6.8	4.7	2.6	1.0	6.1	0.8
	0.5	0.2	0.1	0.5	0.4	0.2	0.1	0.8	0.1
Vegetables	23.8	49.1	77.0	37.8	84.8	79.1	68.7	39.1	64.1
	1.2	2.5	3.6	1.6	3.9	3.6	3.0	2.2	2.8
	0.2	0.4	0.6	0.3	0.7	0.7	0.6	0.3	0.5
Fruits	86.6	70.4	99.6	124.9	136.6	117.2	159.6	44.9	51.5
	0.9	0.8	1.1	1.5	1.6	1.4	1.8	0.5	0.5
	0.4	0.5	0.6	0.9	0.7	0.8	1.2	0.3	0.3
Roots and tubers	431.4	99.5	169.0	118.3	62.2	106.5	203.6	45.3	196.9
	4.3	0.8	4.0	1.9	1.2	2.8	3.6	0.8	4.7
	0.7	0.2	0.2	0.3	0.1	0.2	0.4	0.1	0.3
Cereals	1,021.2	1,620.9	1,027.3	1,027.5	1,629.5	839.6	709.9	1,482.5	1,251.5
	26.5	33.2	30.8	25.3	46.2	24.6	21.2	34.0	36.4
	7.2	5.8	4.0	5.3	9.3	3.5	2.6	5.6	4.4

Malnourishment worldwide

Key words

Food and
Agriculture
Organization
(FAO)

sub-Saharan
Africa

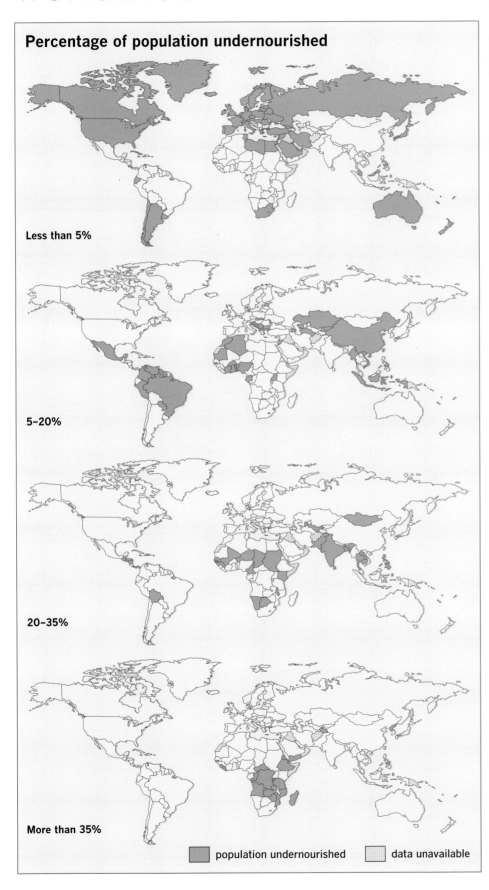

Percentage of population undernourished

Less than 5%

5–20%

20–35%

More than 35%

■ population undernourished   ▨ data unavailable

Calories per person

- Daily calorie consumption varies from high levels in the developed countries, such as Canada, the United States, Europe, Japan, and Australia, to very low levels in poorer countries in Asia and Africa.
- There is currently an average of 2,790 calories of food available each day for every human being on the planet.
- This figure is 23 percent more than in 1961 and more than enough to feed everyone.

Unequal share

- If a third of the cereals fed to livestock were put instead directly onto human plates, the per capita calories available daily would rise to 3,000.
- However, food is not produced or shared in equal quantities around the world.
- Consequently the populations of many of the poorer countries have to live on a calorie intake much lower than that of developed nations.

Fewer calories in Africa

- In 2002 the sub-Saharan African consumed an average of only 2,200 calories a day, significantly less than North Americans who consumed an average of 3,756 calories per day per person.
- Recent figures from the UN Food and Agriculture Organization (FAO) estimate that 316 million Africans, or approximately 35 percent of the continent's total population, are chronically malnourished.

© Diagram Visual Information Ltd.

Food production indexes

- Food production indexes are used by the UN Food and Agriculture Organization (FAO) as a measure of the value of food produced by different countries.
- The indexes are calculated using a formula (called the *Laspeyres formula*) based on the sum of price-weighted quantities of different agricultural commodities produced. ·
- Trade indexes of food products include all commodities that are considered edible and contain nutrients, except animal feed products and alcoholic beverages.
- Certain foods such as coffee and tea are excluded because they contain virtually no nutritional value.

Loss in food production

- Some countries have seen a dramatic fall in food production index value in the last 20 years.
- This can be due to many reasons such as political unrest, natural disasters, or unsuccessful land reforms.
- Singapore has seen the greatest loss in food production index values.
- In 1977 Singapore had a value of 956, which dropped to 850 by 1984, and is currently only 66.6.
- The reason for this is partly urbanization which saw the phasing out of many farms and the country relying far more heavily on imports.

Doubling of food production

- Many countries have managed to double their production index values in the last 20 years.
- These countries include Benin, Kuwait, the United Arab Emirates, and China.
- The many reasons for this include an intensification of farming and a switch to the production of more valuable crops and livestock.

Food production indexes

Countries where food production decreased and increased, 1984–2004

Figures are food production indexes based on the sum of price-weighted quantities produced by each country. These figures are weighed by average international commodity prices for the period 1999–2001. The index is arrived at by dividing the aggregate for a given year by the average aggregate of the 1999–2001 period.

Countries where food production decreased	1984	1994	2004
Bulgaria	174.2	106.6	107.7
Cuba	118.7	74.2	109.6
Finland	113.0	101.8	103.6
Haiti	111.8	95.0	100.6
Japan	108.5	109.0	97.7
Namibia	76.8	110.5	114.0
Puerto Rico	116.8	116.7	98.2
Romania	138.8	107.1	123.2
Singapore	923.5	182.3	70.2

Countries where food production increased	1984	1994	2004
Benin	48.6	70.7	137.4
Burkina Faso	45.0	77.7	115.2
China	45.9	73.3	117.8
Egypt	48.5	73.5	110.9
Ghana	47.0	69.6	121.0
Iran	50.4	84.2	115.4
Jordan	53.5	107.5	118.2
Kuwait	49.4	48.9	125.9
Laos	51.1	69.1	116.8
Malaysia	42.8	81.4	120.0
Nigeria	39.8	82.8	106.2
Pakistan	51.1	80.6	110.6
Paraguay	55.3	79.0	115.0
Saudi Arabia	48.8	97.8	118.6
United Arab Emirates	14.4	36.2	63.7
Vietnam	49.5	73.2	124.4

World, regions, and income categories	1984	1994	2004
Low-income countries	58.0	82.9	107.0
World	70.2	85.3	108.9
Africa sub-Saharan	57.2	82.7	105.7
Developed countries	96.0	95.1	104.3
Developing countries	55.8	79.8	111.5
East and Southeast Asia	63.1	85.0	111.0
Europe	82.6	97.5	104.0
European Union (25)			101.6
Industrialized countries	85.9	92.8	102.6
Latin America and Caribbean	62.2	82.0	112.4
Least developed countries	65.8	80.4	108.1
Middle East	60.4	84.7	108.6
North America, developed	77.8	93.5	106.3
Oceania	67.5	75.1	99.6
South America	58.8	81.1	113.8
South Asia	59.9	82.3	104.8
Western Europe	95.8	93.7	99.6

Food production indexes by country

Key words

fertilizer
herbicide
organic farming
pesticide

sub-Saharan Africa

Indexes by country

Figures are food production indices based on the sum of price-weighted quantities produced by each country. These figures are weighed by average international commodity prices for the period 1999–2001. The index is arrived at by dividing the aggregate for a given year by the average aggregate of the 1999–2001 period. Countries with no data have been omitted

	1984	2004
Albania	75.8	105.9
Algeria	55.5	118.0
Angola	58.4	112.9
Antigua and Barbuda	83.8	107.8
Argentina	68.5	101.4
Armenia		115.2
Australia	64.2	93.3
Austria	90.9	100.4
Azerbaijan		121.3
Bahamas	67.2	105.0
Bahrain	85.1	110.2
Bangladesh	61.4	104.6
Barbados	101.6	94.1
Belarus		115.1
Belgium	0.0	101.5
Belize	44.8	101.3
Benin	48.7	138.0
Bhutan	95.6	94.5
Bolivia	51.1	110.7
Bosnia and Herzegovina		100.5
Botswana	110.1	102.4
Brazil	55.0	123.7
Brunei	48.3	132.9
Bulgaria	177.2	97.7
Burkina Faso	45.1	123.6
Burundi	84.2	104.4
Cambodia	39.3	113.3
Cameroon	51.8	103.0
Canada	71.2	102.2
Cape Verde	36.9	94.5
Central African Republic	57.3	108.2
Chad	47.4	111.8
Chile	53.9	106.7
China	45.9	117.5
Colombia	65.1	106.4
Comoros	62.3	103.4
Congo, Dem Rep	96.9	97.7
Congo, Rep	75.2	108.1
Costa Rica	49.2	94.0
Croatia		102.6
Cuba	120.9	111.6
Cyprus	85.2	105.3
Czech Republic		104.1
Côte d'Ivoire	60.0	90.4
Denmark	94.3	99.7
Djibouti	73.3	107.1
Dominica	88.3	97.3
Dominican Republic	101.4	103.2
Ecuador	52.1	112.5
Egypt	48.1	108.8
El Salvador	73.3	100.4
Equatorial Guinea	61.9	93.4
Eritrea		84.1
Estonia		108.9
Ethiopia		105.9
Fiji	103.3	92.5

	1984	2004
Finland	113.0	106.7
France	98.8	100.0
French Guiana	37.4	103.8
Gabon	74.2	101.1
Gambia	72.4	69.2
Georgia		99.7
Germany	101.2	102.8
Ghana	47.0	121.6
Greece	92.8	96.7
Grenada	125.5	96.5
Guadeloupe	97.4	100.7
Guatemala	55.7	104.4
Guinea	62.6	108.9
Guinea-Bissau	61.5	102.2
Guyana	69.7	105.8
Haiti	111.8	102.3
Honduras	70.9	108.5
Hungary	127.0	110.4
Iceland	111.2	104.3
India	61.0	104.1
Indonesia	62.5	114.8
Iran	50.5	111.9
Ireland	88.6	98.4
Israel	78.9	103.2
Italy	95.5	95.5
Jamaica	83.0	98.8
Japan	108.5	97.9
Jordan	54.3	118.5
Kazakhstan		98.8
Kenya	51.4	101.1
Korea, People's Rep	93.5	109.3
Korea, Rep	67.5	92.5
Kuwait	49.4	124.6
Kyrgyzstan		81.0
Laos	51.2	119.8
Latvia		118.5
Lebanon	60.4	99.8
Lesotho	96.0	105.3
Liberia	100.3	97.4
Libya	67.7	100.9
Lithuania		108.4
Macedonia		95.1
Madagascar	81.7	102.5
Malawi	49.8	95.6
Malaysia	43.0	116.9
Mali	58.9	106.6
Martinique	88.8	100.3
Mauritania	68.6	107.3
Mauritius	86.2	105.8
Mexico	68.9	107.8
Moldova		108.9
Mongolia	91.8	92.3
Morocco	60.0	122.6
Mozambique	70.7	104.2
Myanmar	65.1	116.6
Namibia	77.6	95.7
Nepal	59.4	108.8
Netherlands	96.0	93.0
New Zealand	74.2	115.7
Nicaragua	66.2	127.5
Niger	47.8	118.3

	1984	2004
Nigeria	39.8	105.0
Norway	117.4	99.9
Oman	54.5	91.0
Pakistan	50.7	109.3
Panama	90.3	107.8
Papua New Guinea	71.4	107.8
Paraguay	54.1	110.9
Peru	51.6	90.4
Philippines	66.2	113.5
Poland	112.0	107.2
Portugal	75.5	101.0
Puerto Rico	106.8	100.2
Qatar	27.7	143.9
Romania	139.3	125.4
Russian Federation	107.7	114.3
Rwanda	83.3	112.7
Samoa	114.1	101.4
Saudi Arabia	48.9	108.2
Senegal	46.9	85.3
Serbia and Montenegro		113.5
Sierra Leone	111.7	110.0
Singapore	850.1	66.6
Slovakia		110.7
Slovenia		105.7
South Africa	72.7	104.4
Spain	79.8	103.6
Sri Lanka	88.9	95.2
Sudan	52.6	114.1
Suriname	144.6	105.6
Swaziland	100.0	102.2
Sweden	118.2	101.0
Switzerland	106.0	99.3
Syria	61.8	119.8
Tajikistan		121.4
Tanzania	79.3	103.8
Thailand	74.9	99.8
Togo	61.3	105.3
Tonga	108.3	102.2
Trinidad and Tobago	82.4	117.1
Tunisia	59.0	96.5
Turkey	74.7	105.2
Turkmenistan		109.2
Uganda	61.9	109.0
Ukraine		116.1
United Arab Emirates	14.4	53.1
UK	108.7	98.0
USA	78.6	106.8
Uruguay	66.4	106.6
Uzbekistan		105.2
Venezuela	62.3	99.6
Vietnam	49.7	118.7
Yemen	54.0	106.5
Zambia	67.1	106.8
Zimbabwe	66.6	87.8

Worldwide regional indexes

- From worldwide data it can be seen that the food production index value for the world has increased from 70.2 in 1984 to 108.9 in 2004.
- All regions of the world have seen increases, with the biggest in South America, South Asia, and sub-Saharan Africa.
- The food production index values for poorer countries have increased the most over the past 20 years.
- Developing nations as a whole increased only 8.4 points in 20 years, but some increased by 55.7 over the same period.
- The smallest increases have been seen in Western Europe which increased from 95.8 in 1984 to only 104.3 in 2004.
- These differences between rich and poor regions are thought to be due in part to the availability of better farming technology, as well as from the very low base figures from which the poor countries were starting.

Cuba

- Cuba suffered a severe drop in food production after the collapse of the Soviet Union because tons of herbicides, fertilizers, and pesticides could no longer be imported.
- The country was forced to switch to organic agriculture and to utilize urban as well as rural areas for farming.
- Cuba has managed to increase food production again by adopting and perfecting organic farming techniques.
- Conversely, many other countries have seen large increases in food production index values due to an increase in the land area under cultivation and more intensive farming.

Key words

Food and
Agriculture
Organization
(FAO)

sub-Saharan
Africa

Low-income countries

- Of the 78 low-income countries that cannot produce enough food to feed their populations, over half are in Africa.
- In these African countries, population growth rates are highest and poverty is greatest.
- Soils here tend to be more susceptible to degradation, and advances in modern agricultural technology have had the least impact on food production.

World Food summit

- In 1996, the World Food Summit (WFS) pledged to halve malnutrition by 2015.
- Current data indicates that the number of undernourished people is falling at a rate of only six million each year, far below the rate of 22 million per year needed to reach the WFS target.
- The UN Food and Agriculture Organization (FAO) predicts that in some regions of the world, chronic malnutrition is likely to persist, rising to 30 percent of the population of sub-Saharan Africa by 2010.

Poverty and degradation

- Poverty and hunger frequently cause a cycle of environmental decline that further undermines food security.
- Environmental degradation often occurs when poor nations cannot feed themselves without disregarding the future fertility of the land.
- They overcultivate or overgraze land to meet immediate needs, or annex inappropriate land with infertile, stony, toxic, or poorly drained soils.
- In 1997–99 there were 815 million undernourished people in the world.

The world's undernourished people

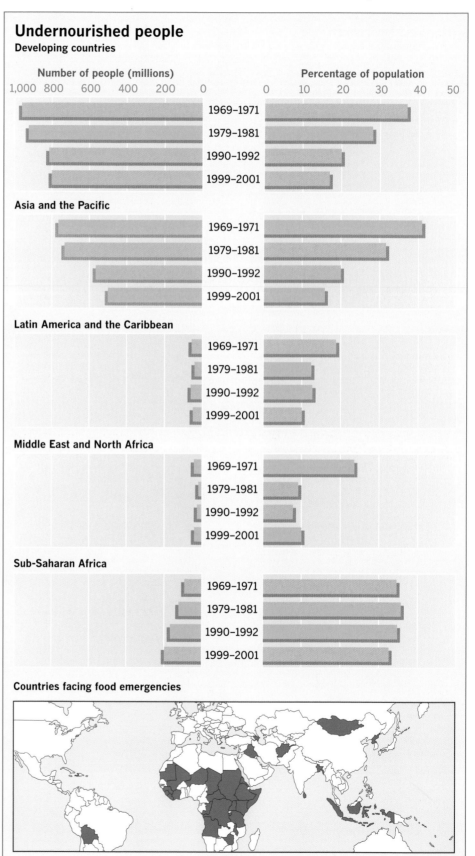

Undernourished people

Developing countries

Global water use and availability

Key words

irrigation
runoff

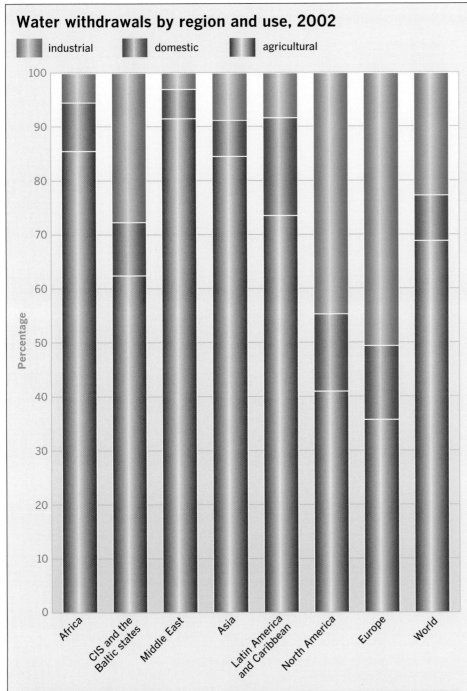

Water withdrawals by region and use, 2002

industrial   domestic   agricultural

Percentage (y-axis: 0–100)

Regions (x-axis): Africa, CIS and the Baltic states, Middle East, Asia, Latin America and Caribbean, North America, Europe, World

Water use by sector in four year periods: China, India, USA
billion cubic meters

	China		India		United States	
	1988–1992	1998–2002	1988–1992	1998–2002	1988–1992	1998–2002
Agricultural	415.0	426.9	460.0	558.4	116.4	197.8
Domestic	35.0	41.5	25.0	52.2	54.0	60.9
Industrial	50.0	162.0	15.0	35.2	33.8	220.7
Total	**500.0**	**630.4**	**500.0**	**645.8**	**204.2**	**479.4**

Potential conflicts

- Throughout the world freshwater sources are dwindling or becoming contaminated.
- Chronic or acute water shortage is increasingly common in many countries, and countries with fast growing populations are becoming potential sources of conflict with their neighbors.

Unequal water distribution

- The distribution of water resources around the globe is highly unequal, even at the continental level.
- Asia has more than 60 percent of the world's population but only 36 percent of the world's river runoff.
- South America has just six percent of the global population but 26 percent of the runoff.
- Canada has more than 30 times as much water available to each of its citizens as China.
- More than 60 percent of the water used in the world is diverted for crop irrigation.
- Asia has two thirds of the world's irrigated land and 85 percent of Asia's water is used for irrigation.

Water usage

- China and India use 22,248 and 22,778 billion cubic feet (630 and 645 billion m³) of water per year respectively.
- The majority of this in each case is used in agriculture for irrigation.
- The United States, which has a much smaller population, still uses around 16,916 billion cubic feet (479 billion m³) of water per year, most of which is used in industry.

Key words

sanitation
sub Saharan Africa

Access to safe water

- Globally, more than one billion people are without access to safe and adequate water supplies.
- Half the total population of the developing nations—2.6 billion people—are without access to adequate *sanitation*.

No convenient access

- Of the estimated five billion people worldwide who do have access to water supply services, only around three billion have the convenience of access through house connections or yard taps.

Worst affected areas

- The people worst affected by lack of access to safe water and sanitation are the rural poor as well as residents of slum areas in the rapidly expanding cities of Africa and Asia.
- However, the quality of drinking water and sanitation facilities has also dropped in some developed nations, such as the former Soviet Union.

Development project

- The Millennium Development Goals (MDG) were set at a United Nations sponsored summit of world leaders in September 2000.
- The goals were adopted by 189 countries, and promised to halve the number of people who do not have safe drinking water and basic sanitation (based on 1990 figures) by 2015.
- A midterm assessment for the MDG was published in 2004.
- It stated that the global target to halve the number of people without sanitation will be missed by half a billion people.
- However, with the exception of sub-Saharan Africa, the target for safe drinking water is well on its way to being met.

Clean water and sanitation

Lack of improved drinking water and sanitation, 2002

Drinking water

Sanitation

Population without improved drinking water (millions)	Region	Population without improved sanitation (millions)
60	Latin America and Caribbean	137
288	sub-Saharan Africa	437
15	Northern Africa	40
15	Developed regions	20
20	Europe and CIS	50
3	Oceania	3
23	Western Asia	38
115	Southeast Asia	208
234	South Asia	938
303	East Asia	749

Availability of improved drinking water and sanitation, 1990–2002

	Population (million)	Improved drinking water		Improved sanitation		
		Urban (%)	Rural (%)	Urban (%)	Rural (%)	
World	5,263	95	63	79	25	1990
	6,225	95	72	81	37	2002
Developed regions	934	100	99	100	99	1990
	993	100	94	100	92	2002
Developing regions	4,048	93	59	68	16	1990
	4,951	92	70	73	31	2002

Waterborne diseases

Major waterborne diseases and poisons

Malaria, yellow fever, dengue, Rift Valley fever

Water-breeding mosquitoes spread malaria, yellow fever, and dengue
- Malaria affects 396 million and kills more than 1.8 million people every year—most of them infants.
- Most malaria deaths occur in sub-Saharan Africa, where malaria accounts for one in five of all childhood deaths.
- Intensified irrigation, dams, and other water-related projects contribute importantly to this disease burden.
- There are 200,000 estimated cases of yellow fever in Africa and Latin America (with 30,000 deaths) per year.
- There are some 50 million cases of dengue every year, some of them of the dangerous dengue hemorrhagic fever type, which can kill 20 percent of sufferers.

Cholera, typhoid, dysentery, diarrhea

Bacterial and viral contamination of drinking water
- Around 1.8 million people die each year from diarrheal disease (including cholera); 90 percent of these deaths are children under five years old.
- Other major diarrheal diseases include typhoid fever and rotavirus.
- Diarrheal diseases impose a heavy burden on developing countries—accounting for 1.5 billion bouts of illness a year in children under five.
- The burden is highest in deprived areas where there is poor sanitation, inadequate hygiene, and unsafe drinking water.
- The polio virus used to be a major waterborne scourge, but has now been virtually eradicated.

Schistosomiasis (bilharzia), river blindness (onchocerciasis), guinea worm, giardiasis, lymphatic filariasis

Parasites in polluted water
- Two billion people are at risk of schistosomiasis in 74 countries of the world.
- Two hundred million people are infected with schistosomiasis, which is caused by a flatworm spread via a freshwater snail.
- Twenty million suffer severe consequences. Basic sanitation reduces the disease by up to 77 percent.
- Worldwide, 120 million people are at risk of onchocerciasis (river blindness), 96 percent in Africa. A total of 18 million people (almost all in Africa) are infected with the disease, a type of filariasis caused by a parasitic worm that lives for up to 14 years in the human body. Of those infected, more than 6.5 million suffer from severe itching or dermatitis and 270,000 are blind.
- Guinea worm (dracunculiasis) is caused by a roundworm which can grow up to three feet (1 m) long. It is the only disease exclusively associated with unhealthy drinking water. Some 85,000 people, all in Africa, contract this debilitating disease every year. The filtering of drinking water prevents transmission.

Trachoma, hookworm

Spread by poor hygiene
- Trachoma, one of the oldest infectious diseases known to mankind, is caused by a microorganism, *Chlamydia trachomatis*, which spreads through poor hygiene and limited access to water and sanitation.
- It provokes an inflammatory reaction in the eye with the formation of follicles in the conjunctiva, which can cause blindness.
- Six million people have been irreversibly blinded by trachoma and 146 million are threatened by blindness.
- Trachoma threatens the health of 500 million people.
- Hookworm infections occur mostly in tropical and subtropical climates and are estimated to infect about one billion people.

Arsenic

Poisoned drinking water
- Arsenic contamination of ground water is a global problem. It has been found in many countries, including Argentina, Bangladesh, Chile, China, India, Mexico, Thailand, and the United States.
- Of a population of 125 million, 35–77 million people in Bangladesh are estimated to be at risk from drinking contaminated water.

Risk to children
- Waterborne diseases remain one of the most significant risks to human health worldwide.
- It is estimated that around 3.4 million people, mostly children, die from water-related diseases annually, and many hundreds of millions more are made sick.

Most severe diseases
- The most severe waterborne diseases, such as malaria, dysentery, and cholera, are directly associated with poor sanitation.
- Most fatalities from diarrheal diseases, including cholera, could be prevented by simple oral rehydration to replace fluids and electrolytes.
- Many parasitic diseases are also spread by poor sanitation, such as schistosomiasis, river blindness, and guinea worm.
- Toxins such as arsenic have contaminated groundwater in some countries through industrial pollution.

Sanitation and infrastructure
- The lack of adequate sanitation to remove sewage, and infrastructure to remove garbage and keep urban areas clean, means some people have to live in close proximity to the causes of disease.
- Open sewers and contaminated water supplies provide opportunities for pathogens to breed and spread easily between people.
- Garbage, such as tin cans and old tires, often provide ideal locations for insect vectors to breed.
- Mosquitoes can breed readily in small pools of water within refuse.

Insect pests: the New World screwworm

Key words

sterile male
  technique

Life cycle

- The New World screwworm *(Cochliomyia hominivorax)* is a serious pest of domestic animals and humans.
- Female screwworm flies lay their eggs at the edges of wounds on living mammals or on natural body openings such as the nostrils, eyes, ears, or mouth. Virtually any wound is attractive.
- Within 24 hours, larvae emerge and immediately begin to feed on the underlying tissues, burrowing into the wound.
- As the worm feeds, the wound is enlarged and deepened, resulting in extensive tissue destruction.
- The larvae reach maturity five to seven days after hatching and leave the wound. They fall to the ground, into which they then burrow to pupate.

Sterile insect technique

- A project to eradicate the screwworm was undertaken by releasing sterilized male screwworms: after the female mates with the sterilized male, it lays unfertilized eggs.
- The screwworm was successfully eradicated from the United States and Mexico by 1991, but since then there have been several outbreaks.
- The Department of Agriculture estimates that the benefit of eradication to the livestock industry is more than $900 million per year.

Spread of the screwworm

- In 1989, the New World screwworm was accidentally introduced to Libya.
- It was eradicated using the sterile male technique.
- The screwworm has now been eradicated from Central America north of Panama, by the maintenance of a permanent barrier of sterile males at the Darien Gap.

Distribution of the screwworm

The northern limits of the New World screwworm are its historical summer limits. Following the success of the sterile insect program, the present northern limit in Central America is the Darien Gap in Panama.

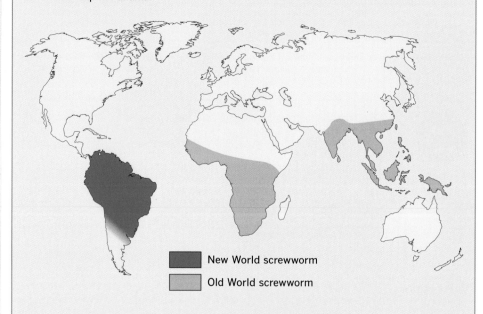

- New World screwworm
- Old World screwworm

Life cycle of the New World screwworm

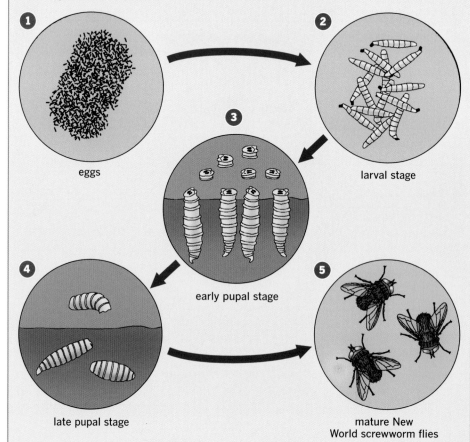

1 eggs

2 larval stage

3 early pupal stage

4 late pupal stage

5 mature New World screwworm flies

Insect pests: the cassava mealybug

Key words

parasitic wasp

The rescue of the cassava crop

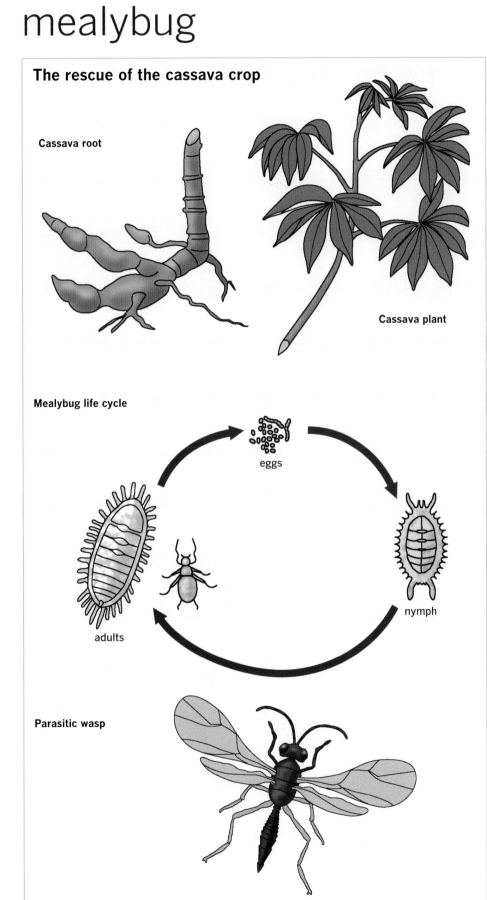

Cassava root

Cassava plant

Mealybug life cycle

eggs

adults

nymph

Parasitic wasp

A staple food in Africa

- Cassava was introduced to Africa from South America in the sixteenth century and it has since become a staple food crop.
- The starchy swollen roots are a source of cheap carbohydrate for 200 million Africans, providing up to 70 percent of their daily energy intake.

Mealybug

- The mealybug, *(Phenacoccus manihoti)* arrived in Africa in the early 1970s on infected plants from South America.
- It spread across the continent to become the worst pest of the cassava crop.
- It damaged cassava plots, drastically reducing leaf and root yields, sometimes by as much as 80 percent.

Parasitic wasp

- Scientists at the International Institute of Tropical Agriculture discovered the mealybug had a natural enemy in South America, a parasitic wasp called *Apoanagyrus lopezi*.
- The wasp uses the mealybug as a host for laying its eggs. The developing larvae eat and kill the mealybug.
- The wasp was brought to Africa, reared in large numbers, and released into the wild in 30 countries.
- Full control was reached between two and four years after the release of the wasps.

Benefits to the economy

- Each dollar spent on the control project was worth $150 to the farmer.
- The overall economic benefit was estimated at between $9 billion and $20 billion.

© Diagram Visual Information Ltd.

Key words

sterile male
  technique
World Health
  Organization
  (WHO)

Insect pests: the tsetse fly

The tsetse fly problem

- The tsetse fly (genus *Glossina*) spreads a parasitic disease, trypanosomiasis, to both cattle (nagana) and humans (sleeping sickness).
- The World Health Organization (WHO) estimates that there are between 300,000 and 500,000 people currently affected by sleeping sickness, with an additional 60 million people at risk.
- The pest prevents the use of livestock across a belt of more than 3.9 million square miles (10 million km²) of Africa.

Life cycle

- There are 22 species of tsetse fly, but all are found only in Africa.
- They breed along rivers and streams, are active during the day, and feed exclusively on blood.
- Unusually for flies, the females do not lay eggs, but give birth to a single live larva.

Sleeping sickness

- Tsetse flies transmit sleeping sickness through their saliva, after first biting a person or animal that is already infected.
- The causal organism of sleeping sickness is a tiny microorganism called a trypanosome.

Eradication

- The tsetse fly has been eradicated from the island of Zanzibar by use of the sterile male technique used against screwworms.
- A joint campaign of the Food and Agriculture Organization (FAO) and the International Atomic Energy Agency (IAEA) was launched in 2001 to eradicate the tsetse fly using sterile insects.

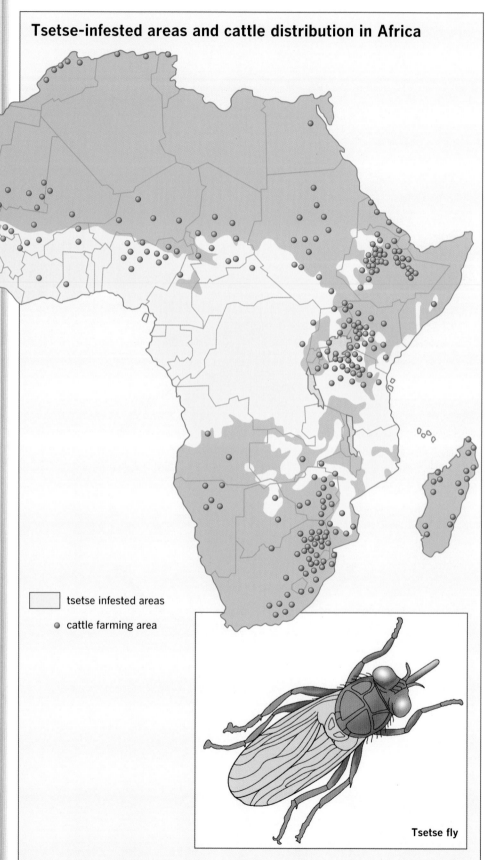

Tsetse-infested areas and cattle distribution in Africa

☐ tsetse infested areas
● cattle farming area

Tsetse fly

Resistant pests

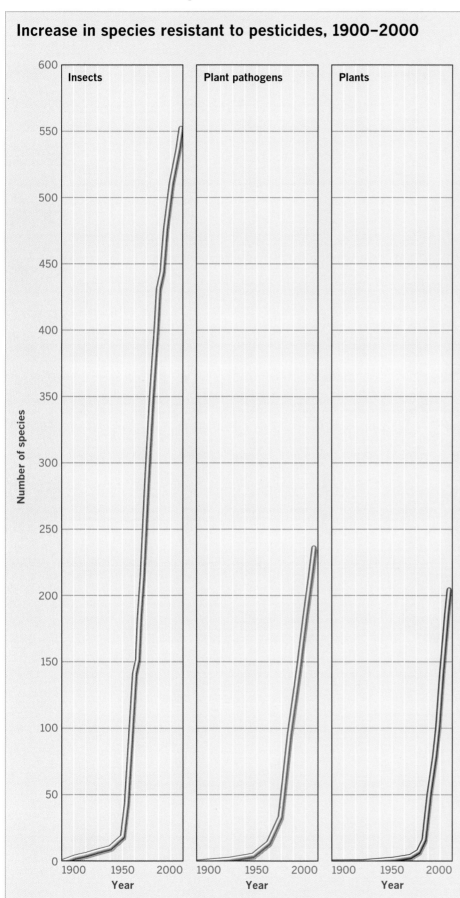

Increase in species resistant to pesticides, 1900–2000

Insects · **Plant pathogens** · **Plants**

Number of species / *Year*

Key words

genetic mutation
integrated pest
  management
  (IPM)

Pesticide use increases

- The use of pesticides increased more than 30 times between 1950 and the end of the 1980s.
- However, pests still cost the world billions of dollars annually in lost agricultural production.

Resistance

- More species of weeds, diseases, and insects are becoming resistant to control measures.
- At least 520 species of insect and mites, 150 plant diseases, and 113 weeds have all become resistant to the pesticides meant to control them.
- Resistance or tolerance arises as a product of natural selection within a population.

Natural selection

- Insects, weeds, or diseases with immunity to a given pesticide are sometimes produced naturally as a result of genetic mutation.
- Those individuals with immunity will be favored in an environment where the pesticides are used, so their genes will spread quickly.
- Before long, a new race of individuals appears with the immunity gene and it becomes harder to control them using the same pesticides.

Avoiding resistant pests

- To help avoid pests becoming resistant to pesticides it is necessary to use an integrated pest management (IPM) approach, involving careful monitoring.
- It may include the use of natural predators, chemical agents, and crop rotations, and usually requires cooperation between crop growers within a region.

Key words

*sustainable
development*

Our Common Future

- In 1987, the United Nations World Commission on Environment and Development released its report *Our Common Future* (the Brundtland Report).
- This report brought the terms *sustainability* and *sustainable development* into widespread use.

Earth Summit, Rio de Janeiro

- At the 1992 Earth Summit in Rio de Janeiro, more than 100 nations signed "Agenda 21"—an international approach toward sustainable development.
- Fundamental to the philosophy of sustainable development is the inseparability of human communities, economies, and the environment.
- There is an interdependence between the way humans manage the environment, the level of cohesion in a community, and economic performance.

Sustainable development

- The concept of sustainable development promotes not only protection of the environment and creation of wealth, but equitable distribution of that wealth within society.
- Sustainable development seeks to ensure the needs of the present are met without compromising the ability of future generations to meet their needs.
- Sustainable development has a number of primary objectives:
- Minimized risk of environmental damage.
- Ecological sustainability and environmental protection.
- Sociocultural sustainability recognizing the needs of all.
- Economic sustainability, maintaining high and stable levels of economic growth and employment.

Sustainable development

Conservation agriculture

One form of sustainable development, "conservation agriculture," aims to conserve, improve, and make more efficient use of natural resources through integrated management of available soil, water, and biological resources combined with external inputs.

Conservation agriculture contributes to environmental conservation as well as to enhanced and sustained agricultural production.

Conservation agriculture maintains a permanent or semipermanent organic soil cover.

This can be a growing crop or a dead mulch. Its function is to protect the soil physically from sun, rain, and wind, and to feed soil *biota*.

The soil microorganisms and soil fauna take over the tillage function and soil nutrient balancing.

Mechanical tillage disturbs this process. Therefore, zero or minimum tillage and direct seeding are important elements of conservation agriculture.

Varied *crop rotation* is also important to avoid disease and pest problems.

Livestock production can be fully integrated into conservation agriculture, by making use of the recycling of nutrients.

The recycling of nutrients reduces the environmental problems caused by concentrated intensive livestock production.

Globally, conservation agriculture is currently practiced on about 140 million acres (58 million ha) of land, from the tropics almost to the Arctic Circle, but mostly in the United States, Brazil, Argentina, Canada, and Paraguay.

The Green Revolution

Key words

Green Revolution
irrigation
per capita

World grain production, 1961–2004

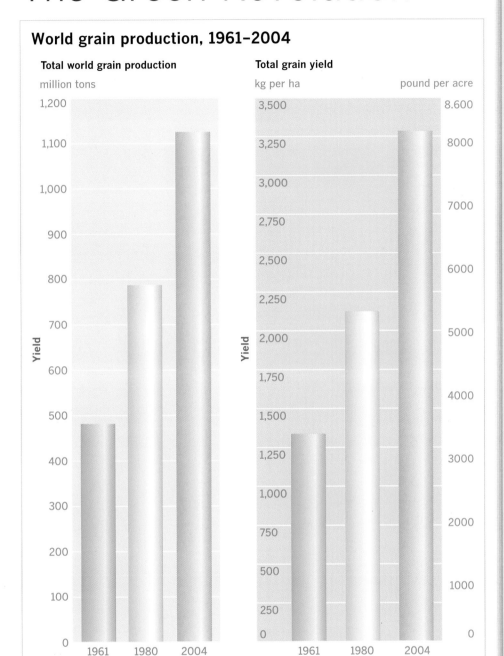

Total world grain production

million tons

Total grain yield

kg per ha | pound per acre

Slowing increase
- Between 1950 and 2000 world total grain production increased on average 2.6 percent per year, well above the rate of population growth.
- Between 1990 and 1996 the increase slowed to 0.7 percent per year, no longer ahead of population growth.

The downside
- The Green Revolution spread a farming method that relies heavily on chemical fertilizers, monocultures, decreased fallow times, and more intensive irrigation and plowing.
- Water supplies became degraded and crop diversity decreased, consequently leading to land degradation and erosion.
- More than half the fertilizers ever produced have been applied to fields since 1984.
- The doubling of agricultural production during the past 35 years has required a 600 percent increase in nitrogen fertilizer and a 250 percent increase in phosphate fertilizer. Consequently, human activity is now the dominant source of fixed nitrogen in the environment.
- The result has been a nitrogen overload on natural ecosystems.

New agricultural age
- The Green Revolution fostered the development of new varieties of food plants, and introduced agricultural practices that greatly increased crop yields.
- It began in 1944 when the Rockefeller Foundation and the Mexican government established a plant breeding station in Mexico, with the goal of boosting grain yields.
- Norman Borlaug, who later won the Nobel Prize for his achievement, developed a new strain of high-yielding wheat.
- With this new strain, Mexico went from importing much of its wheat in 1944 to exporting 0.52 million tons in 1964.
- The wheat also grew well in Africa and Asia. In India production increased from 12 million tons in 1966 to 47 million tons in 1986.

More high-yielding varieties
- Breeders have now produced high-yielding varieties of all major crops.
- Many of these are dwarf varieties, which result because more carbon from photosynthesis is directed to the grain.

The Green Revolution in the developing world
- Gains have been greatest in the developing world, where increased food availability has enabled a rise in per capita calories of 38 percent to 2,660 per person.
- Life expectancy in developing nations increased by ten years in two decades. This was attributed primarily to improved nutrition.

Key words

runoff
soil erosion

Steep slopes

- Soil erosion increases rapidly with hill slopes, and is worst on slopes of 10–25 percent.
- Crops cannot easily be grown on slopes steeper than five percent.
- Many agricultural practices in use can dramatically reduce erosion from hill slopes.

Terracing

- Terracing is widely used in the tropics to grow rice and makes use of water runoff from the hill to increase soil retentiveness and arability.

Contour farming

- Contour farming is the practice of preparing land, planting crops, and cultivating them on a level or nearly level contour around a slope.
- Each crop row serves as a small dam to hold water on the slope and can cut soil losses by as much as 50 percent.

Trees

- Tree planting on higher slopes provides deep roots that hold the soil.
- It also cycles and retains nutrients and provides organic matter to make the soil richer.

Strip cropping

- Strip cropping is the use of alternating strips of different crops.
- It is useful on gentle slopes, and can reduce soil erosion to acceptable levels without banks or drains.

Stone lines

- Stone lines, or stop-wash lines, retain some rainwater and eroded soil on gentle slopes.
- Grass strips can also be used as stop-wash lines.

Using hill slopes

Adapting slopes for agriculture

Terracing

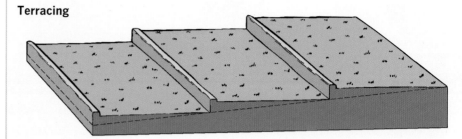

Contour

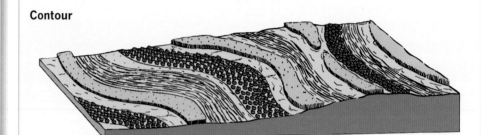

Tree planting

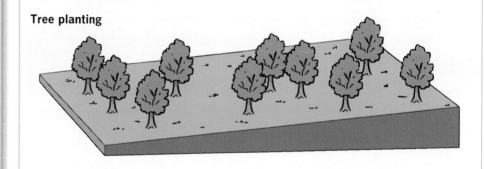

Strip cropping

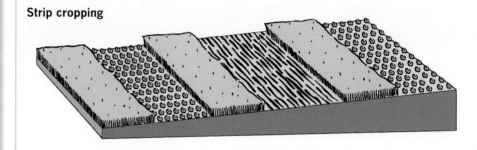

Stone lines

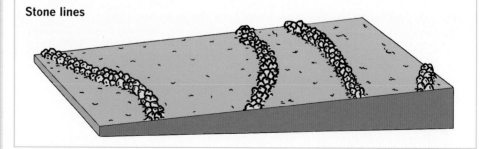

Fertilizer use worldwide

Key words

fertilizer

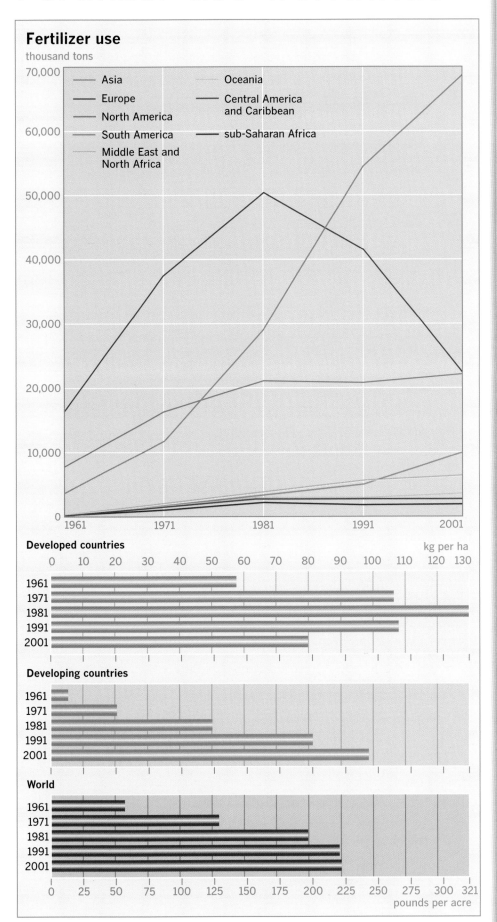

Fertilizer use

thousand tons

Legend:
- Asia
- Europe
- North America
- South America
- Middle East and North Africa
- Oceania
- Central America and Caribbean
- sub-Saharan Africa

Developed countries — kg per ha

Developing countries

World — pounds per acre

The use of fertilizers

- The major chemical requirements of most plants for growth are nitrogen, potassium, phosphorous, calcium, magnesium, and sulfur.
- Fertilizers deliver these nutrients to crops to enable fast and healthy growth.
- Fertilizer was not used heavily until the 1950s but since then its use has greatly increased.
- In 1950 the global fertilizer use was 18 pounds per acre (20 kg ha). By 1990 this had increased to 81 pounds per acre (91 kg ha).

The benefits of fertilizers

- There is considerable potential for increasing world food supply by increasing fertilizer use in low production countries.
- It has been estimated that the developing world could at least triple its crop production by raising fertilizer use to the world average.

The problems with fertilizers

- Agriculture accounts for 86 percent of human-generated nitrogen.
- Over-fertilization is a concern in the developed world, where relatively affluent farmers have the means to over-fertilize, when they may be unaware of the specific nutrient content of soils or the needs of the crops.
- Around half of every ton of fertilizer applied to fields does not reach the plant tissue. It either evaporates or is washed into local watercourses.

The solution

- Better education is needed to time the application of fertilizers, calculate the correct doses, and more accurately deliver it to the crop in the most economical manner.

© Diagram Visual Information Ltd.

Key words

DDT
pesticide

Pesticide usage

- In 1995, world pesticide consumption peaked at 2.8 million tons of active ingredients with a market value of $38 billion.
- Only seven companies now supply about 90 percent of the pesticide market.
- Use of pesticides in the developed world is now decreasing. This is partly due to more powerful new chemicals that are used in much smaller amounts.

Usage in developing nations

- Pesticide usage is still increasing in developing nations and is often used in a way that is environmentally damaging and not sustainable.
- This includes the use of many substances now banned in developed countries because of their severe impact on human health and the environment.
- Many developing world farmers lack the education needed to apply correct pesticides at the correct time in correct doses.

The history of DDT

- DDT is an organochlorine pesticide that was first used in the 1940s.
- It was used worldwide to great effect and was particularly successful in combating insect-borne diseases such as malaria and typhus.
- Insects soon developed resistance to DDT and fears grew over its effects on the environment.
- By 1969 DDT residues and metabolites were found to be causing major environmental damage worldwide.
- DDT was banned in the United States in 1972, but it is still produced and used in many developing countries.

Pesticide use worldwide

World pesticide production, 2002

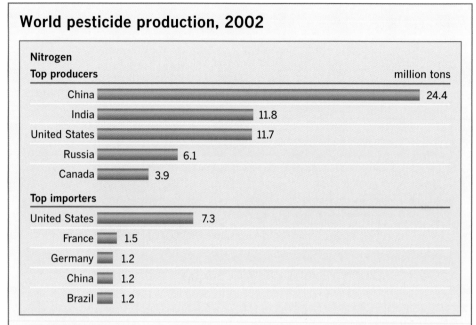

Nitrogen

Top producers — million tons

China	24.4
India	11.8
United States	11.7
Russia	6.1
Canada	3.9

Top importers

United States	7.3
France	1.5
Germany	1.2
China	1.2
Brazil	1.2

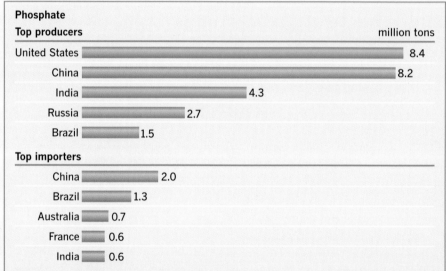

Phosphate

Top producers — million tons

United States	8.4
China	8.2
India	4.3
Russia	2.7
Brazil	1.5

Top importers

China	2.0
Brazil	1.3
Australia	0.7
France	0.6
India	0.6

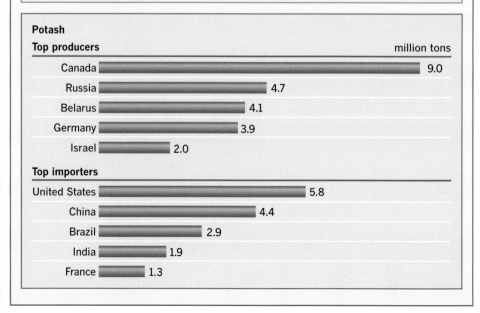

Potash

Top producers — million tons

Canada	9.0
Russia	4.7
Belarus	4.1
Germany	3.9
Israel	2.0

Top importers

United States	5.8
China	4.4
Brazil	2.9
India	1.9
France	1.3

Transgenic crops

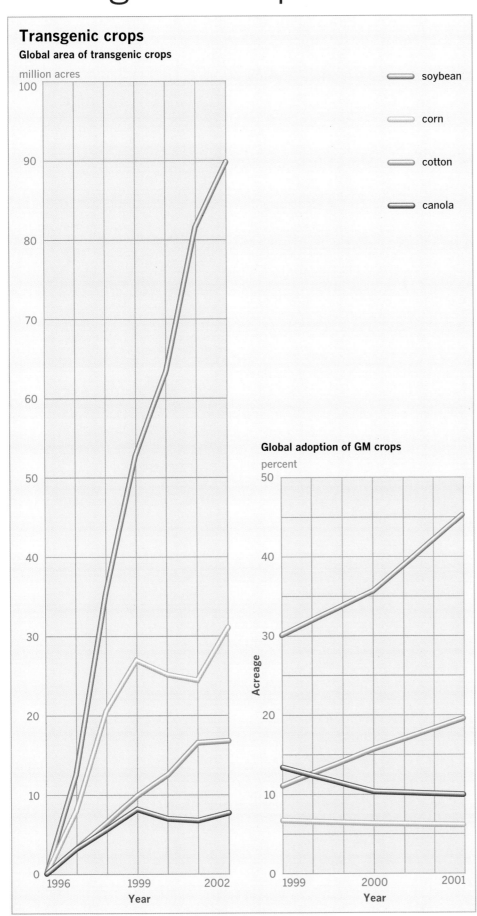

Transgenic crops

Global area of transgenic crops

million acres

Legend: soybean, corn, cotton, canola

Year (1996, 1999, 2002)

Global adoption of GM crops

percent

Acreage

Year (1999, 2000, 2001)

Key words

crossbreeding
genetically
  modified (GM)
  crop
transgenic

Plant breeding

- Plant breeders have been crossbreeding crop plants for centuries in an effort to combine desirable traits.
- Incorporating traits such as improved quality, higher yields, pest or disease resistance, and tolerance of drought, heat, and cold, means that plants will be better suited to grow in some areas than others.
- It is now possible to add desirable traits to crop plants in the laboratory.

Transgenic crops

- A transgenic crop plant contains genes that have been artificially implanted in the plant's genome.
- Transgenic crops are often called genetically modified (GM) crops.
- The inserted gene may come from another unrelated plant, or from a completely different species such as an animal or bacteria.
- This technology enables scientists to bring together, in one plant, genes from a range of living sources.
- The process of making transgenic crops is relatively new to science and is at the cutting edge of human knowledge.

The controversy

- Transgenic technology is viewed by many as "meddling with nature" and many countries have banned the use of transgenic crops altogether.
- Some proponents of transgenic crops claim it will help solve world food shortage problems.

Key words

crossbreeding
herbicide
pesticide
transgenic

Types of transgenic crops

- There are many types of transgenic crops designed for different purposes.
- The most widely used today are soybean, corn, and cotton.

Insect resistant crops

- Some plants have been designed to express pesticides, removing the need to apply synthetic chemicals.
- *Bacillus thuringiensis* (or Bt), is a naturally occurring soil bacteria that contains a toxin lethal to insects.
- Scientists have incorporated the gene for this toxin into different crop plant varieties, so that after insects feed on the plant they die.

Herbicide tolerant crops

- Other plants have been altered to withstand the application of powerful herbicides, so that troublesome weeds die while the crop plants remain alive.

Other transgenic crops

- Tea and coffee varieties are being created that grow without caffeine.
- Genes for vaccines and drugs are being inserted into plants.

The future of transgenic crops

- While the use of transgenic crops increases in some countries, many others are still unsure of its safety. There are fears that:
- Insects might become resistant to certain varieties.
- Crossbreeding might occur between normal and transgenic crops.
- Crops expressing pesticides might the cause contamination and pollution of water supplies, or even the air.

Transgenic crop production

Production of transgenic crops, 2000

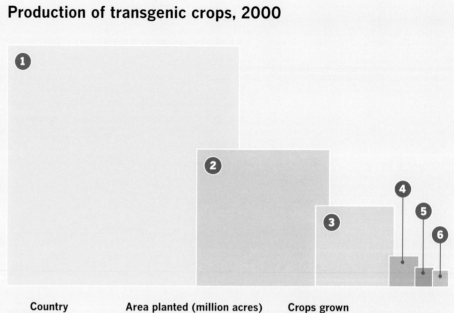

	Country	Area planted (million acres)	Crops grown
❶	USA	74.8	soybean, corn, cotton, canola
❷	Argentina	24.7	soybean, corn, cotton
❸	Canada	7.4	soybean, corn, canola
❹	China	1.2	cotton
❺	South Africa	0.5	corn, cotton
❻	Australia	0.4	cotton
	Mexico	minor	cotton
	Bulgaria	minor	corn
	Romania	minor	soybean, potato
	Spain	minor	corn
	Germany	minor	corn
	France	minor	corn
	Uruguay	minor	soybean

Transgenic crops area planted, 1999
million acres

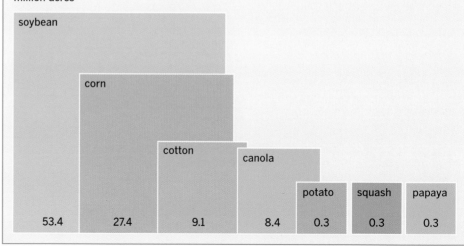

Human casualties of pesticide use

Key words

carcinogen	World Health
DDT	Organization
pesticide	(WHO)

Obsolete pesticides in Africa, 2002

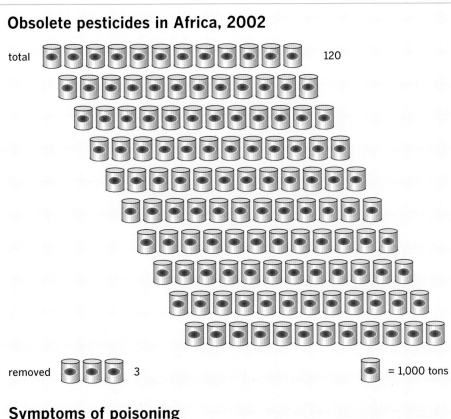

total   120

removed 3   = 1,000 tons

Symptoms of poisoning

Muscular
- reddening of skin
- rashes
- tremors
- muscle twitching
- muscle weakness
- blisters

Digestive
- vomiting
- cramps
- diarrhea

Nervous system
- coma
- headache
- pinpoint pupils
- blurred vision
- excessive tear production
- dizziness

Respiration
- elevated blood pressure
- tightness in chest
- rapid heartbeat
- sweating

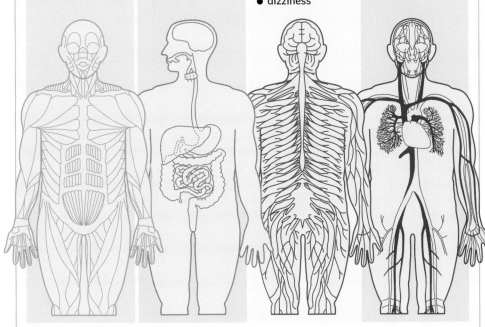

The cost to health

- The World Health Organization (WHO) estimates that each year about three million people suffer severe pesticide poisoning, with more than 20,000 deaths.
- Men and women working in the agricultural sector in developing countries make up 59 percent of the global working population.
- In these countries pesticides cause 14 percent of all known occupational injuries in agriculture and ten percent of all fatalities.

Dangerous chemicals

- About 30 percent of pesticides marketed in developing countries do not meet internationally accepted quality standards.
- Experts have classified the active ingredients of about 160 pesticides as being carcinogenic to some extent, while 118 pesticides have been identified as disrupting hormonal balance.

Obsolete pesticides

- It is thought that there are at least 500,000 tons of unwanted, unused, or obsolete pesticides worldwide.
- In 2002 in Africa alone there were estimated to be about 120,000 tons.
- Between 1992 and 2002 less than five percent of the toxic waste was disposed of safely.
- Adequate hazardous waste destruction facilities do not exist in Africa, so waste has to be shipped to a developed country for high-temperature incineration at an average cost of $3,500 per ton.
- Obsolete pesticides include DDT, Dieldrin, Lindane, and Malathion.
- Dieldrin is said to be five times as toxic as DDT when swallowed and 40 times as toxic when absorbed through the skin.

Key words

Food and Agriculture Organization (FAO)	tilling
	topsoil
soil erosion	

Damaging land use techniques

- Conventional tillage methods with tractors and plows are a major cause of severe soil loss in many developing nations.
- However, if tillage is neglected, the soil becomes unproductive and weedier, so tillage is an essential part of the work of any farmer.
- The UN Food and Agriculture Organization (FAO) estimates that some 40 percent of land degradation around the world is caused by soil erosion.
- Intensive tillage causes more erosion and soil degradation, especially in warmer areas where the topsoil layer is thinner.

Benefits of minimum tillage

- Minimum tillage is a technique used to minimize the amount of soil disturbance while the seedbed is being prepared and maintained.
- The main purpose of using a minimum tillage system is to reduce costs of production while maintaining or increasing yields.
- Special no-till planting machinery pushes seeds directly into the ground.
- Erosion is limited using this method because soil structure is kept intact, moisture is conserved, and plant cover is retained.
- Other benefits include reduced labor requirements, reduced machinery wear, fuel savings, and reduced release of carbon gases.
- However, minimum tillage is not an easy option: it requires commitment, time, and patience from the farmer.

Sustainable land use: minimum tillage

Intensive tillage

Intensive tillage leaves the soil bare and unprotected.

Minimum tillage

Minimum tillage protects the soil against erosion. Special no-till planters cut through crop residues and plant into soil without plowing or disking.

Sustainable land use: intercropping and agroforestry

Key words

agriculture
crop

Agroforestry types

Shade systems
These comprise the intentional manipulation of trees, shrubs, and ground vegetation to produce both timber and shade-requiring nontimber crops.

Silvopasture
Here trees are combined with forage and livestock production.

Sun systems
In sun systems, woody perennials are planted with annual or other crops that require full sunlight.

Timber belts
These consist of multiple rows of trees planted for both environmental protection and the production of crops.

Integrated riparian management
This is the management of areas bordering waterbodies and watercourses to enhance and protect aquatic resources while generating economic benefits.

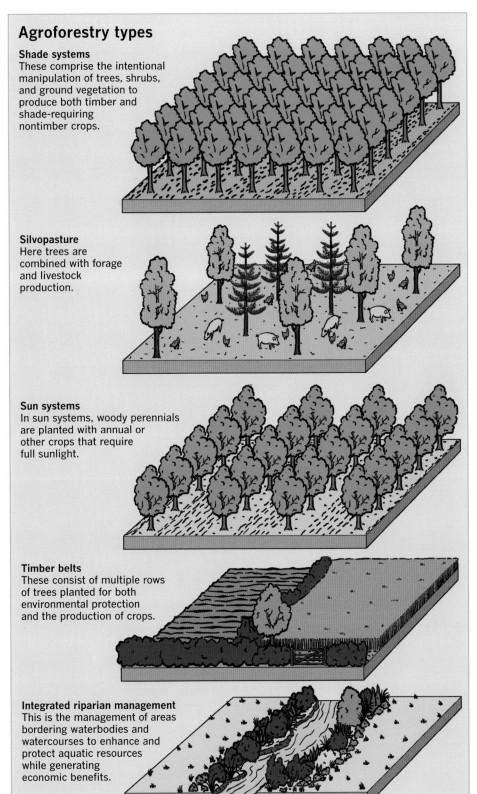

Intercropping

- Intercropping is the growing of two or more crops in proximity to promote interactions between them.
- When two or more crops are grown together, each must have adequate space to maximize cooperation and minimize competition between the crops.
- Intercropping is useful for a number of reasons; for example, a neighboring crop may be more attractive to pests than the main crop and can serve as an attractant.
- Legumes such as peas, beans, and clover fix atmospheric nitrogen using symbiotic *Rhizobium* bacteria for their own use and for that of neighboring plants.
- Some plants exude chemicals that suppress or repel pests and protect neighboring plants.
- Tall or densely canopied plants may protect more vulnerable plants through shading or by providing a wind break.

Agroforestry

- Agroforestry, like intercropping, combines the production of trees with other crops and livestock.
- By blending agriculture and forestry with conservation practices, agroforestry strives to optimize economic, environmental, and social benefits.
- There are five basic types of agroforestry: shade systems, silvopasture, sun systems, timber belts and integrated riparian management.
- Intensive management of trees, agricultural crops and animals, and agricultural land is the key to successful agroforestry.

© Diagram Visual Information Ltd.

Key words

fertilizer
runoff
soil erosion

Terraces

- Terraces are raised mounds of earth with flat tops and sloping sides, constructed across the slope of a cultivated hillside.
- Terracing reduces soil erosion by breaking long slopes into a series of shorter slopes.
- Terraces considerably reduce soil erosion if they are well planned, correctly constructed, and properly maintained.
- The efficiency of a terrace system will also depend on the adoption of other conservation practices.
- The main objectives of terracing are:
- To reduce the velocity of runoff.
- To reduce the volume of runoff.
- To reduce the losses of soil, seed, and fertilizer.
- To increase soil moisture content through improved filtration.

Bunds

- Contour bunding is one of the simplest methods of soil and water conservation and plays an important role in fields with a medium slope.
- Bunds are embankments of earth or stones that act as a barrier to water flow, reducing soil erosion and keeping the soil moist.
- Trees can be planted on bunds so that nutrients are returned to the soil while the root systems bind everything together.
- Cattle can also be grazed on a bund if it is planted with grass.
- Sometimes farmers are reluctant to incorporate bunding as a method of soil and water conservation because they feel that the area under the bund is wasted.

Sustainable land use: terraces and bunds

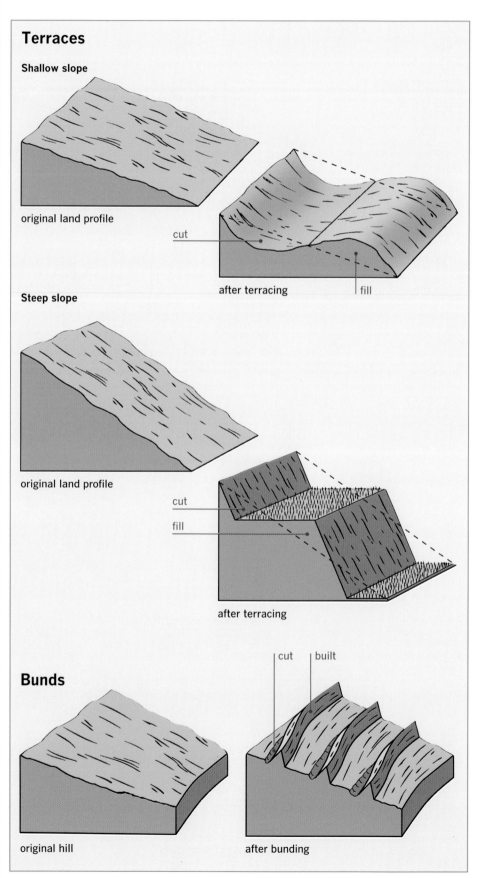

Terraces

Shallow slope

original land profile

cut

after terracing   fill

Steep slope

original land profile

cut

fill

after terracing

Bunds

cut   built

original hill   after bunding

Sustainable land use: soil protection and rejuvenation

Key words

crop
fertilizer
plowing
reforestation

Soil protection

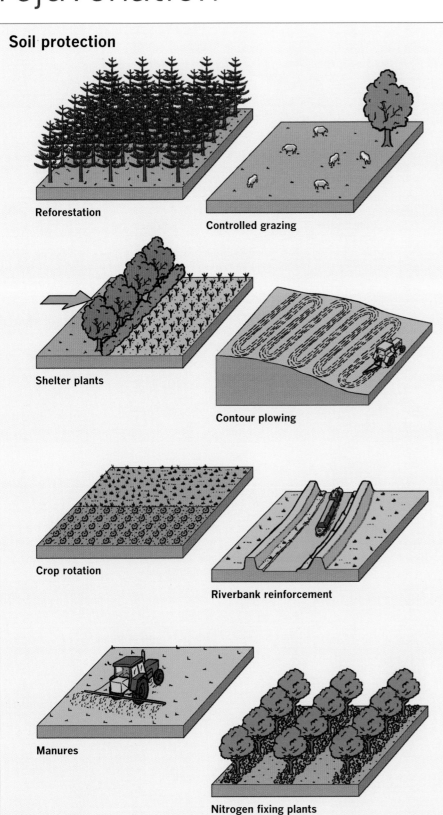

Reforestation

Controlled grazing

Shelter plants

Contour plowing

Crop rotation

Riverbank reinforcement

Manures

Nitrogen fixing plants

Protecting the soil

● With modern destructive farming methods, soil fertility is often lost or greatly reduced.

● There are, however, a number of ways that soil fertility can be both protected and restored.

Reforestation

● *Reforestation*—planting trees—gives soil stability by binding it together so it can retain nutrients and water more easily.

Controlled grazing

● Controlled grazing can be good for soils, but it is important to prevent overgrazing, which leads to a loss of fertility.

Shelter plants

● Shelter plants reduce the effects of wind on soils.

Contour plowing

● Contour plowing prevents gully formation.

Crop rotation

● The use of fallow periods and crop rotation allows soils to recover fertility naturally.

Riverbank reinforcement

● Riverbanks can be reinforced to prevent the loss of topsoil after flooding.

Manures

● Applying manures and crop residues to the soil restores fertility without the use of synthetic fertilizers.

Nitrogen fixing plants

● Plants using *Rhizobium* bacteria such as clover, peas, and beans fix nitrogen and return it to the soil, increasing fertility.

Key words

parasitic wasp

Biological control

- Biological control uses naturally occurring predators, parasites, and diseases to control pests.
- Biological control was pioneered in the 1890s when the cottony cushion scale insect attacked the citrus fruit industry in California.
- A natural predator of the cottony cushion scale, a lady beetle called *Rhodolia cardinalis*, was introduced from Australia to control the pest.
- Lady beetles, lacewings, and parasitic wasps are among the most commonly used biological control agents.

Bacterial control

- Bacteria such as *Bacillus thuringiensis* and viruses are also used to control insect and mite pests successfully.
- A baculovirus was successfully used against the rhinoceros palm beetle *(Oryctes rhinoceros)*, when it devastated Pacific island coconut palms.

Pheromones and viruses

- Synthesized sex pheromones are often used to lure male insects into traps in great numbers.
- The myxoma virus was used to control rabbits in Australia with only partial success.

Results

- To date, of more than 6,000 introductions of alien natural enemies to control pests, only around 25–30 percent have been successful.
- Great care must be taken when introducing alien species to control pests in new environments.
- Sometimes the predator will prefer to prey on species other than the pest and cause great damage to the ecosystem.

Sustainable land use: biological pest control

Pests and biological solutions

Rhinoceros beetle
The rhinoceros beetle, a pest of coconut palms, was successfully controlled by a virus.

Lady beetle
The larva of the lady beetle can eat hundreds of aphids every day, and the adult beetle also eats them.

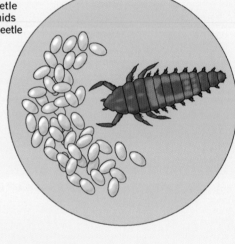

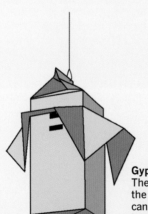

Gypsy moth
The gypsy moth, introduced to the United States from Europe, can defoliate trees and vines, but is controlled by pheromone traps.

Boll weevil and trichogramma

The boll weevil, a pest of cotton growers in the United States, can be controlled by the parasitic wasp trichogramma.
The wasp lays an egg in a bollworm egg; the wasp's larva feeds on the egg, and emerges as an adult wasp eight days later.

Land degradation and habitat destruction

Key words

alkalinization	salinization
deforestation	soil erosion
desertification	
habitat	
irrigation	

Land degradation: the Americas

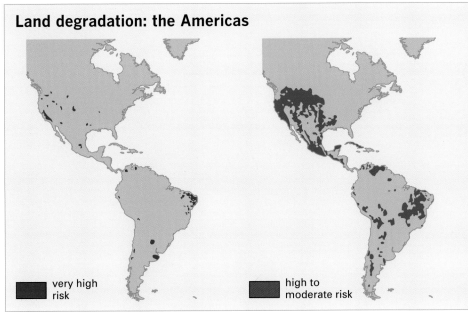

very high risk

high to moderate risk

Land degradation: rest of the world

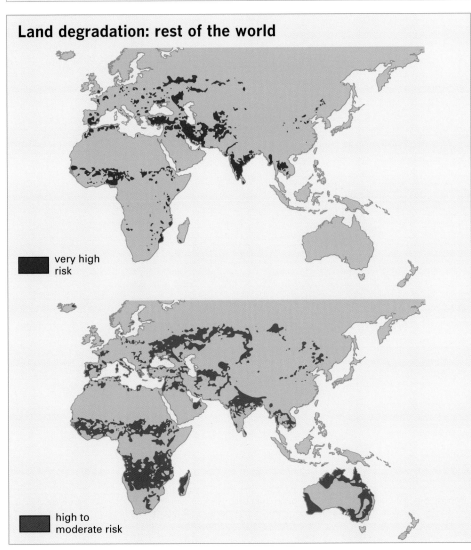

very high risk

high to moderate risk

Introduction

- *Land degradation* is a human-induced or natural process that negatively affects the land's ability to take up, store, and recycle water, energy, and nutrients.
- Land degradation can eventually lead to the destruction of habitats such as tropical forests, coastal environments and Arctic tundra.

Human causes

- There are many causes of land degradation, almost all of which are human-induced.
- Land clearance and deforestation, agriculture, conversion of land for urban developments, irrigation, and pollution are all major causes.

The major stresses

- The major stresses that degrade land are: loss of organic matter and nutrients; destruction of soil structure; alkalinity or acidity increase; salinization; and erosion by wind and water.

The consequences

- As natural habitats become degraded, so their ability to function as part of an ecosystem diminishes.
- Degraded land loses the ability to hold and store nutrients and water and eventually becomes of no use in ecological processes.
- Desertification is land degradation occurring in the arid, semiarid, and subhumid areas of the world.
- More than 25 percent of Earth's land surface has already suffered soil erosion and degradation.

Key words

soil erosion

Causes of erosion

- Wind and water are the primary causes of soil erosion, but their effect on the landscape can be initiated and accelerated by human actions that make the land vulnerable.
- Experts believe that human activity causes ten times more land erosion than all of the natural processes combined.
- Because soil is made at roughly the same rate as natural erosion, it is believed that human activities are stripping soil from Earth's surface faster than nature can replace it.

Wind erosion

- Wind erosion occurs when wind physically removes the lighter, less dense soil particles such as organic matter and silts.
- It removes the most fertile part of the soil, lowering soil productivity and increasing costs.
- Wind erosion is a serious problem in many parts of the world and is especially damaging in arid and semiarid regions.
- Deserts result when wind erosion strips the soil covering an area of land of its vegetation.

Water erosion

- Environments with heavy rainfall are at risk from water erosion.
- This occurs when flowing water or the impact of raindrops causes nutrients and soil particles to be washed away.
- In Brazil, where trees are removed for logging, frequent mudslides occur because the soil becomes unstable without roots to hold it in place.

Wind and water erosion

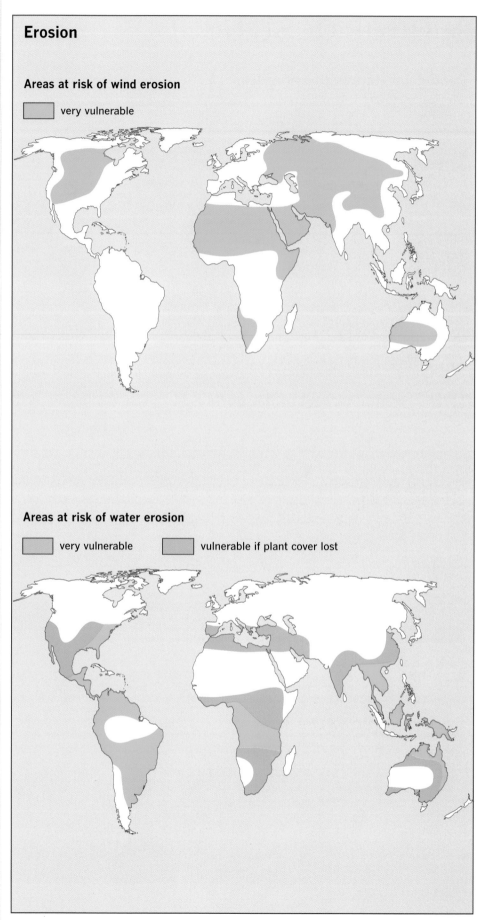

Erosion

Areas at risk of wind erosion

☐ very vulnerable

Areas at risk of water erosion

☐ very vulnerable   ☐ vulnerable if plant cover lost

Human causes of erosion

Human activities causing erosion

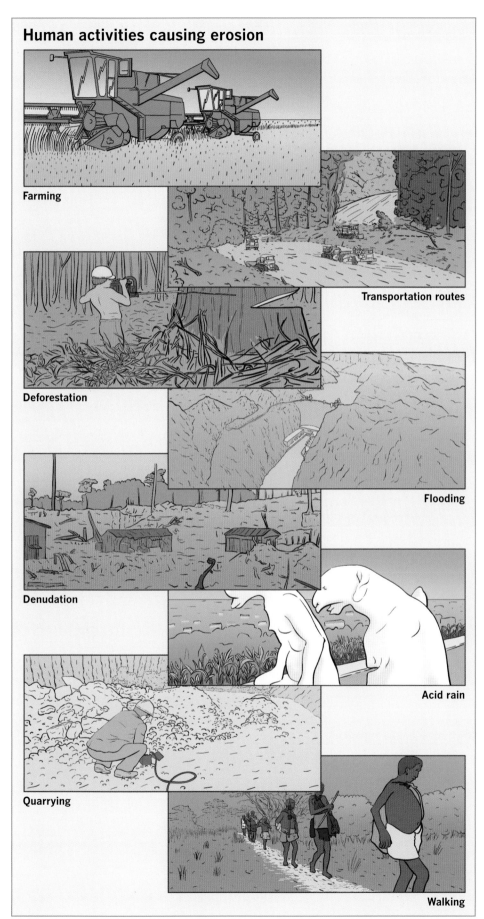

Farming

Transportation routes

Deforestation

Flooding

Denudation

Acid rain

Quarrying

Walking

Key words

acid rain
deforestation

Human activity

- Landscape erosion as a result of human activity can take many forms.
- Human activity often begins the erosion of a landscape and natural systems then accelerate the process.

Farming

- Farming activities continually expose soil to the elements through plowing and tilling. This results in increased erosion.

Transportation routes

- The construction of roads and railroads often allow the elements to begin erosion of the land, and vehicles then accelerate the process.

Deforestation

- Deforestation removes cover for soil from the weather and affects the stability provided by tree roots.

Flooding

- When water levels rise, soils become waterlogged, causing mudslides.

Denudation

- Denudation is the total removal of natural land cover, after which the elements are free to begin eroding the landscape.

Acid rain

- Acid rain corrodes calcium-based rock. This is clearly visible on stone buildings and monuments.

Quarrying

- Open-cast mining and quarrying directly erodes the landscape and affects the stability of surrounding areas.

Walking

- Footpaths can erode the landscape when they are not paved and are much used.

Key words

deforestation
irrigation
soil erosion
topsoil

Primary consequences

- Water and wind action often result in soil erosion.
- Soil may also become unstable due to a lack of vegetation holding it together, resulting in landslides.
- Soils transported by water and wind can build up as deposits in new locations.

Landslides

- Hilly areas that have suffered serious deforestation, and rapid, poorly planned urban expansion onto hillsides, are most at risk of landslides.
- Without trees and vegetation to hold the soil in place, severe rains can wash away massive amounts of mud and topsoil, often causing loss of life.

Secondary consequences

- Loss of soil makes land infertile and renders it unsuitable for farming.
- Unstable land is no longer suitable or safe ground on which to build houses and settlements.
- Deposited soils can clog up irrigation systems, hampering farming productivity.

Tertiary consequences

- People often abandon land that is no longer suitable for farming or settlement.
- The actions of people can therefore eventually result in the loss of their own living space, or that of others.
- The end result can be famine and refugee populations searching for new places to settle.

Consequences of erosion

Effects of erosion

- landslides become more frequent
- silt reduces lifetime of hydroelectric plants and reservoirs
- infrastructure destroyed by floods
- rural populations migrate to the city
- crops grown on unprotected fields
- gully erosion reduces available cropland
- wind erosion affects badly managed pasture
- mud banks reduce river navigability
- flooded village
- fish catch in shallow waters diminishes
- monocrops dominating large areas
- sloped land cultivated without terracing
- deforestation

Repairing damaged land

Repairs to damaged land

Soil reclamation on eroded land

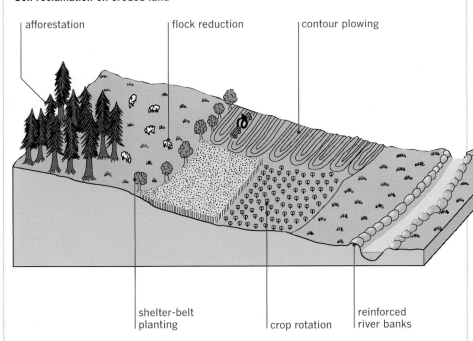

afforestation

flock reduction

contour plowing

shelter-belt planting

crop rotation

reinforced river banks

Drainage

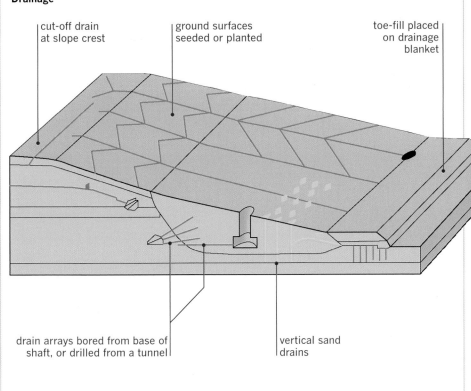

cut-off drain at slope crest

ground surfaces seeded or planted

toe-fill placed on drainage blanket

drain arrays bored from base of shaft, or drilled from a tunnel

vertical sand drains

Key words

soil erosion

Reversing erosion

- Although difficult, it is possible to slow and repair the effects of soil erosion once it has begun.
- The extent of possible repair depends on the area of land to be dealt with, and the level of resources available, such as time, money, manpower, and materials.
- There are a number of different ways to repair and prevent further erosion.

Soil stability

- Deep soils on sloping land need to be stabilized to prevent movement from gravity and water.
- Replanting the soil with trees and shrubs is the best solution.
- The soil can be stapled with stakes while the roots take hold.
- Grass can be used on flatter soils.

Physical prevention

- Drainage channels can be dug to divert groundwater from causing erosion.
- Windbreaks such as walls and hedges can be used to block the wind.

Soil thickness

- Eroded soils can be replaced by importing soil from other locations.
- Imported soil must be stabilized quickly.

Management

- Repairs to damaged land will be quickly undone if management techniques are not changed.
- Rotation systems for arable farming, grazing, and timber felling are often effective at preventing a recurrence of erosion.

© Diagram Visual Information Ltd.

Key words

deforestation
frontier forest
opencast mining

Deforestation

- The removal of forests has become a worldwide cause for concern.
- During the 1990s the global net loss of forests was 232 million acres (94 million ha) or 2.4 percent of the total forest area.
- Fragmentation of tropical forests also accounts for much of the damage because many plant and animal species require large amounts of uninterrupted cover to survive.
- Once an area of forest is destroyed, it is rarely allowed to regrow.
- Often the land is used for short-term commercial farming, after which it is of little use.

Frontier forests

- *Frontier forests* are large, relatively undisturbed, and ecologically intact forests, and are considered the most valuable.
- They are being destroyed at an increasing rate worldwide.

Human encroachment

- Rising populations in developing countries require more space to settle and live.
- In some countries, governments have given incentives to settlers to move into forested areas to build new homes and begin farming.
- New populations require wood for building and fuel for cooking, which increases deforestation further.

Trade, farms, and industry

- Tropical timber can provide a valuable source of income through international trade.
- Land clearance is often required for farms, factories, and opencast mines.
- Transportation routes are often cut through forests to improve communication networks.

Deforestation: a global problem

Global deforestation

Forest cover before human deforestation

Current forest cover

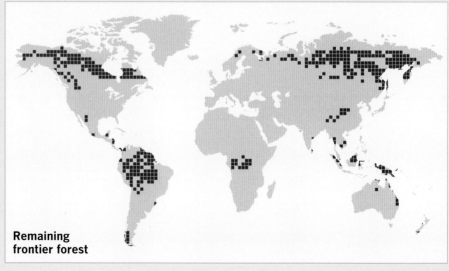

Remaining frontier forest

Deforestation: rate of forest loss

Key words

deforestation

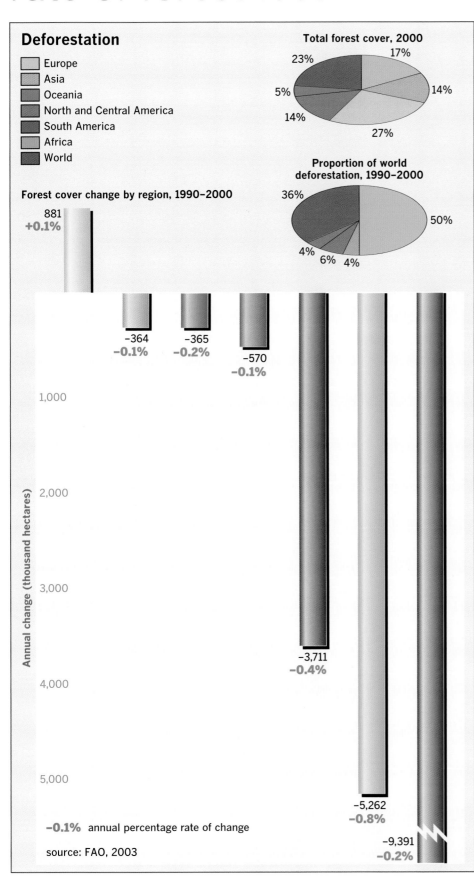

Deforestation

- Europe
- Asia
- Oceania
- North and Central America
- South America
- Africa
- World

Total forest cover, 2000

23% 17% 14% 27% 14% 5%

Forest cover change by region, 1990–2000

Proportion of world deforestation, 1990–2000

36% 50% 4% 6% 4%

881 +0.1%

−364 −0.1%

−365 −0.2%

−570 −0.1%

1,000

Annual change (thousand hectares)

2,000

3,000

−3,711 −0.4%

4,000

5,000

−5,262 −0.8%

−0.1% annual percentage rate of change

−9,391 −0.2%

source: FAO, 2003

Loss of forests

- An estimated 50 percent of Earth's land surface was once forested.
- Today, only 30 percent of the land is covered by forest.
- About 7.5 percent of the total forest cover is tropical forest, which is only about 50 percent of the area of tropical forest that existed 50 years ago.
- The average rate of tropical deforestation worldwide during the 1980s was aproximately 0.8 percent per year.
- The rate of deforestation has remained roughly constant, but as the area of forest has grown smaller it appears to increase.
- The current rate is about 0.9 percent each year and rising.

Collecting data

- Calculating deforestation rates is difficult because absolute figures are collated from thousands of areas of forest lost all over the world.
- Sometimes it is difficult to get data from countries that are geographically inaccessible or politically unstable.
- Some methods of collecting data have proved impractical and inaccurate; deforestation rates are therefore often based on estimates rather than established fact.

Satellite mapping

- Satellite mapping is now the accepted standard technique for making calculations in the twenty-first century.
- It is a relatively accurate means of gathering deforestation data because vast areas of landscape can be analyzed by computer easily.

Key words

habitat

The Amazon basin

- The Amazon River is approximately 4,010 miles (6,450 km) long, the second-longest river in the world.
- Together with its many tributaries it covers eight South American countries: Bolivia, Brazil, Colombia, Ecuador, Guyana, Peru, Suriname, and Venezuela.
- This area is known collectively as the Amazon basin, and holds the largest continuous forest on Earth.

Fire and logging

- The Amazon forest is being cleared at an alarming rate for logging and to make way for roads, settlements, and other developments.
- When trees are felled in the Amazon, the unwanted offcut and vegetation is burned.
- The fires lit for this purpose often get out of control and large areas of virgin forest are burned.
- The result is significant and unnecessary damage to tropical forest.
- The estimated area of forest damaged in this way each year is between 6,500 and 23,000 square miles.

American Corporation Treaty (ACT)

- In 1978 the eight countries that lie within the Amazon basin signed the Amazon Cooperation Treaty (ACT).
- The treaty is recognized by some as an effective instrument for discussion and agreement on policies concerning the future of the Amazon basin.
- However, many experts still view the future of the Amazon basin as bleak unless habitat destruction is brought under control.

The destruction of Amazonia

Destruction of the Amazon rainforest
Annual deforestation in Brazil

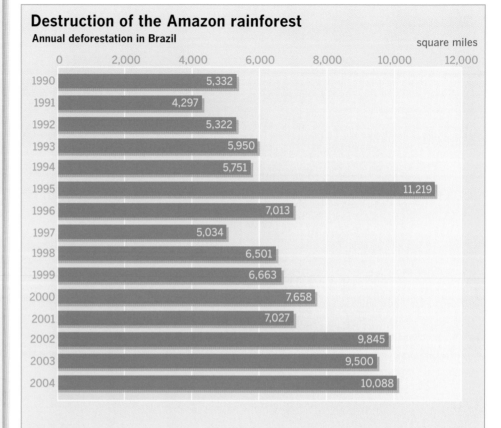

square miles

Year	Deforestation
1990	5,332
1991	4,297
1992	5,322
1993	5,950
1994	5,751
1995	11,219
1996	7,013
1997	5,034
1998	6,501
1999	6,663
2000	7,658
2001	7,027
2002	9,845
2003	9,500
2004	10,088

Tropical forest
The area of tropical forest surrounding the Amazon River is known as the Amazon basin or Amazonia.

Deforestation in Costa Rica

Key words

diversity hotspot
ecotourism
endemic species

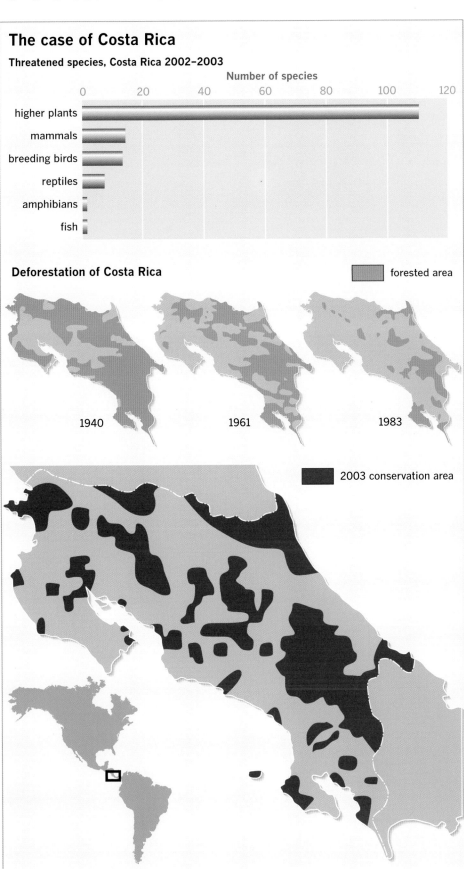

The case of Costa Rica

Threatened species, Costa Rica 2002–2003

Number of species

- higher plants
- mammals
- breeding birds
- reptiles
- amphibians
- fish

Deforestation of Costa Rica

forested area

1940   1961   1983

2003 conservation area

Diversity hotspot

- Costa Rica, despite its small size, is regarded as a diversity hotspot and has one of the highest concentrations of plant and animal species in the world.
- It is home to around 9,000 species of plants, 1,239 species of butterflies, 850 species of birds, 350 species of reptiles and amphibians, and 205 species of mammals.
- Many of these species are endemic to Costa Rica, which further emphasizes how important it is to protect them.

Living space and plantations

- The countries in Central America, including Costa Rica, are all small in area.
- Expanding human populations have resulted in forests being cleared for living and farming space.
- About 65 percent of Central America's forests have been lost in this way since the arrival of Europeans.
- The majority of Costa Rica's forest was destroyed by 1983.

Conservation strategies

- Recent conservation projects in Costa Rica aim to replace as much of the lost tropical forest as possible, and to conserve what remains.
- The country now embraces ecotourism as a way of raising money for conservation.
- Because of Costa Rica's mountainous terrain, some 50 percent of the country is regarded as being suitable only for trees.
- This has helped conservation teams to protect many areas.

© Diagram Visual Information Ltd.

Key words

ecosystem
land reclamation
mangrove forest

Mangrove forests

- *Mangrove forests* are distributed throughout the world's tropical and subtropical ocean coastlines.
- The area with the greatest mangrove diversity is the India–Pacific region.
- Mangroves are composed of salt-tolerant trees and other plant species that are capable of growing in seawater.
- Mangroves have an intricate root system that allows the plants and trees to take root in loose sand or soil.
- They also possess a specialized and unique dispersal mechanism that allows the seeds to remain attached to the parent plant until they germinate.
- Mangroves form the basis of unique and rich ecosystems, but are threatened by human activities.

Threats to mangroves

- Mangroves were once regarded as unproductive and useless environments.
- They were therefore cleared at an alarming rate.
- It is estimated that around 62 million acres (25 million ha) of mangrove forest have been destroyed or grossly degraded in the last 50 years.
- Ecuador, Vietnam, and Thailand have lost more than 50 percent of their original mangroves.
- Shrimp farming accounts for much damage to mangroves in some countries, as does the ever-expanding tourist industry.
- Other causes of destruction are dredging, land reclamation, clearance for agriculture, and salt farming.

Disappearing mangroves

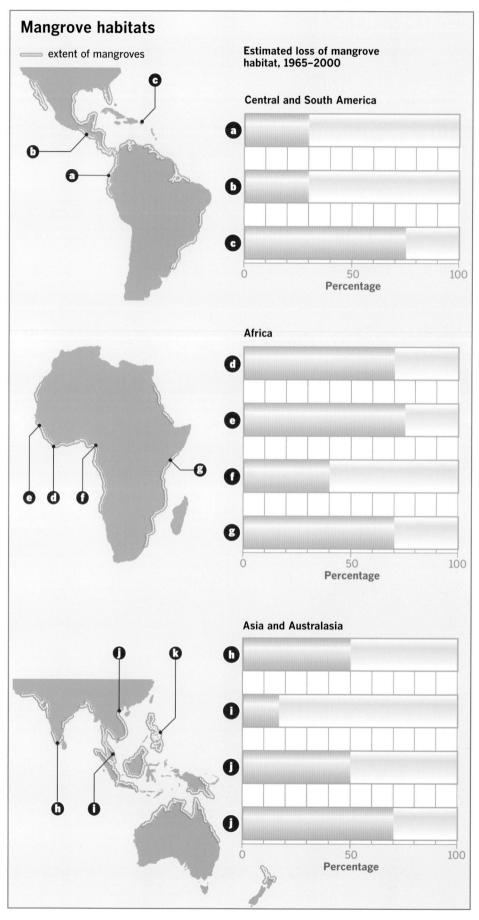

Mangrove habitats

extent of mangroves

Estimated loss of mangrove habitat, 1965–2000

Why mangroves matter

Mangroves as habitats

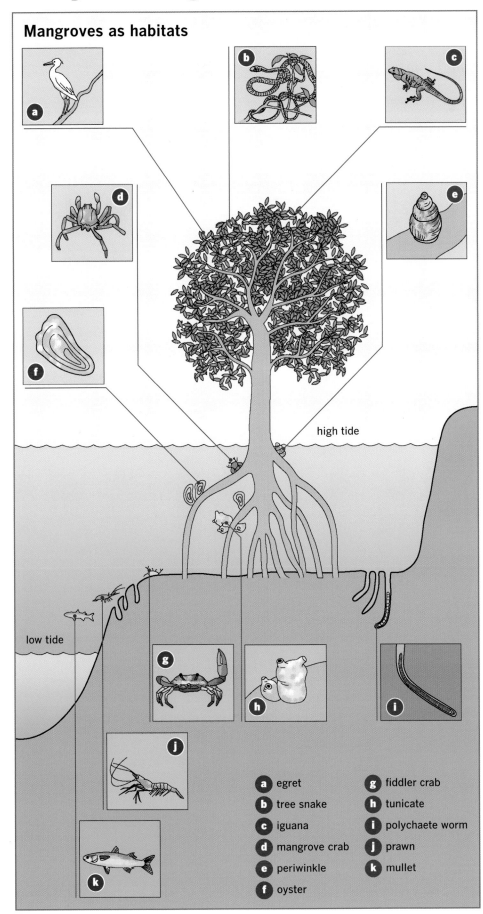

high tide

low tide

a egret	**g** fiddler crab
b tree snake	**h** tunicate
c iguana	**i** polychaete worm
d mangrove crab	**j** prawn
e periwinkle	**k** mullet
f oyster	

Key words

habitat
organic matter
pollution
rhizofiltration

Eco-services

- Mangroves are hugely beneficial to the environment and to people: they provide not only food and livelihoods but also other, less obvious, eco-services.

Natural refuges

- Mangrove wetlands offer a habitat for more than 2,000 species of fish, shellfish, invertebrates, and plants.
- They provide a safe nursery and breeding ground for many species, including sharks and turtles.
- Mangroves are often the starting place of many food webs, with small species of plankton feeding on the organic matter produced.

Pollution control

- Mangroves can also help to control pollution by stopping excess amounts of nitrogen, phosphorous, and petroleum products from entering the ocean environment.
- This is done via a process called *rhizofiltration*.

Protection from the elements

- Mangroves act as a buffer zone by shielding the land from wind and trapping sediment in their roots.
- They also maintain a shallow slope on the seabed that absorbs tidal swells and can protect coastal settlements.
- In 1999 in the Indian state of Orissa, 10,000 people drowned during a cyclone. This disaster was made far worse because many of the state's coastal mangroves had been cut down to make way for shrimp farms.

© Diagram Visual Information Ltd.

Key words

atmosphere	runoff
biodiversity	topsoil
biomass	
biosphere	
greenhouse gas	

Soil degradation
- When trees are removed, topsoil is lost to wind and water erosion because there are no longer any roots to bind it together.
- Surface evaporation increases, reducing the moisture content of the soil.
- The nutrient content of the soil decreases rapidly and no further nutrients are added.

Water loss
- Forests act like a sponge by holding water in the soil and in the biomass of the trees.
- The removal of forests increases rainwater runoff and this in turn leads to the increased probability of floods and droughts.

Lungs of the earth
- Forests act as air purifiers by taking in carbon dioxide and releasing oxygen.
- This is called photosynthesis and is a chemical reaction that takes place in the leaves of trees and plants.
- In this way, it is thought that forests produce up to 40 percent of the world's oxygen.
- Depletion of tree stocks reduces the replenishment of atmospheric oxygen and allows carbon dioxide (CO_2) to build up in the atmosphere.
- The burning of forests contributes to greater atmospheric levels of greenhouse gases (up to 30 percent of the global release of CO_2).

Biodiversity
- It is estimated that more than half the world's plant and animal species live in rainforests, yet these forests cover only about six percent of the planet's surface.
- Deforestation is the primary cause of the loss of biodiversity in the world, as habitats for many species are lost.

The consequences of forest loss

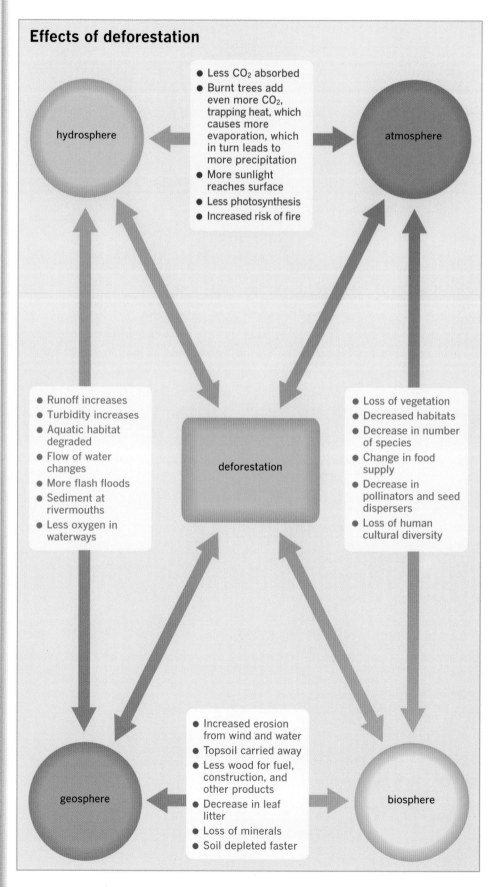

Effects of deforestation

hydrosphere

- Less CO_2 absorbed
- Burnt trees add even more CO_2, trapping heat, which causes more evaporation, which in turn leads to more precipitation
- More sunlight reaches surface
- Less photosynthesis
- Increased risk of fire

atmosphere

- Runoff increases
- Turbidity increases
- Aquatic habitat degraded
- Flow of water changes
- More flash floods
- Sediment at rivermouths
- Less oxygen in waterways

deforestation

- Loss of vegetation
- Decreased habitats
- Decrease in number of species
- Change in food supply
- Decrease in pollinators and seed dispersers
- Loss of human cultural diversity

geosphere

- Increased erosion from wind and water
- Topsoil carried away
- Less wood for fuel, construction, and other products
- Decrease in leaf litter
- Loss of minerals
- Soil depleted faster

biosphere

Causes of wetland loss

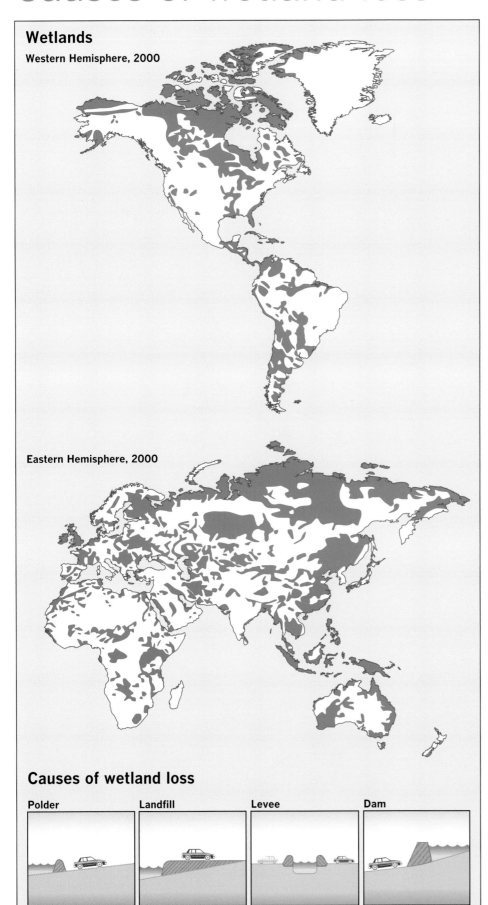

Wetlands

Western Hemisphere, 2000

Eastern Hemisphere, 2000

Causes of wetland loss

| Polder | Landfill | Levee | Dam |

© Diagram Visual Information Ltd.

Wetlands

- Wetlands provide valuable ecosystem services by regulating river flow and filtering pollutants.
- They are important habitats for bird and insect species, and provide spawning grounds for many species of fish.

Land reclamation

- Wetlands are usually found in lowland regions, often where people need more land.
- People drain the water away so that the land becomes dry and can then be developed for settlement and farming.
- This is called land reclamation, which is achieved using a number of different methods.

Polders

- When coastal wetlands, marshes, bogs, lakes, or riverbeds are reclaimed the areas are called *polders*.
- Dams are used to keep the water out and pumps are used to drain the wetland.

Landfill

- Landfill can be used to raise the level of wetland so that it drains naturally.
- Networks of ditches are also used to improve the drainage of this land.

Levees

- The waterlogging of river floodplains is prevented by the construction of levees.
- Levees are ridges built up on either side of a river to contain any rise in water level.

Dams

- Building reservoirs and hydroelectric dams can result in wetland loss.
- The flow of rivers is decreased, so any wetland below the dam dries up.
- Also, the body of water held behind the dam engulfs wetlands.

Key words

habitat
pollution

The Everglades

- The south of the state of Florida is dominated by a large area of wetland known as the Everglades.
- The Everglades is home to many unique species and is a stronghold for the American alligator *(Alligator mississippiensis)*.
- Much of the wetland is being drained and reclaimed so the land can be put to other uses.
- Farming and urban development are the main uses of reclaimed land.
- A significant proportion of the Everglades wetland is also being lost to pollution.
- Agricultural and industrial chemicals from the surrounding lands are killing plant and animal life.
- Flood control operations are also causing areas of wetland to dry up.

Yellowstone National Park

- The states of Wyoming, Montana, and Idaho all contain parts of the Yellowstone National Park.
- The park covers a huge area and contains many different habitat types including wetland areas such as rivers, lake fringes, and thermal springs.
- Water pollution is a major threat to these habitats in some areas, as more and more settlements and industrial sites are built.
- The pollution comes from sewage, waste, and mining operations.
- Ongoing mining practices have degraded Henderson Mountain, which lies just three miles northeast of Yellowstone National Park.
- Acid mine pollution and heavy metal contaminants have polluted the headwater sources of numerous rivers in the park and caused significant damage.

Wetland loss: Yellowstone and the Everglades

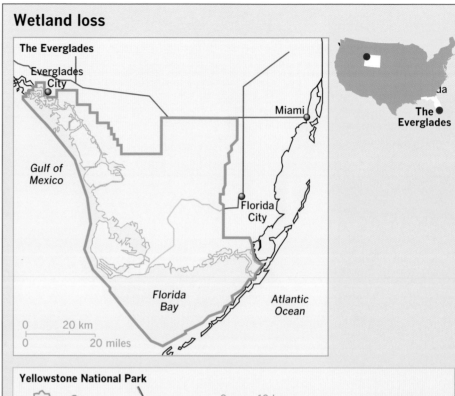

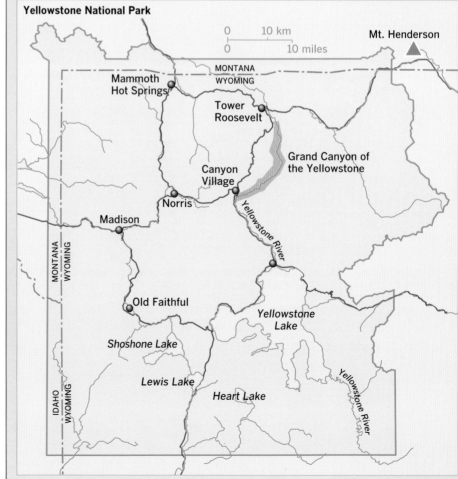

Why wetlands matter

The value of wetlands

a valuable ecological resource

food and jobs for people

a foundation for food chains

wetland

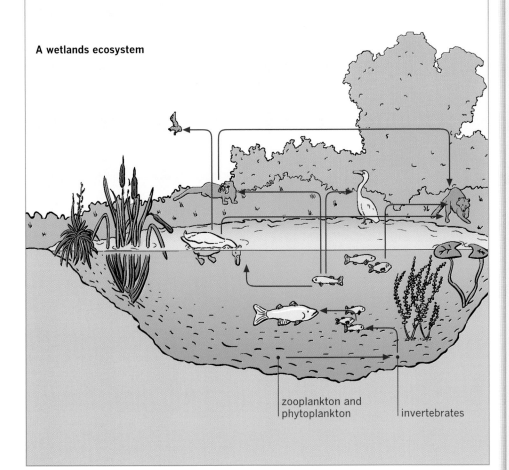

A wetlands ecosystem

zooplankton and phytoplankton

invertebrates

Key words

biodiversity
biomass
ecosystem
runoff

Importance of wetlands

- Wetlands provide many benefits, including habitat and food for fish, flood protection, shoreline erosion control, water quality improvement, and many opportunities for recreation, education, and research.
- Wetlands are also some of the most biologically productive natural ecosystems in the world.
- They provide great volumes of biomass and nutrients as leaves and stems break down in the water.
- The biomass becomes food for many animals, including insects, crustaceans, and foraging fish, and the nutrients are used by wetland plants and algae.

Ecological services

- Wetlands function as natural tubs or sponges, storing water and slowly releasing it.
- This reduces the likelihood of flood damage to crops in agricultural areas, helps control increases in the rate and volume of runoff in urban areas, and buffers shorelines against erosion.
- Wetlands increase the quality of water, including that of drinking water, by intercepting surface runoff and removing or retaining its nutrients, processing organic wastes, and reducing sediments before they reach open water.

Biodiversity

- All wetlands, especially those in the tropics, are extremely diverse and abundant.
- They are highly productive systems and often support the ecosystem of a much wider area.
- The loss of or damage to wetlands can have a negative effect on a whole region.

Desertification worldwide

© Diagram Visual Information Ltd.

The causes of desertification

- Desertification is the degradation and gradual conversion of healthy, fertile soils in arid, semiarid, and dry subhumid areas into desert.
- Loss of topsoil and soil fertility results in a decline in the production of crops and livestock.
- The problem is often caused by excessive pressure being applied to delicate soils and ecosystems where there is little rain and the soil is already fragile.
- Desertification mostly arises from the demands of increasing numbers of people who settle on land in order to grow crops and graze animals.

Impact of desertification

- The United Nations Environment Program (UNEP) refers to desertification as "one of the most serious global environmental problems."
- Desertification currently threatens the health and livelihoods of more than one billion people.
- These are mostly poor people living in rural environments in developing countries.

The Great Plains dust bowl

- In the 1930s, parts of the Great Plains in the United States were turned into a "dust bowl" as a result of poor farming techniques and drought.
- Millions of people were forced to abandon their homes in search of more productive areas.
- Improved agricultural practices and water conservation measures have ensured that this has not happened in this region again.

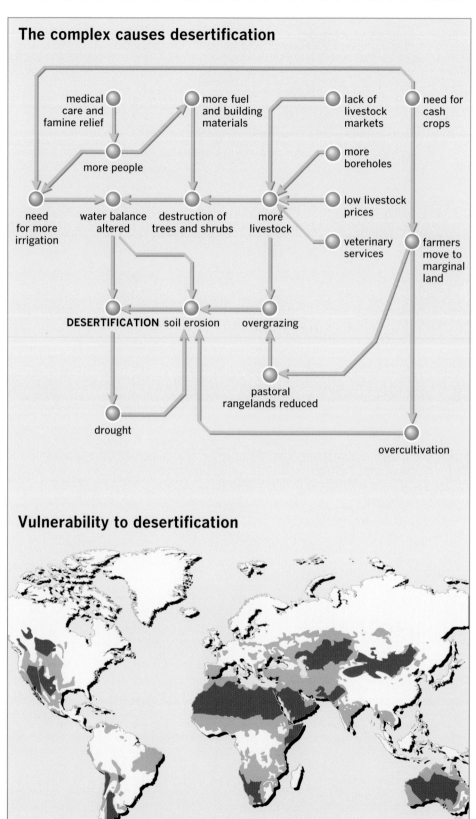

The complex causes desertification

Vulnerability to desertification

arid areas   highly vulnerable areas

Desertification in Africa

Vulnerability to desertification in Africa

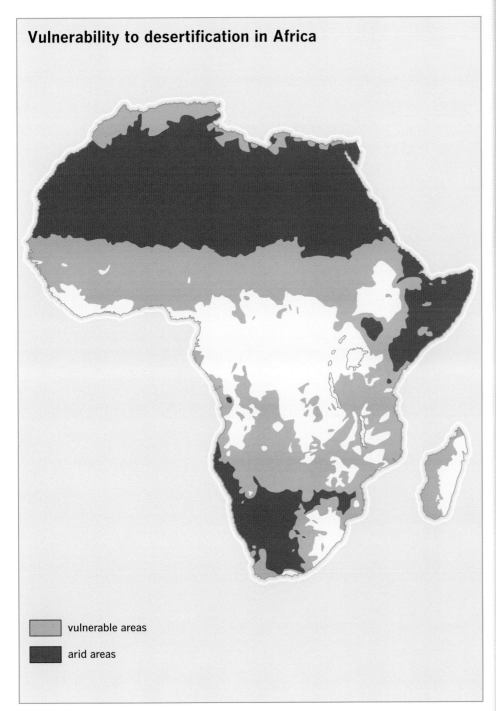

vulnerable areas

arid areas

Key words

desertification
soil degradation

The situation in Africa

- Desertification has had its greatest impact in Africa, where 60 percent of the continent is already desert or drylands and droughts frequently occur.
- Over the past 50 years, an area the size of Somalia has become desert along the Sahel—the southern fringe of the Sahara.
- Desertification now threatens more than 33 percent of the African continent.
- The Sahel countries are home to approximately 22 million people, and are particularly vulnerable.
- A further 330 million people (more than 40 percent of the African population) live in areas of high or moderate vulnerability.

Expanding desert

- The Sahara Desert extends south by an average of three miles every year.
- Around 180 tons of soil per acre may be blown away from denuded land around the Sahara every year.

Causes in Africa

- The main cause of desertification in Africa is not drought but the mismanagement of land.
- Overgrazing and the felling of trees and brushwood for fuel are prime causes.

Worldwide desertification

- Susceptible drylands cover around 40 percent of Earth's surface.
- Desertification puts at risk more than one billion people who are dependent on these lands for survival.
- More than 25 percent of Earth's land surface has already suffered erosion and soil degradation.

Key words

climate change
salinization
soil degradation
soil erosion

Climate change

- Recent shifts in world climate have caused many parts of the world to become much drier.
- Prolonged periods of drought mean that vegetation dries out and dies.

Water and wind erosion

- Without plants to hold and bind the soil together, it dries up and becomes vulnerable to erosion.
- As the soil turns to dust it can be blown away, leaving the land degraded.
- Sudden rainfall then washes away any remaining nutrients.

Farming and irrigation

- Intensive farming on drylands can be very damaging to the soil structure and helps speed up degradation.
- Salinization of soils often results from irrigation, which further damages the land.
- The combined effects of natural elements and human activity eventually exhaust the land.
- The degraded land that results is ultimately left to the process of desertification.

Preventing land degradation

- Degradation of land can be prevented or slowed in a number of ways.
- In farms, more efficient use of irrigation and water resources, and the control of salinization are effective means of improving arid lands.
- Wind velocity can be reduced over the soil surface by planting more trees and shrubs.
- This also helps bind the soil together, further reducing the risk of degradation.

Land degradation in dryland regions

Land degradation in dryland regions

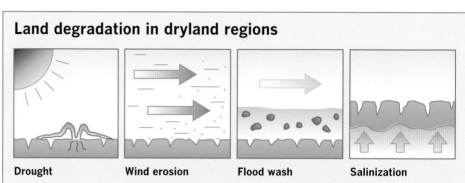

Drought   Wind erosion   Flood wash   Salinization

Main causes of dryland soil degradation by region, 2000

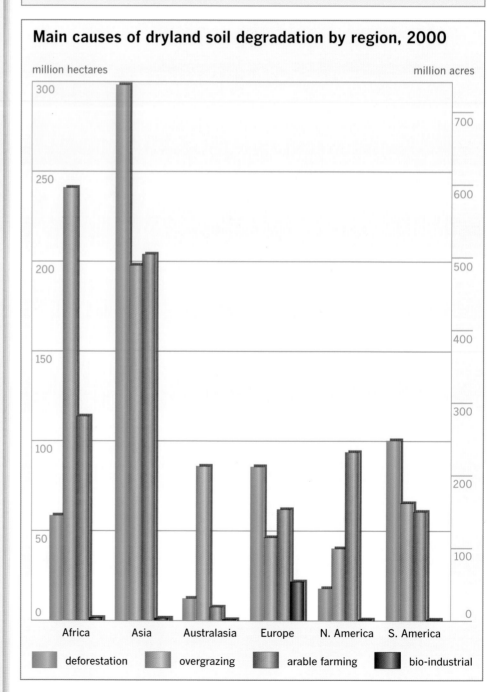

deforestation   overgrazing   arable farming   bio-industrial

Soil degradation worldwide

Key words	
fertilizer	soil degradation
herbicide	
irrigation	
pesticide	
salinization	

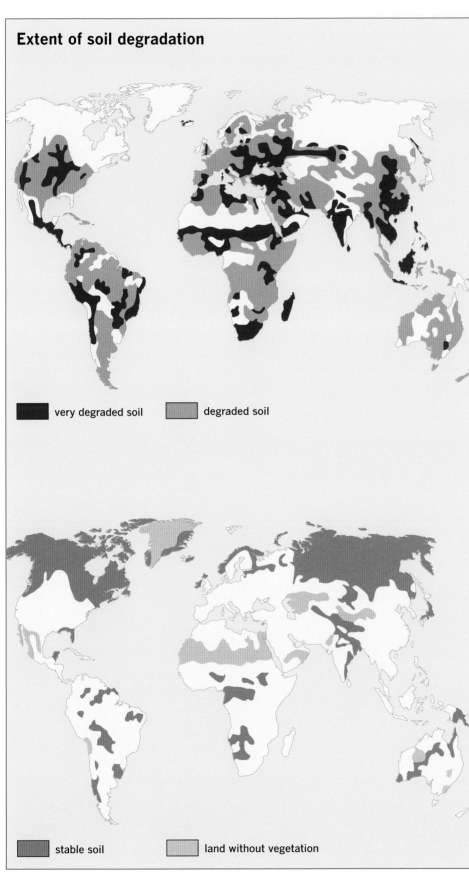

Extent of soil degradation

very degraded soil   degraded soil

stable soil   land without vegetation

Soil degradation in poor countries

- Soil degradation is a common feature of landscapes in developing and poor nations.
- For many countries in Africa, Asia, and South America, the combination of poverty and climate results in soils becoming exhausted of nutrients and minerals and often contaminated with pollutants.
- Degradation of soils also occurs where intensive farming methods have been used or population densities are very high and the demands on the soil are great.
- The soils become exhausted because they are too often used for growing crops and never given the chance to recover.

Chemicals

- In many countries, chemicals in the form of herbicides, pesticides, and fertilizers are continually applied to soils.
- The overuse of chemicals in this way can cause massive soil damage, rendering it infertile.
- Additionally, watering by irrigation tends to bring salts to the surface of the soil.
- Excessive salts can literally sterilize the land; if this happens the land must be abandoned.
- Other symptoms of salinization are less obvious but usually result in reduced crop yields.

Worldwide problem

- The maps show the global nature of the problem: very little populated land can now be classified as stable.

Key words

irrigation

The scale of irrigation

- The irrigation of agricultural land is practiced in many parts of the world, although only about 17 percent of all croplands are under irrigation.
- However, this small proportion of land produces more than 33 percent of the world's food.
- About 70 percent of all freshwater used every year throughout the world is used for agricultural irrigation.
- Less than half of the water withdrawn for irrigation reaches the intended crops.
- The rest soaks out of pipes into unlined irrigation canals, or evaporates on its way to the fields.

Surface irrigation

- Surface irrigation is one of the oldest and most traditional methods.
- It involves the use of ditches and channels to drain and direct water from the source to the crops.
- Modern variants use pipes and tanks to prevent water evaporating or soaking away.

Sprinkler irrigation

- Sprinkler irrigation uses a device to sprinkle or spray water onto the crop.
- This is more efficient than surface irrigation but still loses a lot of water to evaporation.

Direct irrigation

- In direct irrigation a water supply is applied direct to the crop in order to conserve as much water as possible.
- Small pipes lead from a larger conduit and drip water to the roots of the plants.

Localized irrigation

- Localized irrigation involves the slow release of water from a buried container near the roots of the plant.

Irrigation: types and problems

Water used and lost in irrigation

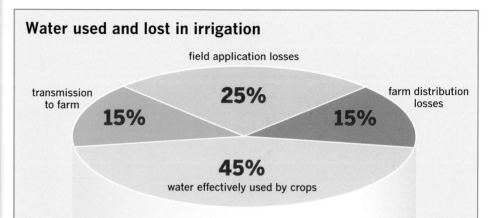

field application losses

transmission to farm

25%

farm distribution losses

15%

15%

45%

water effectively used by crops

Types of irrigation

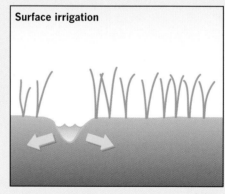

Surface irrigation

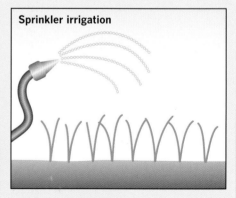

Sprinkler irrigation

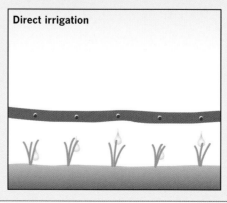

Direct irrigation

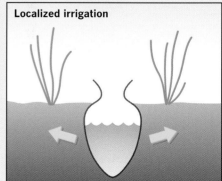

Localized irrigation

Trends in irrigation

Key words

groundwater
irrigation

Irrigation trends

Irrigated land as a percentage of total agricultural land, 1965–2002

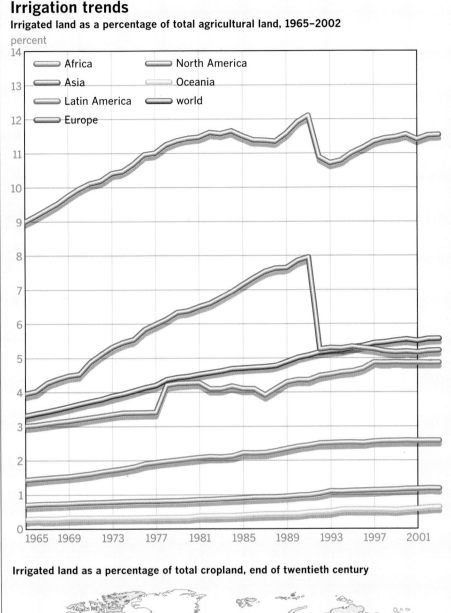

percent

Legend:
- Africa
- Asia
- Latin America
- Europe
- North America
- Oceania
- world

Irrigated land as a percentage of total cropland, end of twentieth century

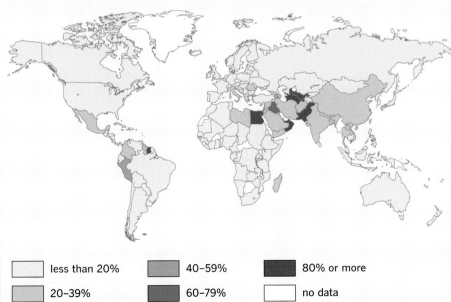

- less than 20%
- 20–39%
- 40–59%
- 60–79%
- 80% or more
- no data

Irrigation

- Irrigation involves the conveyance of water from a source of supply to an area of land where it is needed for the cultivation of crops.
- In recent years there has been an increase in the use of irrigation to facilitate cultivation in arid and semiarid regions.
- Between 1970 and 1990 the total area of irrigated land in the world rose by 36 percent and today it accounts for almost six percent of all cultivated land.
- Irrigated agriculture is highly productive and provides more than 33 percent of the world's food.
- Crop yields on irrigated land are significantly higher than those achieved on rain-fed lands with similar soils and similar climatic conditions.
- It is unlikely that there will be a significant expansion of irrigated land in the future, mainly due to a shortage of suitable available water.
- The current emphasis is on increasing the efficiency of irrigation methods, which, through leakage and evaporation, often result in the loss of up to 60 percent of water.

Sources of irrigation water

- In semiarid and arid regions irrigation systems rely on the import of surface water.
- Water is drawn from rivers and reservoirs in surrounding areas where rainfall is high and transported by pipeline.
- Groundwater may also be a suitable source of supply, depending upon availability and the cost of pumping it to the surface.
- Groundwater must be well managed, especially in coastal regions where a drop in the level of the water table will cause an influx of seawater to groundwater aquifers.

© Diagram Visual Information Ltd.

Key words

irrigation
salinization

Salinization

- *Salinization* is the build-up of salts in the soil.
- It occurs mainly in areas where excessive quantities of water have been applied to the land, usually by irrigation.
- The water dissolves salts beneath the soil and brings them to the surface as it evaporates, a process called *leaching*.
- The salt levels at the surface of the soil therefore increase each time the land is irrigated.
- This salinization eventually interferes with the crops and can cause the land to become sterile.

The problems

- High levels of salts in the soil prevent the roots of plants from acquiring nutrients by osmosis (**1**).
- This is because the water outside the roots has a higher concentration of solute than that inside.
- As a result the plants lose water (**2**) and are unable to feed from the soil; eventually they die (**3**).
- Also, the salts kill off beneficial soil microorganisms (**4**).
- Salt levels of 3,000–6,000 parts per million are enough to have an adverse effect on most cultivated plants.

The solutions

- The salts originate from deep within the ground and from rainwater.
- When salinization occurs the only solution is to flush the soil with more water so that the salts are transported away.
- This requires large amounts of freshwater and may result in the salts contaminating local rivers and lakes.
- Globally, about 20 percent of irrigated farmland is affected by salinization.

The salinization problem

Salinization
Regional distribution of salt-affected soils

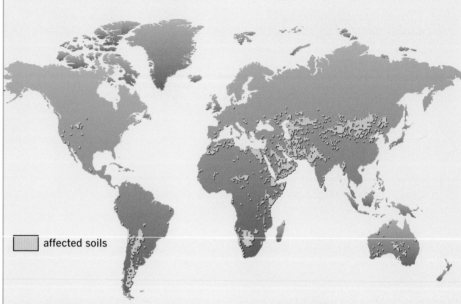

affected soils

The total area of saline soils is about 980.5 million acres worldwide.

The salinization problem

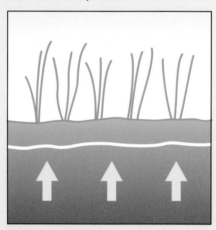

1 Salt rises with water.

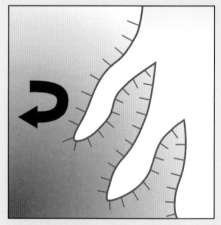

2 Osmosis in plant cells is halted or reversed.

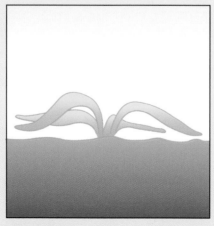

3 Plants begin to die.

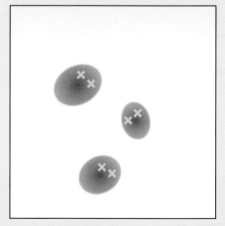

4 Beneficial microorganisms are killed.

Terrestrial and marine pollution

Key words

crude oil   pollution
fertilizer
fossil fuel
pesticide
phosphate

Estimated emissions of organic water pollutants

liter per worker per day

less than 0.2	0.37–0.52	
0.2–0.37	more than 0.52	no data

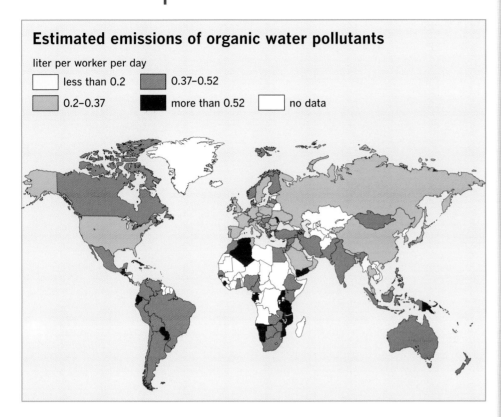

Sources of pollutants from human activities entering the sea

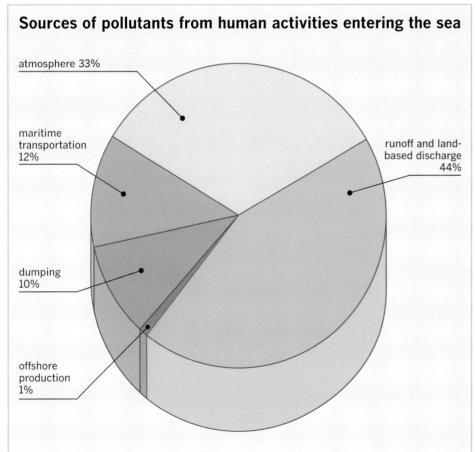

atmosphere 33%

maritime transportation 12%

runoff and land-based discharge 44%

dumping 10%

offshore production 1%

History of pollution

- During the last 50 years global consumption of commercial energy has risen more than fourfold, far outpacing the rise in population.
- Industrial and chemical pollutants are predicted to increase if the global economy expands, as expected, four- or fivefold over the next 50 years.

Fossil fuels

- The extraction and use of fossil fuels has caused extensive land and sea pollution.
- Disasters such as the Exxon Valdez oil spill in 1989 have had a grave impact on the environment. In that spillage 11 million gallons (41.8 million l) of crude oil were released, contaminating 1,300 miles (2,080 km) of coastline.

Chemicals

- Many pollutants such as pesticides, industrial solvents, and vehicle emissions are created by human activities.
- Fertilizers containing phosphate are a major pollutant in watercourses and cause the overproduction of algae and waterweeds.
- Other pollutants, including arsenic and ultraviolet radiation, occur naturally in the environment, though they are often increased by human activities.

Diseases linked to pollution

- Many diseases are linked to environmental problems such as polluted drinking water, polluted air, poor waste disposal, and exposure to mosquitoes and other carriers of disease.
- An estimated three million premature deaths, mainly from acute and chronic respiratory infections, are now being attributed to pollution each year.

© Diagram Visual Information Ltd.

Key words

climate change
fossil fuel
global warming
greenhouse gas
Kyoto Protocol

Global energy

- Global energy production has increased nearly 70 percent since 1971, and is projected to increase at more than two percent annually for the next 15 years.
- This increase is predicted to raise greenhouse gas emissions 50 percent higher than current levels unless a concerted effort takes place to increase the energy efficiency of fossil fuels.
- Scientists believe that an increase of this amount of greenhouse gases will speed up climate change and global warming.
- Fossil fuels account for about 80 percent of the world's primary energy consumption and supply roughly 90 percent of the world's commercial energy requirements.

Kyoto Protocol

- At the Earth Summit in Rio de Janeiro in 1992, world leaders agreed that emissions of greenhouse gases needed to be reduced in order to combat climate change.
- In 1997 in Kyoto, Japan, it was agreed that 1990 levels of greenhouse gas emissions should be cut by five percent between 2008 and 2012.
- This agreement was then named the *Kyoto Protocol*.
- The five percent reduction was set as a global aim and different countries were given different targets.
- The United States was set a target of seven percent and the European Union eight percent.
- The Kyoto Protocol came into effect on February 16, 2005.
- The United States—the world's biggest producer of greenhouse gases—has as yet refused to ratify the treaty, citing economic reasons.

World energy production and the Kyoto Protocol

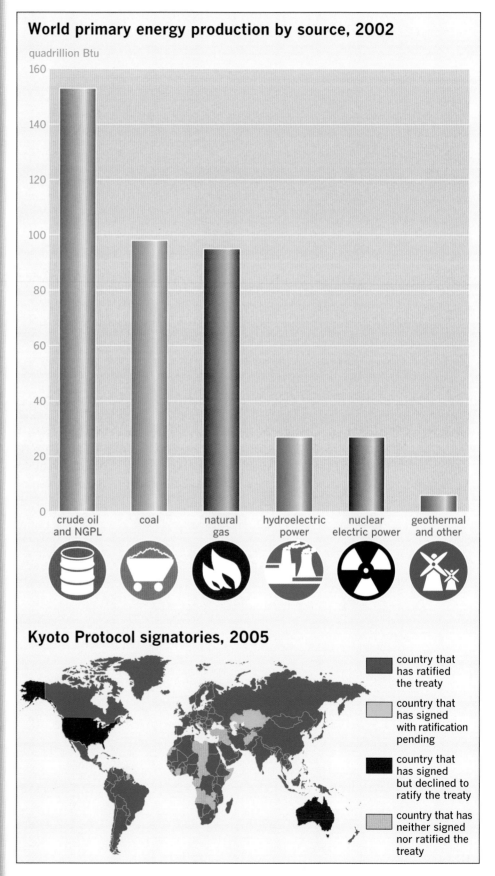

World primary energy production by source, 2002

quadrillion Btu

crude oil and NGPL	
coal	
natural gas	
hydroelectric power	
nuclear electric power	
geothermal and other	

Kyoto Protocol signatories, 2005

- country that has ratified the treaty
- country that has signed with ratification pending
- country that has signed but declined to ratify the treaty
- country that has neither signed nor ratified the treaty

Carbon dioxide emissions

Key words

carbon dioxide
fossil fuel

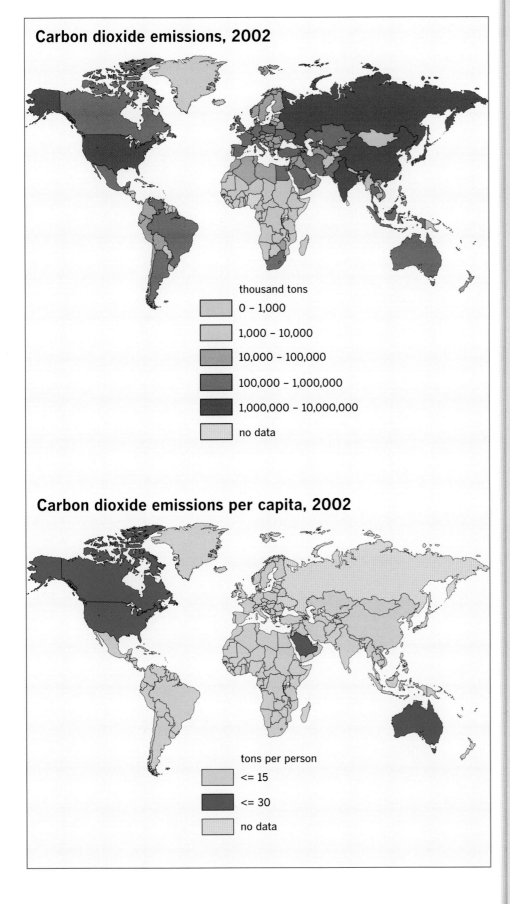

Carbon dioxide emissions, 2002

thousand tons

- 0 – 1,000
- 1,000 – 10,000
- 10,000 – 100,000
- 100,000 – 1,000,000
- 1,000,000 – 10,000,000
- no data

Carbon dioxide emissions per capita, 2002

tons per person

- <= 15
- <= 30
- no data

Carbon dioxide

- Large quantities of carbon enter the atmosphere each year as a result of the burning of carbon-based fuels.
- These fuels are mainly coal, natural gas, and oil.
- On average, coal combustion emits about twice as much carbon dioxide (CO_2) as natural gas; oil levels lie in-between.

Future impact

- Energy-related emissions account for more than 80 percent of the carbon dioxide released into the atmosphere each year.
- If all economically recoverable conventional fossil fuel were burnt over the next 100 years, this would lead to long-term global warming of more than 6.3°F (3.5°C).

Carbon from the United States

- The United States currently leads the world in carbon emissions.
- About one third of carbon emissions caused by humans in the United States comes from motor vehicles, another third from electricity power plants, and the final third from households and commercial sites.
- In 2002 the United States emitted about 6.4 billion tons of carbon dioxide, which was 0.8 percent higher than in 2001.
- U.S. carbon dioxide emissions have grown by an average of 1.2 percent annually since 1990.

Waste production

- The European Environment Agency estimates that Europe produces more than 250 million tons of municipal waste each year and more than 850 million tons of industrial waste.
- Since 1985 it is estimated that the annual average rate of increase of these wastes in the OECD European area is about three percent.

Waste disposal

- Two of the most common methods of disposal are *landfill* and *incineration*, both of which pose serious environmental risks if not carried out to the highest standards.
- Increasingly, more and more waste products now contain substances recognized to be toxic or highly toxic.
- Some wastes, such as polychlorinated biphenyls (PCBs), take many years to become harmful. Others, such as those from the nuclear industry, are hazardous from the moment of their production and will remain so forever.
- Improper management and illegal dumping of waste, particularly hazardous and toxic waste, pose increasing threats to the environment and human health.

Dangerous pesticides

- In many countries of the world there are dumps of dangerous and obsolete pesticides, which frequently expose communities to poisons in the air, food, and water.
- To date, just 3,500 tons have been removed from Africa and the Eastern Mediterranean at a cost of $24 million.
- It is estimated that a further 20,000 tons remain in Africa, 80,000 in Asia and Latin America, and up to 200,000 tons in Eastern Europe.

Industrial and hazardous waste

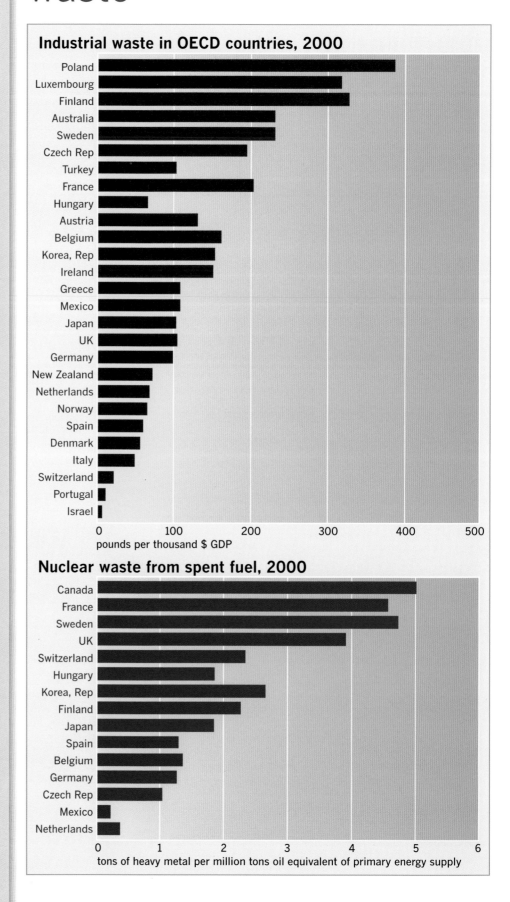

Industrial waste in OECD countries, 2000

pounds per thousand $ GDP

Nuclear waste from spent fuel, 2000

tons of heavy metal per million tons oil equivalent of primary energy supply

Environmental impact of industrial processes

Key words

DDT
environmental
  persistence
Industrial
  Revolution

pesticide

Heavy metal production ranked in order of toxicity

High toxicity

Mercury

- batteries
- agrochemicals
- photographic processing
- pharmaceuticals

Cadmium

- pigment production
- cement
- batteries
- agrochemicals
- electrodes

Copper

- metal plating
- agriculture
- wire manufacture

Zinc

- alloys
- electroplating
- paper manufacture
- glass manufacture

Nickel

- metal plating
- iron and steel manufacture

Lead

- batteries
- leaded gasoline
- cables

Chromium

- metal plating
- iron and steel manufacture
- pigment manufacture

Low toxicity

Industrial pollution
- Since the Industrial Revolution, textile, steel, glass, and soap manufacturers have all been dependent on readily available basic chemicals such as sulfuric acid and the alkali sodium carbonate.
- Our present standards of living would be impossible without power generation and the industries that manufacture such materials as steel, nonferrous metals, and chemicals.
- However, these processes have had a profound effect on the environment and human health.
- Earth's soil, atmosphere, and water are permeated with waste metals and organic chemicals that reach us through our food, drinking water, and the air we breathe.

Chlorine
- One chemical that has had a particularly strong impact on the environment is chlorine.
- The chlorine industry grew rapidly following World War II, with products such as pesticides, solvents, dry cleaning fluids, and PVC plastic.
- In the 1960s and 1970s it was recognized that many chlorine compounds were toxic and had high environmental persistence.

Chlorine in pesticides
- Pesticides have always represented a small, but significant proportion of world chlorine production.
- The deliberate release of pesticides increases their environmental impact.
- Pesticides still contain chlorine and many of the more damaging, such as DDT and Dieldrin, are now banned in most developed countries.

© Diagram Visual Information Ltd.

Key words

pesticide
polychlorinated
    biphenyl
    (PCB)

What is hazardous waste?

- Although precise definitions vary, hazardous waste is essentially waste that contains dangerous properties that may render it harmful to human health or the environment.
- Hazardous waste includes wastes that are toxic, poisonous, explosive, corrosive, flammable, and infectious.
- Worldwide, more than 440 million tons of hazardous waste are generated each year, three quarters by OECD countries.

Waste production

- The main sources of hazardous waste are chemical production, energy production, pulp and paper factories, mining industries, and leather and tanning processes.
- About 75 percent of pesticide use and hazardous waste generation occurs in developed nations.

Most hazardous substances

- Some of the most hazardous substances are arsenic, lead, mercury, vinyl chloride, benzene, polychlorinated biphenyls (PCBs), and cadmium.
- Arsenic is used specifically because of its toxic properties: its main uses are in insecticides, fungicides, and sheep and cattle dips.
- The use of arsenical compounds has been greatly reduced over the years in favor of less persistent and less toxic synthetic organic compounds.

Nuclear problem

- Perhaps the most potentially damaging form of hazardous waste is nuclear.
- Since the 1960s, more than 200,000 tons of spent nuclear fuel have been produced by 400 reactors in 31 countries and every year 10,000 tons are added.

Generation of hazardous waste

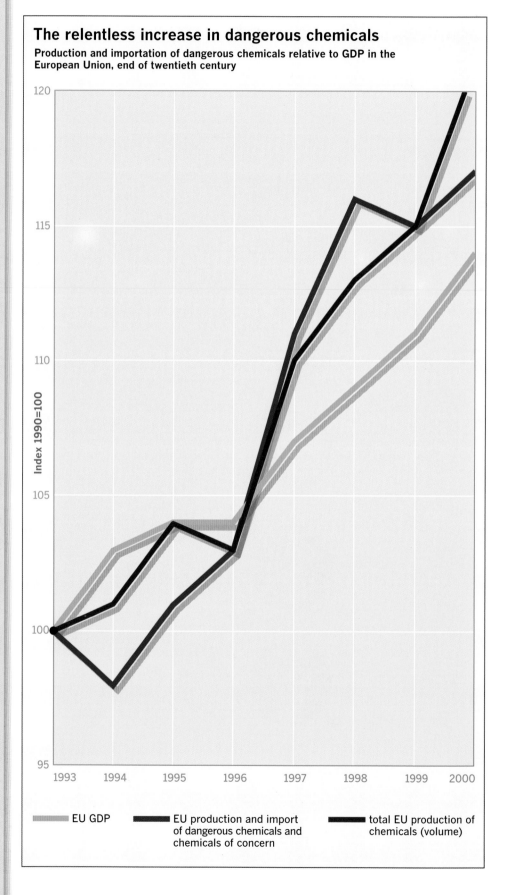

The relentless increase in dangerous chemicals

Production and importation of dangerous chemicals relative to GDP in the European Union, end of twentieth century

Index 1990=100

- EU GDP
- EU production and import of dangerous chemicals and chemicals of concern
- total EU production of chemicals (volume)

Disposal of hazardous waste

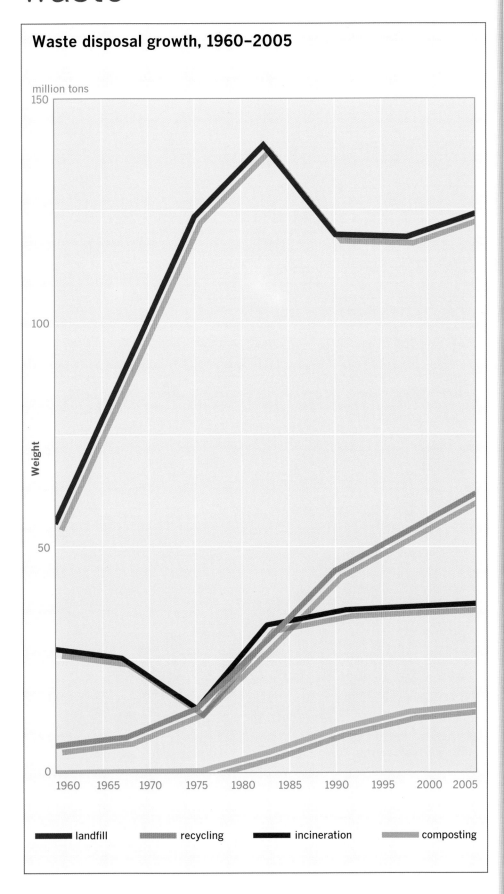

Waste disposal growth, 1960–2005

million tons

Weight

landfill ▬▬▬ recycling ▬▬▬ incineration ▬▬▬ composting ▬▬▬

Key words

food chain   recycling
greenhouse gas
incineration
landfill
pollution

Waste disposal methods
● There are four basic methods of waste disposal: incineration, landfill, dumping at sea, and recycling.

Incinerators
● Incinerators reduce the volume of solid waste, but they do not make the problem of toxic substances in the waste disappear.
● Incinerators emit a wide range of pollutants in their stack gases, ashes, and other residues; for example, they are still the primary source of dioxin pollution worldwide.

Landfill
● Landfill is not a completely safe disposal strategy for toxic and radioactive wastes.
● Many types of waste are capable of producing large quantities of methane, a potent greenhouse gas.
● The environmental disadvantages of the burial of nuclear waste include the spread of radioactivity into the surrounding environment.
● Obsolete weapons are another source of hazardous waste, particularly nerve gas, chemical weapons, and nuclear weapons that were never designed with safe disposal in mind.

Dumping at sea
● The oceans have long served as a dumping ground for waste, but direct dumping at sea is one of the fastest ways for toxic compounds to enter the food chain.

Recycling
● Recycling is the most ecologically friendly way of processing hazardous wastes.
● Many types of waste can now be made safe using modern processes.

Key words

bioaccumulation
Environmental
  Protection
  Agency (EPA)

The Toxics Release Inventory

- The Toxics Release Inventory (TRI) is a publicly available database run by the Environmental Protection Agency (EPA).
- It contains information on toxic chemical releases and other waste management activities that must be reported annually by manufacturing facilities.
- The goal of the TRI is to provide information that will enable the public to hold companies and local governments accountable for the management of toxic chemicals.

Expanding coverage

- The TRI program has expanded greatly since it began in 1987.
- There are plans to expand the number of toxic chemicals and chemical compounds on the list to 650.
- Facilities must report the quantities of each chemical that they have released into the air and water or onto the land each year.
- New industrial areas have been added to expand coverage beyond the industries originally covered .
- The reporting thresholds for certain pesticides with toxic and bioaccumulation properties have also been reduced.

Results from the TRI 2003

- In 2003, 23,811 facilities reported to the TRI Program.
- These facilities reported 4.44 billion pounds of on-site and off-site disposal of the almost 650 toxic chemicals.

The Toxics Release Inventory

Toxics Release Inventory

Total disposals and other releases by type, 2003

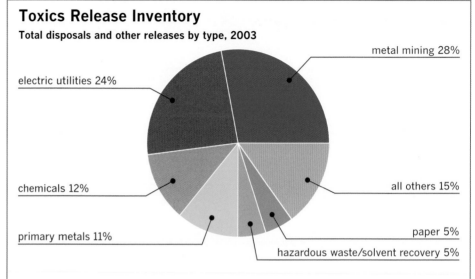

metal mining 28%

electric utilities 24%

all others 15%

chemicals 12%

paper 5%

primary metals 11%

hazardous waste/solvent recovery 5%

Annual total disposals and other releases, 1988–2003

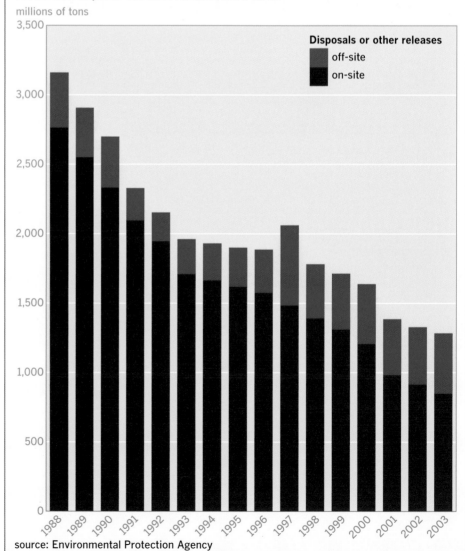

millions of tons

Disposals or other releases
off-site
on-site

source: Environmental Protection Agency

Spending on pollution control

Pollution abatement

- Pollution abatement and control (PAC) activities are defined as procedures aimed at the prevention, reduction, and elimination of pollution.
- They are generally undertaken by the public sector, business sector, and private households as a direct result of legislation to reduce pollution.
- Pollution abatement excludes expenditure on natural resource management and nature protection.
- Collectively, however, these are all referred to as "environmental protection."

Types of expenditure

- There are a number of different ways of investing in pollution abatement measures.
- Investment expenditure is a measure of money spent on equipment and land used for pollution abatement.
- Internal expenditure is the cost of using energy, materials, and specialized personnel in an effort to protect the environment.
- Sometimes the by-products of pollution abatement processes have an economic value and can be sold to reduce the overall cost of the process.

Abatement in the United States

- Pollution abatement capital expenditures in the United States amounted to $6 billion annually by the end of the twentieth century.
- Of this, $3.5 billion was attributed to air, $1.8 billion to water, $362 million to solid waste, and $182 million to multimedia.

Pollution abatement and control

Expenditure on pollution abatement and control by country, 1999

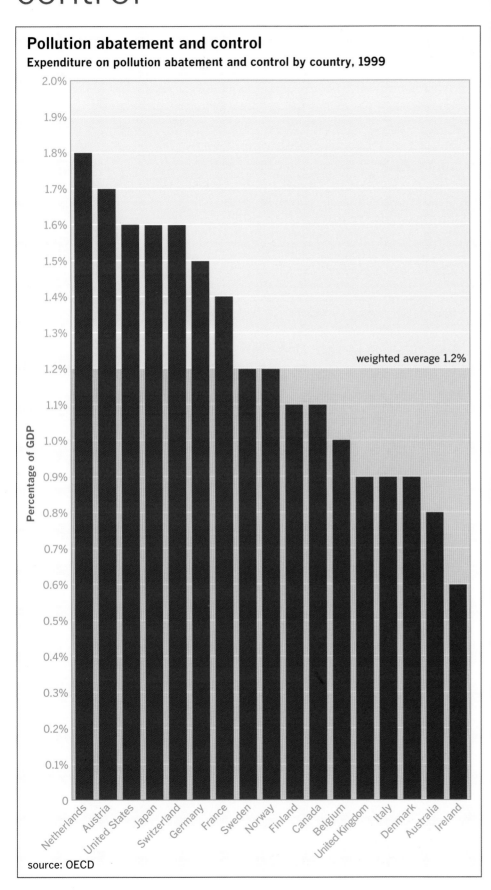

weighted average 1.2%

source: OECD

Key words
heavy metal
persistent
organic
pollutants
(POPs)

Moving hazardous waste

- Trade in hazardous wastes has become a global problem demanding global solutions.
- About a tenth of all the hazardous waste generated around the world each year crosses national frontiers.
- A large proportion of this waste continues to move from OECD (industrialized) countries to non-OECD (developing) countries, where disposal costs are lower and procedures usually subject to less regulation.

Illegal trade in waste

- Officially, less than 1,000 tons of hazardous waste per year is traded to developing nations.
- However, illegal traffic in waste poses a severe threat to the environment and human health.
- There have been cases of the large-scale illegal trafficking of hazardous wastes that also involved money laundering and illegal arms trading.
- There have also been cases of ships transporting hazardous waste sailing around the world in search of ports to discharge their cargoes at.

Basel Convention

- This "toxic trade" led to the creation by the UN of the "Basel Convention on the Control of Transboundary Movements of Hazardous Wastes and Their Disposal," which came into force in 1992.
- Two groups of hazardous chemicals, *heavy metals* and *persistent organic pollutants* (POPs), receive particular attention.
- Although the emissions of some of these substances are falling, their concentrations in the environment remain cause for concern.

International movement of hazardous waste

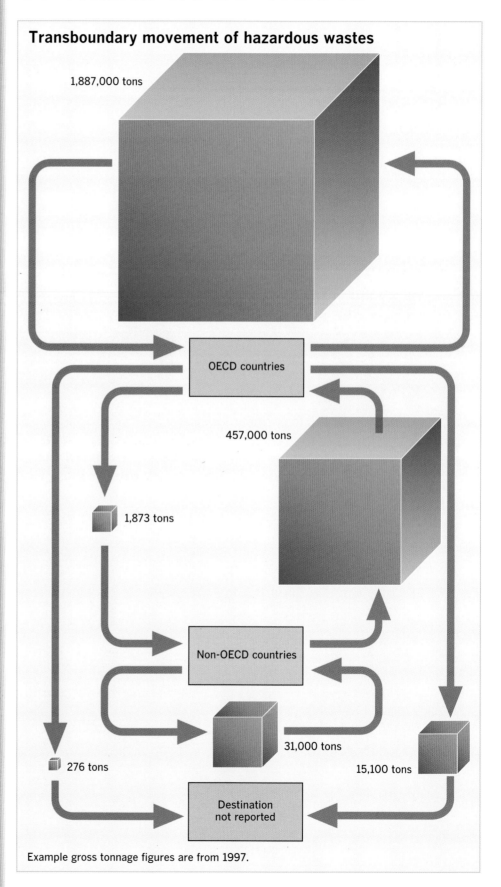

Transboundary movement of hazardous wastes

1,887,000 tons

OECD countries

457,000 tons

1,873 tons

Non-OECD countries

276 tons

31,000 tons

15,100 tons

Destination not reported

Example gross tonnage figures are from 1997.

Landfill, seepage, and leakage

Key words

bedrock
greenhouse gas
groundwater
landfill
runoff

Seepage and leakage

Urban landfill

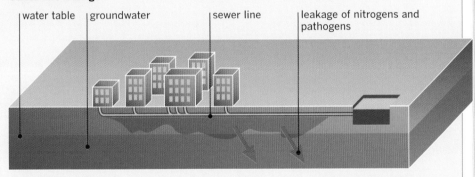

water table | groundwater | landfill | leakage and seepage of organic compounds and other contaminants

Sewer line leakage

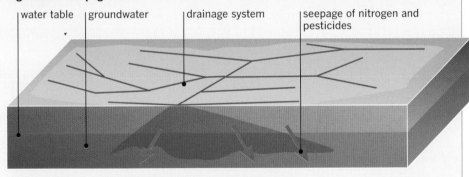

water table | groundwater | sewer line | leakage of nitrogens and pathogens

Agricultural seepage

water table | groundwater | drainage system | seepage of nitrogen and pesticides

Occurrence of seepage and leakage

A cross-section of a clay-lined landfill site on a slope leading down to a river illustrates how both seepage and leakage can occur.

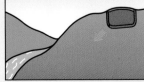

Leakage of pollutants

Seepage of pollutants

Gases and liquids leak into the atmosphere

Pollutants permeate bedrock

Pollutants may contaminate surface water

Landfill sites

- Landfill sites are depressions excavated in the ground into which wastes are deposited.
- It is necessary to situate landfill sites in the correct locations to prevent waste from escaping, and to avoid any connection between the waste and the surrounding environment, particularly groundwater.
- Landfill sites are usually constructed on top of solid impermeable bedrock to minimize the damage if seepage does occur.
- It is also important not to situate landfill sites on top of mines or quarries, since these frequently contact groundwater and can act as conductors of pollutants.
- Landfill sites can be artificially sealed to contain wastes using clay, plastic, or composites.

Seepage and leakage

- Leakage of pollutants can occur when the landfill container develops holes or cracks, allowing waste material to escape into the environment.
- Seepage takes place when pollutants escape because the lining material of a container is porous or permeable and allows the passage of pollutants.
- Gaseous pollutants can seep or leak into the environment and behave in a similar way to liquids, though they may be heavier or lighter than air.
- Pollutants underground can permeate and even break down bedrock. Eventually they may dissolve into the groundwater and harm the environment.
- Above ground, liquid pollutants can contaminate surface runoff water and drain into river systems.
- Certain gaseous pollutants may mix with the air, further adding to greenhouse gases in the atmosphere.

Key words

bioaccumulation
DDT
food chain
heavy metal

persistent
organic
pollutants
(POPs)
pesticide

Bioaccumulation

- Species at the top of food chains are particularly vulnerable to pesticides and other poisons as a result of *bioaccumulation*.
- Bioaccumulation is a process by which chemical contaminants become more concentrated in the tissues of organisms as they pass higher up the food chain.
- Contaminants such as heavy metals and pesticides such as DDT are stored in the fatty tissues of animals and are passed from animal to animal as predators hunt and eat their prey.
- Eventually, these compounds accumulate at dangerous levels at the top of the food chain and it is the top predators that suffer the most: there is abundant evidence that carnivores such as ospreys, falcons, and eagles, have suffered serious declines in fecundity and population size as a result of the bioaccumulation of environmental poisons.

Food chain

- When marshes are sprayed with DDT to control mosquitoes, plankton takes up trace quantities of the chemical.
- Filter feeders such as clams feed on the plankton and take in the DDT, which accumulates within them.
- Gulls, which feed on the clams, may accumulate DDT levels 40 times higher than the amount present in their prey.

Human populations

- Human populations can be affected too, particularly indigenous groups such as the Inuit, who rely heavily on sea mammals for their food.
- Seals, whales, and walruses, which are the staple food of the Inuit diet, have become deposits for many persistent organic pollutants (POPs). These collect in the animals' fat and are passed on to people as they are eaten.

Poisoned food chains

Bioaccumulation of DDT in a food chain

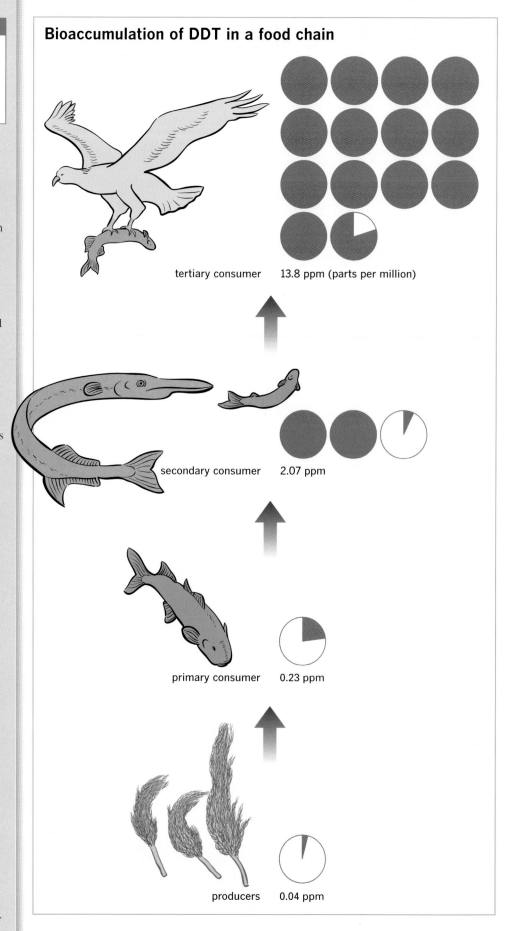

tertiary consumer   13.8 ppm (parts per million)

secondary consumer   2.07 ppm

primary consumer   0.23 ppm

producers   0.04 ppm

Bioaccumulation: Clear Lake, California

Key words

DDT
pesticide
resistance

Bioaccumulation at Clear Lake, California

The western grebe provided the first identification of the process of bioaccumulation in food webs.

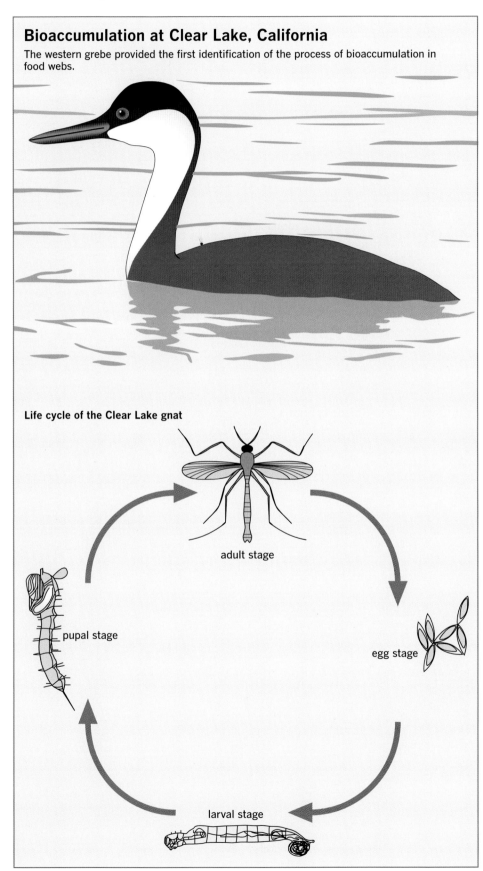

Life cycle of the Clear Lake gnat

adult stage

egg stage

larval stage

pupal stage

Gnat control program

- In the 1940s and 1950s an estimated 120,000 gallons of the pesticide DDD and methyl parathion were applied to Clear Lake in California in an attempt to eradicate the Clear Lake gnat (*Chaborus astictopus*).
- DDD is a chlorinated hydrocarbon pesticide related to DDT.
- The control program failed, with complete resistance to the pesticide evolving in the gnats within ten years.

The western grebe

- The pesticide had devastating effects on Clear Lake's bird population, especially the western grebe (*Aechmorphus occidentalis*).
- The grebe was affected through eating lake fish contaminated by the pesticides.
- Five years after the initial DDD applications, 100 grebes were found dead in one season.
- Analysis of their fat tissue revealed extremely high concentrations of DDD (1,600 parts per million).
- Clear Lake fish were found to have excessively high DDD concentrations of between 40 and 2,500 parts per million.

Population crash

- The western grebe populations crashed from over 1,000 to 25 breeding pairs in ten years.
- Other fish-eating birds, such as the osprey, disappeared entirely.

Slow recovery

- In recent years, attempts have been made to clean up Clear Lake.
- By 1999, 20 pairs of grebes had again nested at Clear Lake, along with bald eagles.
- Large amounts of DDD remain in the lake, but are buried beneath layers of sediment.

Key words

alga
eutrophication

Kaneohe Bay

- Kaneohe Bay on the island of Oahu, Hawaii, was once known for its thriving, highly diverse coral reefs.
- After 1945, the human population increased tenfold and sewage discharge into the bay led to a huge increase in the nutrient content of the water.

Eutrophication

- High nutrient levels in the bay led to "green bubble algae" *(Dictyosphaeria cavernosa)* spreading rapidly over the coral and caused extensive mortality.
- This process, by which bodies of water become enriched with dissolved nutrients, is called *eutrophication*. It results in an increased growth of algae and other microscopic plants.
- Filter-feeding organisms multiplied as a result of the increased plankton.
- Many of these organisms bored into the calcium carbonate of the coral causing further degradation and breakdown of the reef.
- As a result of the death of large parts of the reef other organisms that relied upon it for food and shelter died off.

Sewage diverted

- The sewage was eventually diverted to offshore discharge sites, which has reduced the amount of organic material entering the bay.
- Some areas have now recovered, though nutrient sediments were still relatively high in 2001 because more people were living in the bay area by then.
- Corals require the cleanest water quality of any coastal system and have evolved to live in water that is low in nutrient levels.
- Any artificial rise in nutrient levels from sources such as sewage can cause significant damage.

Bioaccumulation: Kaneohe Bay, Hawaii

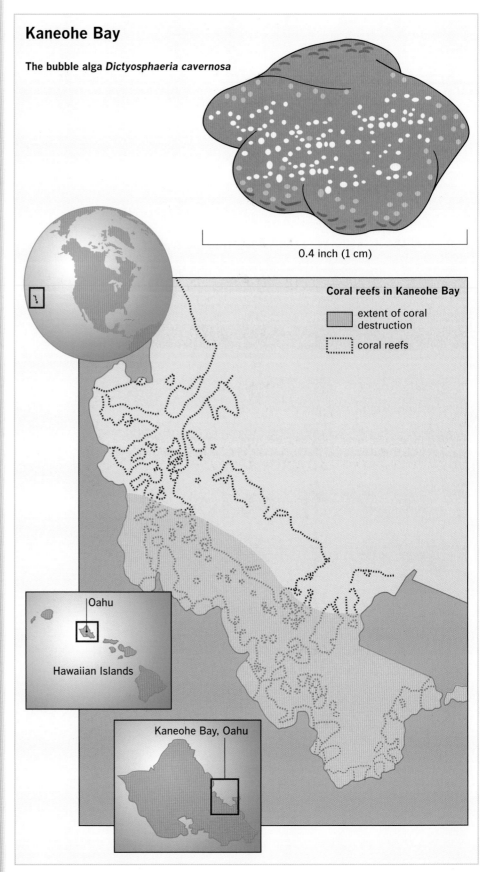

Kaneohe Bay

The bubble alga *Dictyosphaeria cavernosa*

0.4 inch (1 cm)

Coral reefs in Kaneohe Bay

- extent of coral destruction
- coral reefs

Oahu

Hawaiian Islands

Kaneohe Bay, Oahu

Metal concentrations: the Rhine

Key words

fertilizer
heavy metal

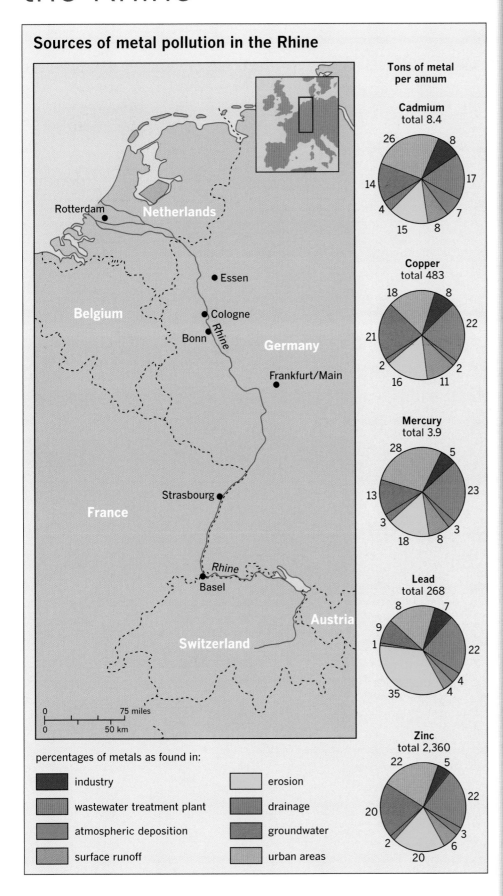

Sources of metal pollution in the Rhine

Tons of metal per annum

Cadmium total 8.4

26 8 17 7 8 15 4 14

Copper total 483

18 8 22 2 11 16 2 21

Mercury total 3.9

28 5 23 3 8 18 3 13

Lead total 268

8 7 22 4 4 35 1 9

Zinc total 2,360

22 5 22 3 6 20 2 20

percentages of metals as found in:

- industry
- wastewater treatment plant
- atmospheric deposition
- surface runoff
- erosion
- drainage
- groundwater
- urban areas

The Rhine

- The Rhine is the longest river in western Europe, measuring approximately 820 miles (1,320 km).
- It begins at the Rheinwaldhorn Glacier in the Swiss Alps and flows through or borders on Switzerland, Liechtenstein, Austria, Germany, France, and the Netherlands, before entering the North Sea at Rotterdam.
- Its important tributaries are the Aare, Neckar, Main, Moselle and Ruhr rivers.
- The population of the Rhine basin is approximately 50 million people.

River pollution

- The Rhine and its tributaries are polluted by a number of heavy metals, including cadmium, copper, mercury, lead, and zinc.
- This pollution comes from towns, cities, and industries on the banks of the river in Switzerland, France, Germany, and the Netherlands.
- The Rhine is also polluted by fertilizers that have been responsible for high levels of nitrogen and phosphorous in the water.
- By 1975 biologists could find only 29 species of fish remaining in the Rhine.
- Salmon had been completely absent since 1958.

Recovery

- Between 1983 and 1997, total heavy metal loads decreased, mainly due to reduced industry emissions in Germany.
- This followed the introduction of the "Rhine Action Plan against Chemical Pollution" adopted by the European Community in 1987.
- Following the introduction of a project to bring salmon back to the Rhine, oxygen levels in some areas have returned to normal and adult salmon have been found.

Key words

bioaccumulation	pesticide
ecosystem	runoff
food chain	
heavy metal	
herbicide	

The Great Lakes

- The Great Lakes—Superior, Michigan, Huron, Erie, and Ontario—and their channels form the largest freshwater surface system on Earth.
- Covering more than 94,000 square miles (151,000 km²) and draining more than twice as much land, they hold an estimated six quadrillion gallons (23 quadrillion l) of water.
- The Great Lakes basin provides freshwater for the 33 million people who live in the region. The lakes are crucial to the local ecosystem and economy.
- Combined, the lakes contain around one fifth of the world's surface freshwater supply, making them of great global importance.

Pollution factors

- Humans have greatly affected the quality of the lake water in recent years.
- The area has been used as a dumping ground for toxic chemicals from industry and agriculture.
- Pollutants have ranged from sewage disposal to industrial toxic contamination with heavy metals and runoff from agriculture, including pesticides and herbicides.

Suffering wildlife

- Wildlife has suffered greatly as a result of the pollution.
- Through a process of bioaccumulation, these toxic substances have moved up through the food chain resulting in tumors and death for predatory animals such as trout, herring, birds, and even humans.
- Studies in the region have found that local cormorants suffer a high incidence of crossbilled syndrome and terns exhibit birth defects many times higher than normal.

Toxic pollutants in the Great Lakes

Phosphorous concentrations in the Great Lakes

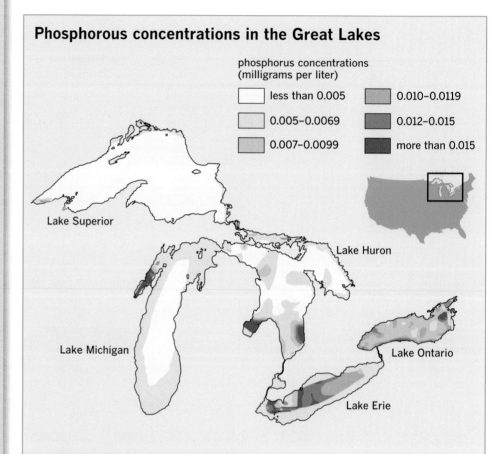

phosphorus concentrations (milligrams per liter)

less than 0.005	0.010–0.0119
0.005–0.0069	0.012–0.015
0.007–0.0099	more than 0.015

Lake Superior

Lake Huron

Lake Michigan

Lake Ontario

Lake Erie

Organic chemicals in the aquatic food chain

Persistent organic chemicals, such as PCBs, bioaccumulate. The degree of concentration in each level of the Great Lakes aquatic food chain for PCBs is shown in parts per million (ppm). The highest levels are reached in the eggs of fish-eating birds such as herring gulls.

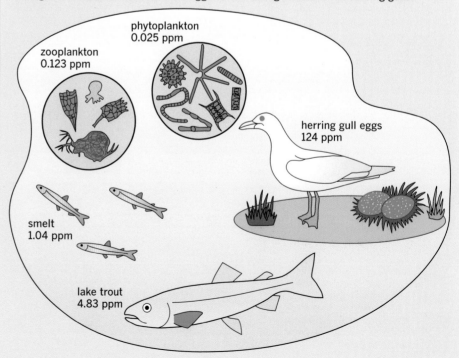

phytoplankton
0.025 ppm

zooplankton
0.123 ppm

herring gull eggs
124 ppm

smelt
1.04 ppm

lake trout
4.83 ppm

American rivers at risk

Endangered rivers

Southwest

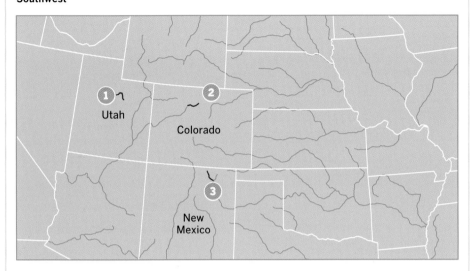

West Coast

East Coast

1. Price River
2. Fraser River
3. McCrystal Creek
4. Skykomish River
5. Tuolumne River
6. Santa Clara River
7. Susquehanna River
8. Little Miami River
9. Roan Creek
10. Santee River

Key words

indicator species
pollution

American rivers

- Although pollution levels have fallen in recent years, many American rivers are still at risk.
- Animals such as the Pacific salmon, the Missouri River's piping plover, and the Southwestern willow flycatcher are considered indicator species of ecological change.
- When sensitive animals such as these begin to decline it is seen as an indicator of the worsening health of the whole waterway.
- Experts predict that around four percent of freshwater species will become extinct every ten years.
- At this rate of extinction North America's rivers are losing species as fast as the tropical forests.

The Susquehanna River

- American Rivers, an environmental organization, named the Susquehanna River in New York, Pennsylvania, and Maryland as the most endangered in 2005.
- The main threats to this river are thought to be sewer pollution and dam construction.
- Over the entire Susquehanna River basin, sewer systems empty large quantities of raw or poorly treated sewage into the waterways.
- It is thought that unless more money is invested in prevention and cleanup, the Susquehanna River and Chesapeake Bay into which it drains, will eventually become a dead zone.

Other rivers under threat

- McCrystal Creek, New Mexico is threatened by coal bed methane drilling operations.
- More than half of the water from Fraser River, Colorado has been pumped away to help fuel development elsewhere.

Key words

eutrophication
fertilizer
organic

Eutrophication

- In cases of eutrophication, bodies of water become so rich in nutrients that natural wildlife cannot survive.
- High levels of nutrients in the water provide food for algae and foreign species.
- As the algae die and decompose, high levels of organic matter and decomposing organisms starve the water of available oxygen.
- This causes the death of fish and other wildlife.
- Eutrophication is a slow and natural process, but human influence greatly accelerates it, often causing much environmental damage.

Farming

- One common cause of eutrophication is intensive farming, in which inorganic fertilizers rich in very soluble nitrates as well as phosphates and potassium are widely used.
- When it rains, these chemicals are washed over and through the soil into nearby waterways.
- The unnaturally high levels of nutrients in the water cause excessive algal growth, which has detrimental effects on other wildlife.
- This can be avoided by the use of organic fertilizers and manures, which are high in nutrients but less destructive to the environment.

Sewage

- Untreated sewage is a good source of food for microorganisms that thrive on decaying matter.
- When sewage is pumped directly into a river or lake, these organisms multiply causing eutrophication.
- Proper treatment of sewage is required before it is discharged into rivers to prevent this.

Eutrophication

Eutrophication

Water rich in oxygen
Water with few nutrients is rich in oxygen and supports a variety of animal and plant life.

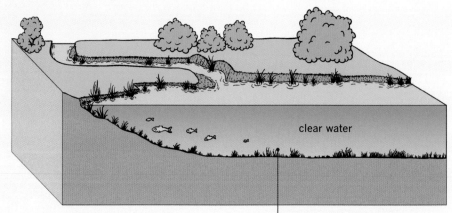

clear water

sunlight penetrates deep into the water, thus allowing water plants to grow

Water low in oxygen due to eutrophication
Water with high concentrations of nutrients is low in oxygen, and few animals or fish can live in it.

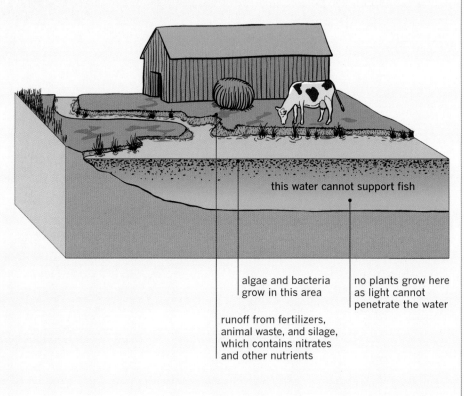

this water cannot support fish

algae and bacteria grow in this area

no plants grow here as light cannot penetrate the water

runoff from fertilizers, animal waste, and silage, which contains nitrates and other nutrients

Nuclear waste disposal

Key words

nuclear waste

Nuclear waste

A nuclear fuel route

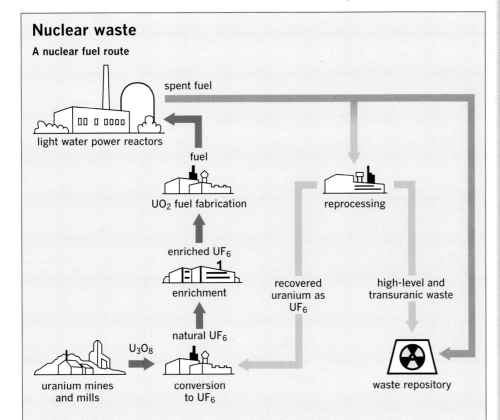

spent fuel

light water power reactors

fuel

UO_2 fuel fabrication

reprocessing

enriched UF_6

enrichment

recovered uranium as UF_6

high-level and transuranic waste

natural UF_6

U_3O_8

uranium mines and mills

conversion to UF_6

waste repository

Radioactive waste dumped at sea around the United States, 1946–93

(PBq=Petabecquerel [Peta=10 to the power of 15])

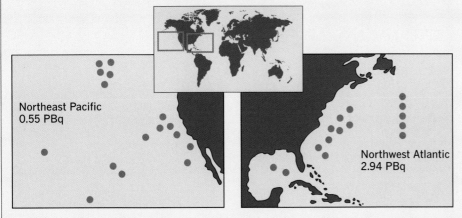

Northeast Pacific
0.55 PBq

Northwest Atlantic
2.94 PBq

Proposed Yucca Mountain Repository

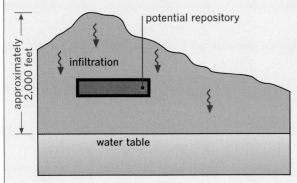

potential repository

approximately 2,000 feet

infiltration

water table

- Yucca Mountain has been approved as a repository for nuclear waste in the United States.
- The repository will be approximately 1,000 feet (300 m) below the top of the mountain, and 1,000 feet (300 m) above the water table.
- This will limit the risk of water reaching the waste and carrying radioactive material to the water table.
- It will be able to store about 70,000 tons of nuclear waste.

Nuclear waste problem

- Since the 1960s, more than 200,000 tons of spent fuel have been produced by more than 400 reactors in 31 countries.
- Each year another 10,000 tons are added and it is estimated that by 2050, production will have risen to 450,000 tons.

Waste disposal on land

- One method of disposing of nuclear waste is burial.
- The most accepted method is to package the waste into canisters of corrosion-resistant metals, such as stainless steel or copper, and to bury these in stable rock structures deep underground.
- However, it is well known that if a leak occurred, the environmental consequences would be catastrophic.
- Some radioactive elements have a half-life of up to 100,000 years, so in the event of a disaster, contamination would be irreversible and permanent.
- Other methods considered for disposal include polar ice sheet burial, hot rock disposal, and launching waste into space.

Waste disposal at sea

- Disposal of nuclear waste at sea was allowed for 48 years until it was banned by the London Convention on Dumping in 1993.
- During this time, 14 countries used more than 80 sites to dispose of around 85 Petabecquerel (PBq) of radioactive waste.
- Around 53 percent of the dumped waste was classified as low level packaged waste.
- Another 43 percent of the nuclear waste was associated with the dumping of reactors and spent nuclear fuel.

© Diagram Visual Information Ltd.

Key words

eutrophication
landfill

Toxic waste dumps on land

- Europe produces more than 2.5 million tons of solid waste a year.
- Most countries still use landfill sites to dispose of their waste.
- Landfill sites are possible sources of toxic chemicals and produce large quantities of methane gas.
- They must be managed so that pollutants do not seep into groundwater.

Tires

- Tires are a major problem as they are virtually non-degradable and spread noxious fumes when burned.
- Western Europe, the United States, and Japan produce around 580 million tires a year.
- Often, tires are left in huge dumps because they are almost impossible to recycle or destroy safely.
- These tire dumps are serious fire hazards since once alight they can take years to extinguish.

Toxic waste dumping at sea

- Large quantities of oil, plastics, and other debris including chemical contaminants are dumped or discharged at sea.
- The main source of marine pollution is from land-derived pollutants such as industrial effluent and sewage and to a lesser extent from sulfur and nitrogen oxides returning to the sea from the rain.
- Other sources are oil and gas extraction and mining, garbage, industrial waste, and waste associated with the deliberate or accidental discharge of oil.
- High levels of organic matter discharged into the sea can cause the eutrophication of coastal waters and damage to the environment.

Toxic waste disposal

Sources and methods of land pollution

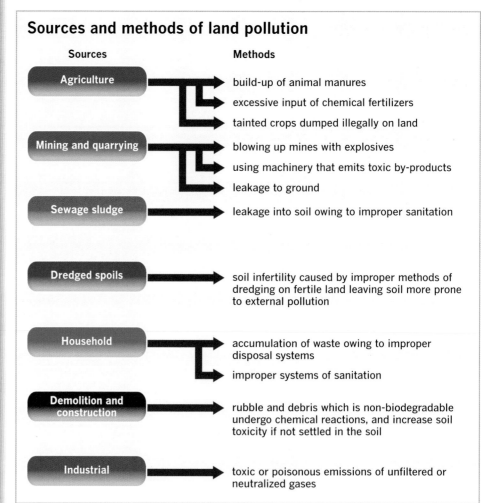

Sources	Methods
Agriculture	build-up of animal manures
	excessive input of chemical fertilizers
	tainted crops dumped illegally on land
Mining and quarrying	blowing up mines with explosives
	using machinery that emits toxic by-products
	leakage to ground
Sewage sludge	leakage into soil owing to improper sanitation
Dredged spoils	soil infertility caused by improper methods of dredging on fertile land leaving soil more prone to external pollution
Household	accumulation of waste owing to improper disposal systems
	improper systems of sanitation
Demolition and construction	rubble and debris which is non-biodegradable undergo chemical reactions, and increase soil toxicity if not settled in the soil
Industrial	toxic or poisonous emissions of unfiltered or neutralized gases

Nutrient pollution

Pollution of the seas by nutrients is a serious problem. Dissolved inorganic nitrates and phosphates from municipal sewage plants, agricultural runoff, and industrial effluent all enter coastal waters, where they can cause sudden explosions in populations of algae. The algae in turn can produce toxins that affect fish or shellfish, and reduce the oxygen content of water, stressing marine organisms. The main inputs of inorganic nutrients into the Northeast Atlantic for 1995 are shown in the table below.

Sources of nutrient pollution

country	phosphorus (tons)			nitrogen (tons)		
	sewage	agriculture	industry	sewage	agriculture	industry
Belgium	4,800	1,500	3,400	28,200		18,000
Denmark	700	530	120	2,700	50,000	1,200
France	NI	21,000	NI	NI		NI
Germany	9,900	13,500	4,500	148,500	270,000	40,500
Netherlands	3,700	6,400	6,800	31,500		8,500
Norway	510	160	60	9,960	8,450	1,500
Sweden	190	200	85	5,100		900
Switzerland	1,000	NI	30	17,000	NI	1,000

NI = No Information available

Sewage pollution

Key words

ecosystem
pathogen

Sewage as pollution

Main constituents of sewage

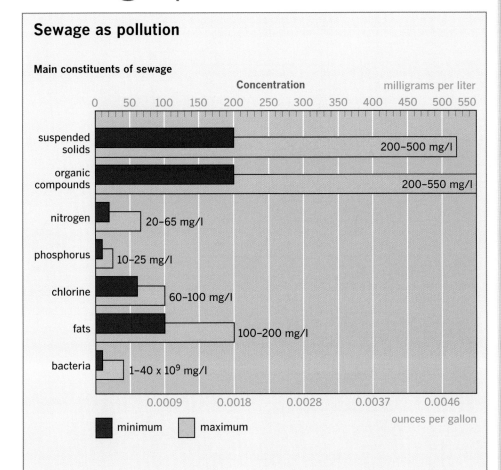

Concentration — milligrams per liter

suspended solids	200–500 mg/l
organic compounds	200–550 mg/l
nitrogen	20–65 mg/l
phosphorus	10–25 mg/l
chlorine	60–100 mg/l
fats	100–200 mg/l
bacteria	1–40 x 10⁹ mg/l

ounces per gallon

■ minimum   ☐ maximum

Heavy metals in sewage

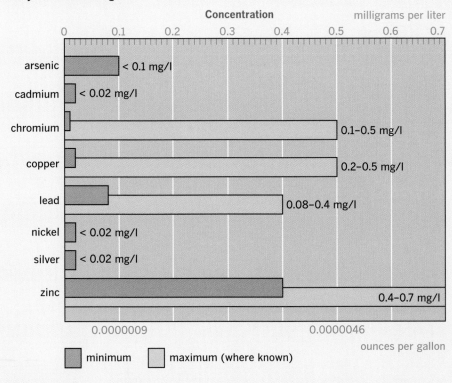

Concentration — milligrams per liter

arsenic	< 0.1 mg/l
cadmium	< 0.02 mg/l
chromium	0.1–0.5 mg/l
copper	0.2–0.5 mg/l
lead	0.08–0.4 mg/l
nickel	< 0.02 mg/l
silver	< 0.02 mg/l
zinc	0.4–0.7 mg/l

ounces per gallon

■ minimum   ☐ maximum (where known)

Sewage pollution

- Sewage is defined as waste matter from domestic or industrial establishments that is carried away in sewers or drains.
- It is usually 99 percent water with one percent impurities amounting to around 0.01 ounces per gallon (1,000 milligrams per liter).
- Many countries release quantities of sewage directly into water bodies.
- For example, it is estimated that roughly 300,000 gallons (1.1 million l) of raw or partially treated sewage is discharged into the sea around the coastline of the United Kingdom every day.
- The natural system can easily cope with small quantities of sewage containing fecal matter and other organic components.
- However, high concentrations of industrial and domestic waste entering the freshwater and marine environment can disrupt and damage ecosystems.

Sewage treatment

- The sewage treatment process removes impurities so that the remaining waste water can be safely returned to the river or sea and become part of the water cycle again.
- A sewage treatment plant separates solids from liquids by physical processes and then purifies the liquid using biological processes.

Risks to health

- In some countries there is insufficient treatment of sewage, or sewage treatment plants may occasionally break down and be unable to cope with large volumes of wastewater.
- When this happens, toxins and pathogens may be introduced to drinking water, with possible health risks.

© Diagram Visual Information Ltd.

Key words

bleaching
deforestation
ecosystem
soil erosion

Water as an industrial coolant

- The main cause of thermal pollution is the use of water as a cooling agent for industrial facilities such as nuclear power plants.
- About half of all water withdrawn in the United States each year is used for cooling electric power plants.
- Often the easiest and cheapest method is to take water from a convenient body of surface water, pass it through the plant, and return the heated water to the same body of water where it can cause damage to entire ecosystems.

Deforestation and soil erosion

- The deforestation of shorelines also contributes to thermal pollution.
- Deforestation increases soil erosion, which makes water muddy; this in turn increases the amount of sunlight absorbed, which raises the temperature of the water.

The consequences

- As water gets warmer, the amount of oxygen dissolved in it decreases while the rates of photosynthesis and plant growth increase.
- Warmer water causes aquatic organisms to increase their respiration rates and consume oxygen faster.
- It also increases their susceptibility to disease, toxins, and parasites.
- For example, heated water discharged into shallow water near the shore of a lake can disrupt spawning and kill young fish.
- Higher seawater temperatures can destroy coral reefs through a phenomenon known as bleaching.
- A small but sudden rise in water temperatures can directly kill plants and animals and damage fragile ecosystems.

Thermal pollution

Direct effects of heat discharges on marine life

Organism	algae	mangroves
Critical water temperature	93.2°F (34°C)	100.4°F (38°C)
Effect	major change in community structure	reduction in photosynthesis

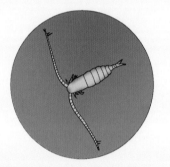 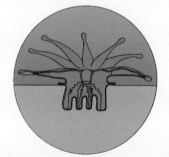

Organism	copepods	corals
Critical water temperature	95–104°F (35–40°C)	95–104°F (35–40°C)
Effect	mass mortality	high mortality

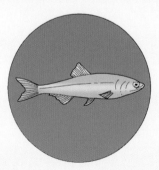

Organism	fish
Critical water temperature	93.2–118.4°F (34–48°C)
Effect	death

Environmental impact assessment

Key words

sustainable development

Environmental impact assessment (EIA)

This flowchart for an environmental impact asessment of macroeconomic reforms, devised by the World Wildlife Fund/World Wide Fund for Nature (WWF), shows the environmental impact of certain fiscal reforms.

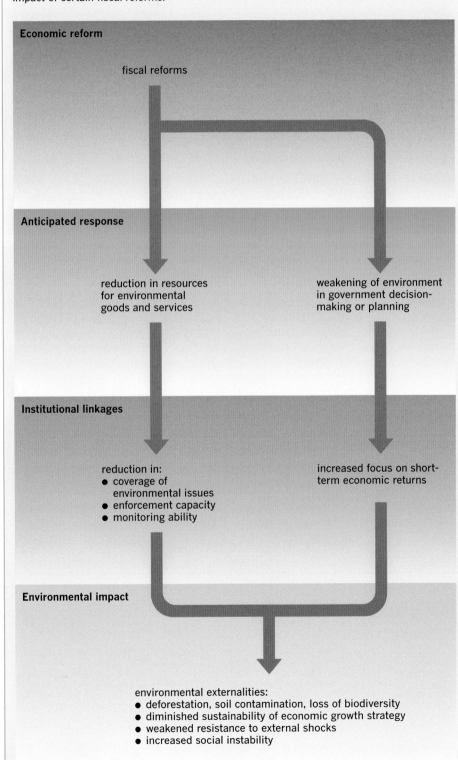

Economic reform

fiscal reforms

Anticipated response

reduction in resources for environmental goods and services

weakening of environment in government decision-making or planning

Institutional linkages

reduction in:
- coverage of environmental issues
- enforcement capacity
- monitoring ability

increased focus on short-term economic returns

Environmental impact

environmental externalities:
- deforestation, soil contamination, loss of biodiversity
- diminished sustainability of economic growth strategy
- weakened resistance to external shocks
- increased social instability

Sustainable development

- Economic, social, and environmental changes are inherent in the development of nations and societies.
- While development aims to bring about positive change, it can also lead to conflicts.
- In the past, the promotion of economic growth as the motor for increased wellbeing was the main priority of development, with little sensitivity to adverse social or environmental impact.
- The need to avoid adverse effects and to ensure long-term benefits led to the concept of *sustainability*.
- Sustainability has become accepted as an essential component of development if the aim of increased wellbeing and greater equity in fulfilling basic needs is to be met for this and future generations.

Environmental impact assessment

- To predict the environmental impact of any development activity and to provide an opportunity to mitigate negative impacts and to enhance positive impacts, the environmental impact assessment (EIA) procedure was developed in the 1970s.
- An EIA may be defined as a formal process to predict the environmental consequences of human development activities and to plan appropriate measures to eliminate or reduce adverse effects and to augment positive effects.
- EIA has three main functions: to predict problems; to find ways of avoiding them; and to enhance the positive effects.

Key words

atmosphere	heavy metal
chlorofluoro-	particulate
carbons	pollution
(CFCs)	
greenhouse gas	

Types of pollutant

- The many different types of air pollutants can be broadly classified as suspended particulate matter, gases, and vapors.
- Some atmospheric gases have been detected well out into space, but 99 percent of the mass of the atmosphere lies below an altitude of 16–18.5 miles (25–30 km).
- Most air pollution occurs in this lower half of the atmosphere with the greatest concentration to be found below three miles (5 km).

Gaseous pollutants

- The principal gaseous air pollutants are: oxides of nitrogen (NO_2), ozone (O_3), carbon monoxide (CO), sulfur dioxide (SO_2), ammonia (NH_3) and volatile organic compounds.
- Chlorinated fluorocarbons (CFCs) and other *greenhouse gases*, lead, other *heavy metals*, and radon, are also air pollutants.

Particulate matter

- Particulate matter affects more people through time than any other pollutant.
- The main components of particulate matter are coarse particles, such as soil and mineral ash, the fine particles found in wood smoke, and engine exhausts.

Effects of pollution

- Acidification of the environment is becoming a global problem as more countries industrialize.
- Approximately half of the world's population now lives in urban areas, and this is expected to increase by two percent each year between 2005 and 2010.
- The use of energy from fossil fuels will largely govern future levels of atmospheric pollution.

Atmospheric pollution

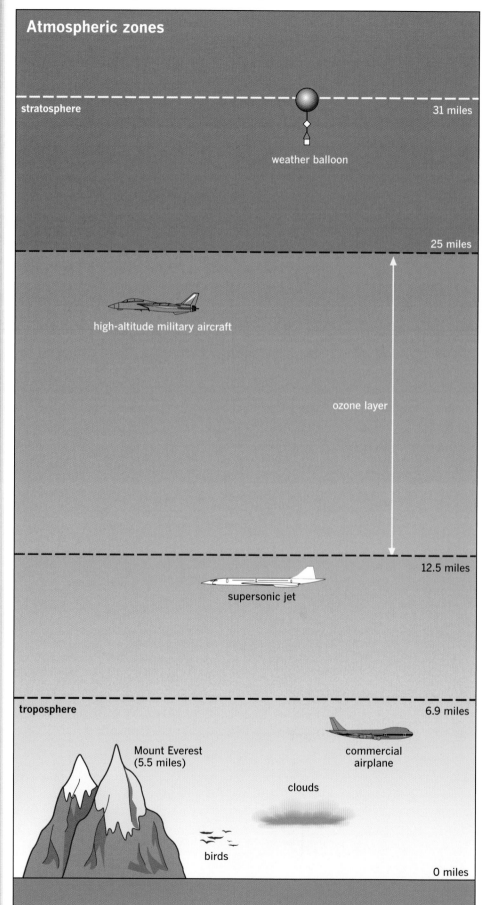

Atmospheric zones

- weather balloon
- stratosphere — 31 miles
- 25 miles
- high-altitude military aircraft
- ozone layer
- supersonic jet — 12.5 miles
- troposphere — 6.9 miles
- commercial airplane
- Mount Everest (5.5 miles)
- clouds
- birds
- 0 miles

Sustainable energy

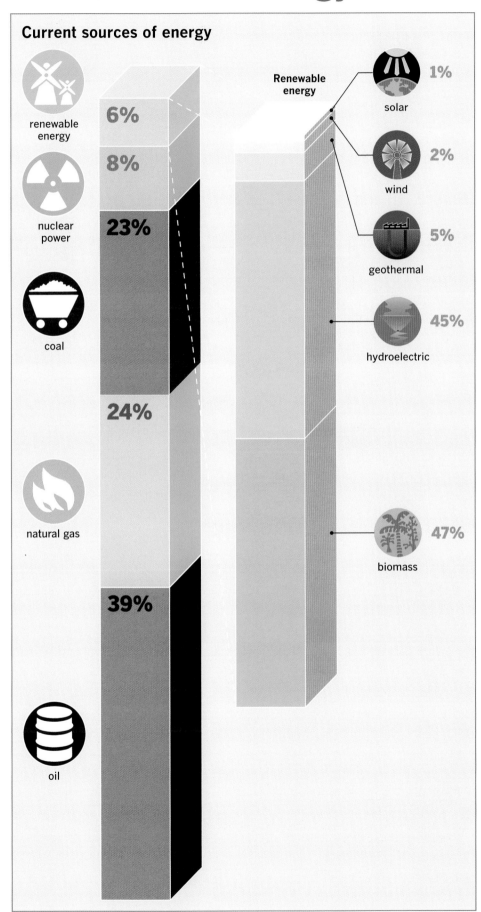

Current sources of energy

renewable energy **6%**

nuclear power **8%**

coal **23%**

natural gas **24%**

oil **39%**

Renewable energy

solar **1%**

wind **2%**

geothermal **5%**

hydroelectric **45%**

biomass **47%**

Key words

fossil fuel
greenhouse gas
hydroelectric
  power
renewable energy

Alternative energy sources
● The use of renewable energy is gradually decreasing the dependence on fossil fuels.
● Used in place of *fossil fuels*, renewable energy substantially reduces emissions of greenhouse gases and other pollutants.

Geothermal
● *Geothermal energy* is contained in the rock and the fluid in Earth's crust.
● It plays a significant role in the power supplies of some emerging economies.
● Geothermal energy is the largest source of non-hydropower renewable energy in the United States.

Wind
● Wind power is the process by which wind turbines convert kinetic energy in the wind to electricity.
● Installed wind power generation capacity has increased more than ten-fold over the last decade, growing at an average annual rate of 30 percent.

Solar (photovoltaic)
● Semiconductors, which convert solar energy into electricity, are called photovoltaic (PV) devices or *solar cells*.

Hydropower
● *Hydropower* is energy derived from flowing water. *Hydroelectric power* is electrical hydropower.
● Hydroelectric power involves the exploitation of tidal energy as well as dammed rivers.

Biomass
● Energy crops, such as sugarcane or corn, can be converted into ethanol for fuel.
● Domestic, agricultural, and industrial wastes and crop residues can be burned or gasified to produce energy.

Key words

acid rain	particulate
fossil fuel	
global warming	
greenhouse effect	

Vapors

- Vapors are vaporated liquids, including gasoline, acetone, methanol, alcohol, turpentine, and water, that enter the atmosphere as air pollutants.

Particulates

- Particulates are tiny particles from burning or internal combustion engines carried by convection and dispersed into the environment.

Methane (CH_4)

- Methane is a naturally occurring substance produced by the decomposition of organic materials.
- It is the chief constituent of natural gas and is also produced in the digestive tracts of animals such as cows.

Sulfur dioxide (SO_2)

- Sulfur dioxide is a poisonous gas with a strong odor.
- It is manufactured industrially by burning sulfur in air so that it oxidizes, and is used in chemical processes.
- It is one of the chemicals responsible for acid rain.

Carbon dioxide (CO_2)

- Carbon dioxide is a colorless, odorless gas produced by burning carbon-rich, fossil fuels or timber.
- Increased quantities in the atmosphere contribute to the greenhouse effect and global warming.
- High levels can also contribute to acid rain by producing carbonic acid (H_2CO_3) when it dissolves in atmospheric water droplets.

Nitrogen dioxide (NO_2)

- Nitrogen dioxide is a reddish-brown poisonous gas produced when various metals are dissolved in nitric acid (HNO_3) during industrial processes.
- Another important source is the exhausts of gasoline engines.

Major air pollutants: 1

Air pollutants

Sources	Pollutant gases			Sources	Pollutant gases			
power stations	CO_2	SO_2	NO_x	domestic burning	CO_2	NO_x	SO_2	CH_4
factories	CO_2	SO_2	NO_x	fertilizers	NO_x			
burning tropical forests	CO_2	NO_x	CH_4	rice paddies	CH_4			
automobiles	CO_2	NO_x		livestock	CH_4			
airplanes	CO_2	NO_x		garbage dumps, landfill	CH_4			
ships	CO_2	NO_x						

Methane **CH_4**

burning tropical forests · domestic burning · rice paddies · livestock · garbage dumps, landfill

Sulfur dioxide **SO_2**

domestic burning · power stations · factories

Carbon dioxide **CO_2**

burning tropical forests · domestic burning · power stations · factories · automobiles · airplanes · ships

Nitrogen dioxide **NO_2**

burning tropical forests · domestic burning · power stations · factories · automobiles · airplanes · ships · fertilizers

Major air pollutants: 2

Air pollutants (continued)

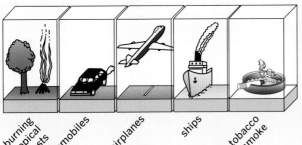

Carbon monoxide **CO**

burning tropical forests · automobiles · airplanes · ships · tobacco smoke

Chloroflourocarbons **CFCs**

refrigerators aerosols

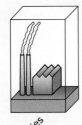

Dioxins

factories

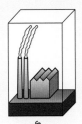

Nitric oxide **NO**

factories

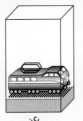

Ozone **O₃**

electric motors

Ozone depleters

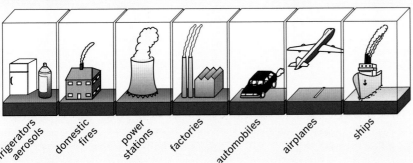

refrigerators aerosols · domestic fires · power stations · factories · automobiles · airplanes · ships

Natural composition of the air

Gas	Volume percentage
Nitrogen (N₂)	78
Oxygen (O₂)	21
Argon (Ar)	0.94
Carbon dioxide (CO₂)	0.03
Helium (He)	0.01
Neon (Ne)	0.01
Xeon (Xe)	0.01

Gas	Volume percentage
Krypton (Kr)	0.01
Methane (CH₄)	trace
Ammonia (NH₂)	trace
Hydrogen sulphide (H₂S)	trace
Carbon monoxide (CO)	trace
Nitrous oxide (N₂O)	trace

Key words

chloroflouro-carbons (CFCs)
fossil fuel
herbicide
ozone

Carbon monoxide (CO)

- A colorless, odorless, poisonous gas produced by the incomplete combustion of fossil fuels and organic compounds.
- Sources include fossil-fuelled power stations, gasoline engines, forest fires, and tobacco smoke.

Chlorofluorocarbons (CFCs)

- *Chloroflourocarbons (CFCs)* are gases manufactured by replacing the carbon atoms in hydrocarbon compounds with those of elements from the halogen group, usually fluorine and chlorine.

Dioxins

- Dioxins are highly toxic complex compounds produced as by-products of some chemical processes such as herbicide production and paper bleaching.

Nitric oxide (NO)

- An industrial by-product formed when nitric acid is reduced by a chemical reaction.
- As an air pollutant nitric oxide produces nitrogen dioxide.

Ozone (O₃)

- An unstable, poisonous, bluish gas with a pungent smell, often associated with electrical motors.
- In the atmosphere ozone readily decomposes into molecular oxygen, but in the stratosphere it forms the protective layer of ozonosphere.

Ozone depleters

- A group of gaseous chemicals that cause ozone depletion.
- Gases that deplete ozone include chlorofluorocarbons (CFCs), methyl chloroform, carbon tetrachloride, methyl bromide, and nitric oxide.

Key words

pollution
smog
WHO

Smogs and killer fogs

- In 1880, 2,200 people died in London, England, when coal smoke from home heating and industry combined to form a toxic smog of sulfur dioxide and airborne combustion particles.
- Both the 1948 "killer fog" in the small town of Denora, Pennsylvania, that killed 50, and the London "fog" of 1952, in which some 4,000 died, were catalysts for government efforts to tackle urban air pollution.
- Southeast Asia has recently experienced smog episodes caused by Indonesian forest fires. During these fires, air pollution levels in Sarawak reached record levels of 831 mg/m³, posing a serious risk to human health.

Impact on health

- A recent assessment by the European Environment Agency found that 70 percent of European cities surveyed failed WHO air quality standards for at least one pollutant.
- Worldwide, the WHO estimates that as many as 1.4 billion urban residents breathe air with pollutant levels exceeding their safety limits.
- In the United States, an estimated 80 million people live in areas that do not meet U.S. air quality standards, which are roughly similar to WHO standards.
- On a global basis, estimates of mortality due to outdoor air pollution run from around 200,000–570,000 annually, representing about 0.4–1.1 percent of total annual deaths.
- The health impact of urban air pollution seems likely to be greater in some of the rapidly developing countries, where pollution levels are highest.
- The World Bank has estimated that exposure to particulate levels exceeding the WHO limits accounts for roughly 2–5 percent of all deaths in urban areas in the developing world.

Air pollution in the urban environment

Relative importance of urban pollutants

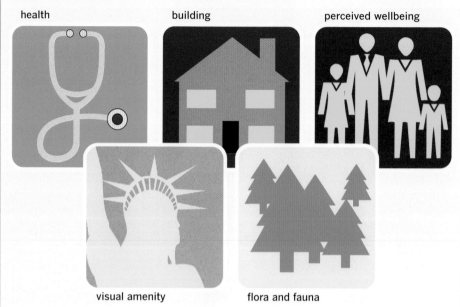

health   building   perceived wellbeing

visual amenity   flora and fauna

Pollutant effects

Pollutant	Health	Visual amenity	Buildings	Flora and fauna	Perceived wellbeing
CO	low	low	low	low	low
NO_x	medium	medium	low	low	medium
SO_x	medium	medium	high	low	high
VOCs	high	high	medium	low	medium
particles	high	high	medium	medium	high
lead	high	low	low	low	medium

NO_x: nitrous oxides; SO_x: sulfur oxides; VOC: volatile organic compound

Temperature inversion

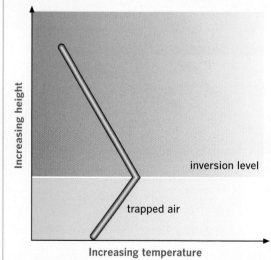

Increasing height

inversion level

trapped air

Increasing temperature

- Temperature inversion occurs when the temperature of the atmosphere increases with altitude in contrast to the normal decrease with altitude.
- When a temperature inversion occurs, cold air lies beneath warmer air at higher altitudes.
- During a temperature inversion, air pollution released into the atmosphere's lowest layer is trapped and becomes concentrated and can only be removed only by strong winds blowing horizontally.
- High pressure systems often combine temperature inversions with low wind speeds, which can lead to prolonged periods of severe smog over industrial and residential areas.

Indoor air pollutants

Key words

industrialized
  country

Domestic air pollutants

Cleaning products

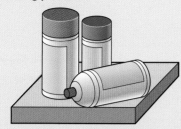

Air fresheners, moth repellents, and dry cleaning fluids may contain para-dichlorobenzene or tetrachloroethylene, both potential carcinogens.

Insecticides

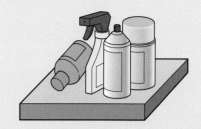

Insecticides contain toxic chemicals that can accumulate inside the body.

Cigarettes

Tobacco smoke produces toxic gases such as benzopyrene and carcinogens.

Wood board

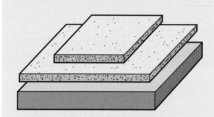

Wood board and other insulating materials emit formaldehyde which causes eye, skin, throat, and lung irritations.

Paint products

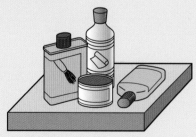

Paint thinners and strippers contain poisonous solvents that persist in the air.

Cookers

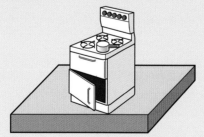

Badly ventilated gas and kerosene cookers release carbon monoxide and nitrogen oxides.

Carpets

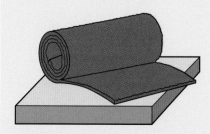

Some carpets and plastics can emit styrene which can cause kidney damage.

Refrigerators

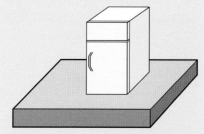

Old refrigerators must be disposed of carefully because of the chlorofluorocarbon (CFC) contained in their coolant systems.

Developed nations

- In industrialized countries, there are many sources of air pollutants in the home.
- Do-it-yourself work such as painting may lead to temporary increases in pollutants, such as volatile organic compounds (VOCs), in enclosed spaces.
- Another significant source of indoor pollution is the burning of fuels in flueless appliances, such as portable gas heaters, gas stoves, or ovens.
- In faulty appliances, incomplete combustion may result in the release of carbon monoxide, a highly poisonous gas.
- Carbon monoxide also builds up when people smoke cigarettes indoors.
- Dirty homes or houses in a state of disrepair may be a source of dustmites and mold spores.

Developing nations

- More than three billion people worldwide rely on wood, dung, crop waste, or coal to meet their basic energy needs.
- Cooking and heating with such solid fuels on open fires or stoves without proper ventilation leads to indoor air pollution.
- Indoor smoke contains many health damaging pollutants, including small soot or dust particles that can penetrate deep into the lungs.
- Exposure is highest among women and children, who spend the most time near the domestic hearth.
- A study in Mexico showed that women who had been exposed to wood smoke for many years faced 75 times greater risk of acquiring chronic lung disease than unexposed women.
- There is evidence that consistent exposure to indoor air pollution can lead to respiratory infections in children and chronic pulmonary disease and lung cancer in adults.

© Diagram Visual Information Ltd.

Key words

*chlorofluoro-
    carbons (CFCs)*
fossil fuel
greenhouse gas

Rising emissions

- Oxides of sulfur and nitrogen, methane, and CFCs are some of the most damaging pollutants produced by human activities.
- Between 1800 and the 1990s, the world population increased by a factor of six, while global CO_2 emissions rose by a factor of 800, most notably from the burning of fossil fuels.
- Since 1751 roughly 290 billion tons of carbon have been released into the atmosphere from the consumption of fossil fuels.
- Half of these emissions have occurred since the mid-1970s.
- The increase in emissions has been caused by new fuel burning technologies, particularly those for generating electricity and powering the internal combustion engine.

Global emissions

- The 2002 global fossil fuel CO_2 emission estimate was 6,975 million tons of carbon.
- This represented an all-time high and a two percent increase from 2001.
- North America emits the highest level of fossil fuel CO_2 with 1.65 billion tons of carbon emitted in 2000.
- Since 1997 Canada has experienced a 9.5 percent decline in fossil-fuel CO_2 emissions while the United States shows a 2.8 percent increase.
- The increasing industrialization of the developing world means that emissions on a global scale are still rising and are likely to continue to rise for many years to come.

Major emissions of pollutant gases

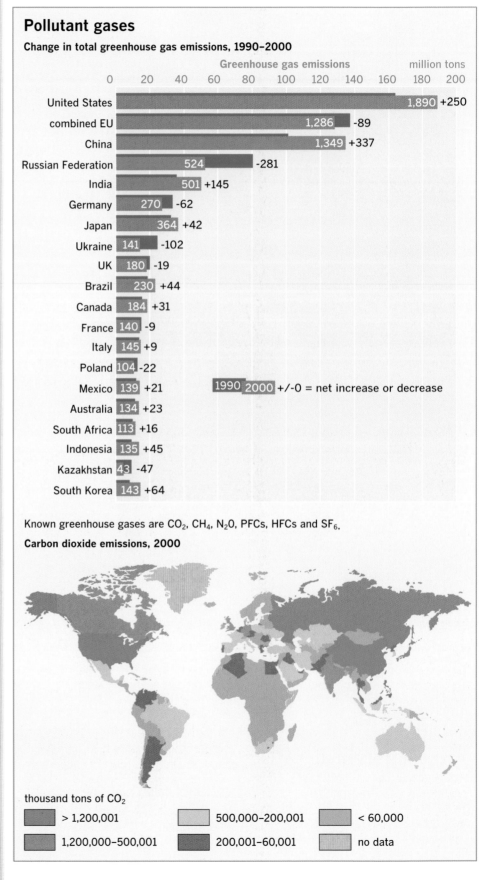

Pollutant gases

Change in total greenhouse gas emissions, 1990–2000

Greenhouse gas emissions — million tons

Country	1990/2000	+/-
United States	1,890	+250
combined EU	1,286	-89
China	1,349	+337
Russian Federation	524	-281
India	501	+145
Germany	270	-62
Japan	364	+42
Ukraine	141	-102
UK	180	-19
Brazil	230	+44
Canada	184	+31
France	140	-9
Italy	145	+9
Poland	104	-22
Mexico	139	+21
Australia	134	+23
South Africa	113	+16
Indonesia	135	+45
Kazakhstan	43	-47
South Korea	143	+64

1990 2000 +/-0 = net increase or decrease

Known greenhouse gases are CO_2, CH_4, N_2O, PFCs, HFCs and SF_6.

Carbon dioxide emissions, 2000

thousand tons of CO_2

- > 1,200,001
- 1,200,000–500,001
- 500,000–200,001
- 200,001–60,001
- < 60,000
- no data

Emissions of nitrogen oxides

Key words

acid rain	fertilizer
Environmental	fossil fuel
Protection	ozone
Agency (EPA)	
eutrophication	

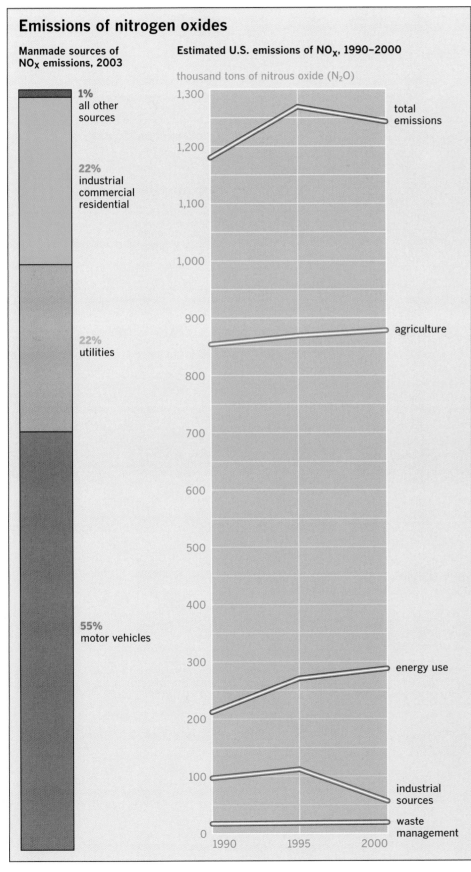

Emissions of nitrogen oxides

Manmade sources of NO_X emissions, 2003

- 1% all other sources
- 22% industrial commercial residential
- 22% utilities
- 55% motor vehicles

Estimated U.S. emissions of NO_X, 1990–2000

thousand tons of nitrous oxide (N_2O)

- total emissions
- agriculture
- energy use
- industrial sources
- waste management

Nitrogen oxides

- The nitrogen oxides (NO_X) normally found in the atmosphere include nitrous oxide (N_2O), nitric oxide (NO), and nitrogen dioxide (NO_2).
- N_2O in the atmosphere is broken down by sunlight, and some is removed by soils.
- N_2O is a stable gas with anaesthetic characteristics and is sometimes called "laughing gas."

Effects

- NO_X are highly toxic to various animals as well as to humans. High levels can be fatal, while lower levels affect the delicate structure of lung tissue.
- NO is a precursor to the formation of NO_2 and an active compound in ozone (O_3) formation.
- Nitrogen oxides in the air are a potentially significant contributor to a number of environmental effects such as acid rain and eutrophication.

Reducing emissions

- Reducing fossil fuel use, preventing the burning of tropical forests, and reducing our dependence on nitrogen-based chemical fertilizers could stabilize N_2O concentrations in the atmosphere.
- Nitrogen oxides can travel long distances, causing health and environmental problems in locations far from their source of emission.
- Since the 1970s, the Environmental Protection Agency (EPA) has required motor vehicle manufacturers to reduce NO_X emissions.
- Since 1995, NO_X emissions from highway vehicles have decreased by more than five percent, while vehicle miles traveled increased significantly.
- The EPA also helped devise a two-phased strategy to cut NO_X emissions from coal-fired power plants in an attempt to reduce acid rain.

Key words

acid rain
anthropogenic
climate change
WHO

Sources of sulfur dioxide

- Sulfur dioxide (SO_2) belongs to the family of sulfur oxide (SO_x) gases.
- These gases are formed when fuels that contain sulfur, such as coal and oil, are burned during metal smelting and other industrial processes.
- The highest recorded concentrations of SO_2 have been in the vicinity of large industrial facilities.

Effects of sulfur dioxide

- Sulfur emissions are an important constituent of acid rain and a contributor to global climate change.
- More than 600 million people live in urban areas where sulfur dioxide levels exceed WHO guidelines.
- High concentrations of SO_2 can result in temporary breathing impairment for asthmatic children and adults who are active outdoors.

Sources and trends

- Coal burning is the single largest anthropogenic (human-made) source of sulfur dioxide, accounting for about 50 percent of annual global emissions, with oil burning accounting for a further 25–30 percent.
- While anthropogenic SO_2 emissions in Europe and North America have been decreasing since 1980, the anthropogenic SO_2 emissions from China, Asia, and the tropics have been increasing.

Reducing emissions

- Switching from high- to low-sulfur coals has reduced sulfur emissions in some cases.
- In the United Kingdom total sulfur dioxide emissions fell by 74 percent between 1990 and 2003.
- In the United States, SO_2 emissions decreased by 31 percent between 1993 and 2002.

Sulfur dioxide emissions

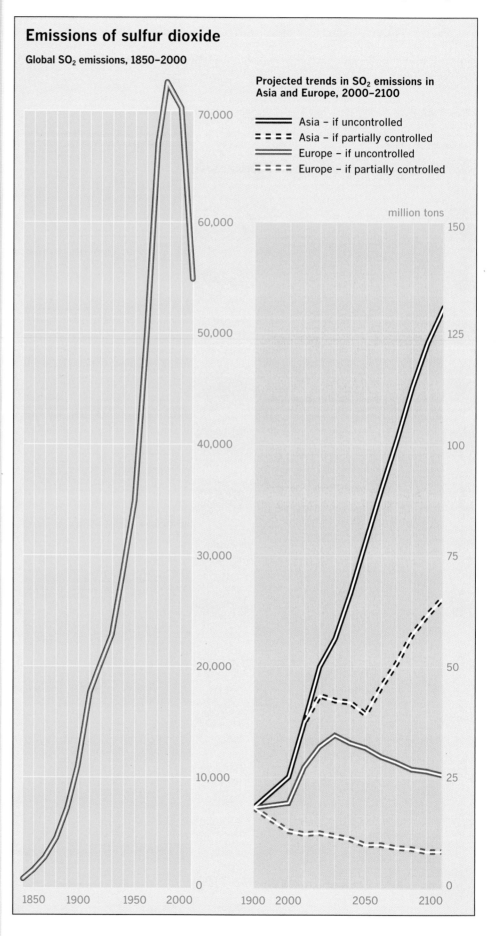

Emissions of sulfur dioxide

Global SO_2 emissions, 1850–2000

Projected trends in SO_2 emissions in Asia and Europe, 2000–2100

— Asia – if uncontrolled
= = = = Asia – if partially controlled
— Europe – if uncontrolled
= = = = Europe – if partially controlled

million tons

Rise in carbon emissions

© Diagram Visual Information Ltd.

Emissions of sulfur dioxide

Increase in atmospheric CO_2 levels recorded at Mauna Loa Observatory, Hawaii

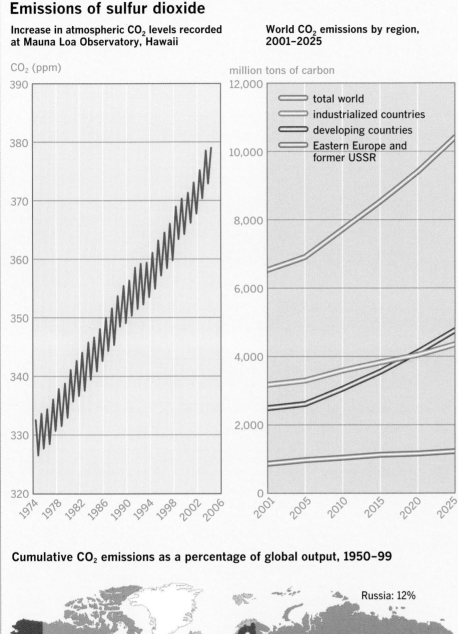

CO$_2$ (ppm)

390 380 370 360 350 340 330 320

1974 1978 1982 1986 1990 1994 1998 2002 2006

World CO_2 emissions by region, 2001–2025

million tons of carbon

12,000 10,000 8,000 6,000 4,000 2,000 0

- total world
- industrialized countries
- developing countries
- Eastern Europe and former USSR

2001 2005 2010 2015 2020 2025

Cumulative CO_2 emissions as a percentage of global output, 1950–99

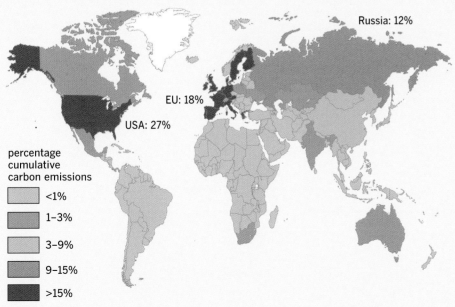

Russia: 12%

EU: 18%

USA: 27%

percentage cumulative carbon emissions

- <1%
- 1–3%
- 3–9%
- 9–15%
- >15%

Sources of carbon

- Roughly 75 percent of global CO_2 emissions are from the burning of fossil fuels.
- These emissions, together with CO_2 from land use changes and the emissions of methane (CH_4), nitrous oxide (N_2O), hydrofluorocarbons (HFCs), perfluorocarbons (PFCs), and sulfur hexafluoride (SF_6) are the main contributors to climate change.

Worldwide emissions

- The 2002 global fossil fuel CO_2 emission estimate of 6.87 billion tons of carbon, represented an all-time high and a two percent increase from 2001.

Industrialized nations

- North America is the highest fossil fuel CO_2 emitting region of the world, with 1.65 billion tons of carbon emissions in 2000.
- This 2000 total was an all-time high for North America and represented a 1.5 percent increase from 1999.
- The United Kingdom's CO_2 emissions recently increased for two consecutive years: 2.2 percent in 2003 and 1.5 percent in 2004.
- New targets require European Union countries to reduce their CO_2 emissions by 15–30 percent by 2020.

Developing nations

- Population growth, rising personal incomes and standards of living, and further industrialization in developing countries are expected to have a much greater influence on levels of energy consumption than in industrialized countries.

Key words

anthropogenic
biosphere
carbon cycle
fossil fuel
greenhouse gas

Carbon cycle

- Numerous processes collectively known as the *carbon cycle* naturally regulate the concentration of carbon dioxide in the atmosphere.
- Natural processes such as plant photosynthesis allow the movement, or flux, of carbon between the atmosphere, the land, and oceans.
- While these natural processes can absorb some of the vast quantities of anthropogenic carbon dioxide emissions produced each year, an estimated 3.2 billion tons is added to the atmosphere annually.
- The oceans, vegetation, and soils actively exchange CO_2 with the atmosphere and are significant reservoirs of carbon.
- Terrestrial vegetation and soils contain about three and a half times as much carbon as the atmosphere; the exchange is controlled by photosynthesis and respiration.
- Ocean uptake of carbon is limited by the solubility of CO_2 in seawater and the slow rate of mixing between surface and deep-ocean waters.

Carbon in the atmosphere

- Earth's positive imbalance between emissions and absorption results in the continuing growth in greenhouse gases in the atmosphere.
- The terrestrial biosphere has historically been a source of carbon to the atmosphere, but today it is a net sink.
- The current terrestrial carbon sink is caused by land management practices, higher carbon dioxide levels, nitrogen deposition, and possibly by recent changes in climate.
- Human burning of fossil fuels and changes in land use continue to disturb the carbon cycle, increasing the concentration of carbon dioxide in the atmosphere.

The carbon cycle

The global carbon cycle

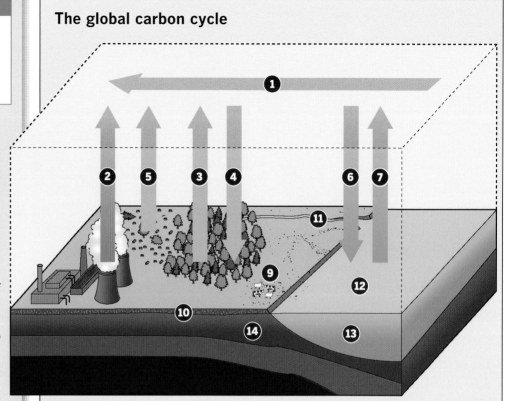

Billions of tons of carbon annually transferred or stored

- **1** atmosphere (750)
- **2** fossil fuel burning (6)
- **3** respiration (60)
- **4** photosynthesis (62)
- **5** deforestation (1)
- **6** rainfall (92)
- **7** evaporation (90)
- **8** fossil fuels (5,000)
- **9** plants and animals (610)
- **10** soil and plant debris (1,600)
- **11** rivers (1)
- **12** surface ocean (1,000)
- **13** intermediate/deep ocean (38,000)
- **14** rocks (75,000,000)

Carbon dioxide annually emitted (+) or absorbed (−)

Human emission sources

fossil fuel burning and cement production	+5.5
tropical deforestation	+1.6

Sinks

absorption by the oceans	−2.0
forest regrowth in the Northern Hemisphere	−0.5
carbon dioxide and nitrogen fertilization, climatic effects	−1.3
balance accumulated in the atmosphere	+3.3

Global methane emissions

Key words

biomass
landfill

Natural sources of atmospheric methane

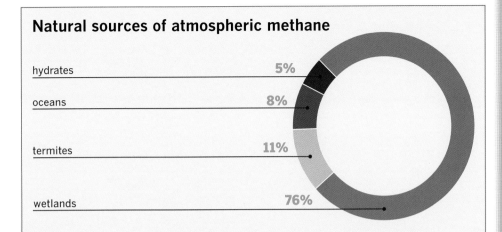

hydrates **5%**

oceans **8%**

termites **11%**

wetlands **76%**

Human-related sources of methane in the United States

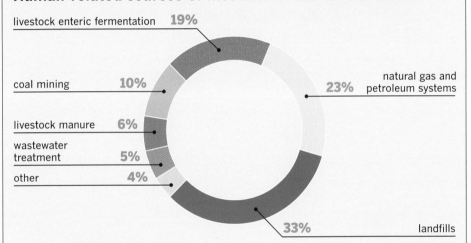

livestock enteric fermentation **19%**

coal mining **10%**

livestock manure **6%**

wastewater treatment **5%**

other **4%**

natural gas and petroleum systems **23%**

landfills **33%**

U.S. methane emissions

Source category	Gigagrams (Gg) of methane				
	1990	1998	1999	2000	2001
Landfills	10,999	9,639	9,701	9,798	9.663
Natural gas systems	5,810	5,903	5,728	5,772	5,588
Enteric fermentation	5,612	5,557	5,551	5,509	5,468
Coal mining	4,149	3,235	3,033	2,902	2,893
Manure management	1,490	1,858	1,852	1,820	1,850
Wastewater treatment	1,147	1,318	1,341	1,348	1,350
Petroleum systems	1,309	1,090	1,029	1,010	1,011
Rice cultivation	339	376	395	357	364
Stationary sources	388	342	351	363	353
Mobile sources	236	217	214	211	204
Petrochemical production	56	78	80	79	71
Field burning of agricultural residues	33	37	36	37	36
Silicone carbide production	1	1	1	1	<0.5
Total	30,669	29,651	29,312	29,207	28,851

source: EPA

Sources of methane

- Atmospheric methane is produced both from natural sources such as wetlands and from human activities such as flaring and venting of natural gas, coal mining, biomass burning, livestock farming, rice farming, and landfills.
- In the United States, the largest methane emissions come from the decomposition of wastes in landfills, ruminant digestion, and manure management. These are associated with domestic livestock, natural gas, oil systems, and coal mining.

Human-made sources

- It is estimated that 60 percent of global methane emissions are related to human activities.
- Globally, ruminant livestock produce about 79 million tons of methane per year, accounting for about 28 percent of global methane emissions from human-related activities.
- Methane is also produced during flooded rice cultivation by the anaerobic decomposition of organic matter in the soil.
- Landfills are the largest human-related source of methane in the United States, accounting for 34 percent of all methane emissions.

Natural sources

- Natural sources of methane include wetlands, gas hydrates, permafrost, termites, oceans, freshwater bodies, non-wetland soils, and other sources such as wildfires.
- Global emissions of methane by termites are estimated to be about 20 tetragrams (Tg) per year, and account for approximately 11 percent of the global methane emissions from natural sources.

© Diagram Visual Information Ltd.

Sources of lead

- Lead is a highly toxic heavy metal that was used for many years in products found in and around the home.
- Alkyl-lead is used primarily as a fuel additive to reduce "knock" in combustion engines.
- Industrial processes, primarily the processing of metals, are the major source of lead emissions to the atmosphere.

Effects on human health

- Unlike metallic forms of lead, alkyl-lead is easily absorbed through the skin.
- Once it enters the body lead interferes with normal cell function and with a number of physiological processes.
- It primarily affects the peripheral and central nervous systems, the blood cells, and metabolism of vitamin D and calcium, and also causes reproductive toxicity.
- Lead may cause a range of health effects, from learning and behavioral problems, to seizures and death. Infants younger than six years old are most at risk, because their bodies are growing fastest.
- Today, lead poisoning remains the single most significant preventable disease associated with an environmental or occupational toxin.

Reduction lead use

- Since the 1980s, the Environmental Protection Agency (EPA) and its federal partners have phased out lead in gasoline, reduced lead in drinking water, and banned or limited lead use in consumer products, including residential paint.
- In 1990, the Clean Air Act Amendments completely prohibited the use of leaded gasoline as fuel for on-road automotive use in the United States.

Lead emissions

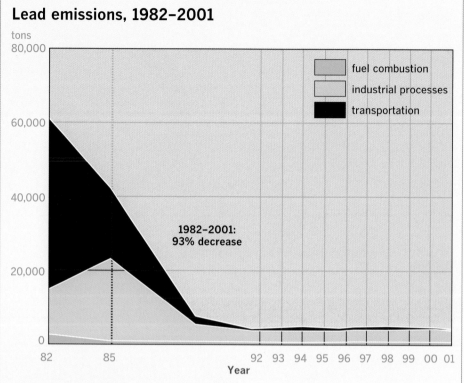

Lead emissions, 1982–2001

1982–2001:
93% decrease

- fuel combustion
- industrial processes
- transportation

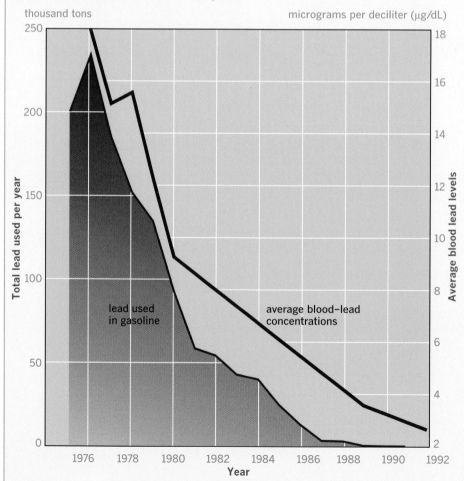

Gradual phaseout of lead in gasoline correlated with children's blood–lead concentration, USA

lead used in gasoline

average blood–lead concentrations

Sulfur emissions

Sulfur emissions, 1850–1990

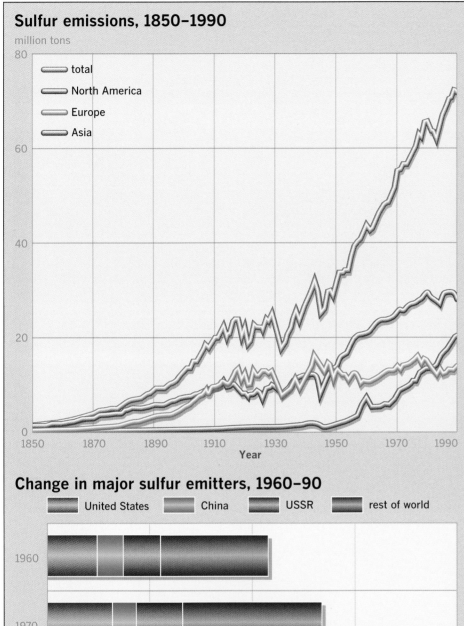

million tons

Legend: total, North America, Europe, Asia

Year axis: 1850, 1870, 1890, 1910, 1930, 1950, 1970, 1990

Change in major sulfur emitters, 1960–90

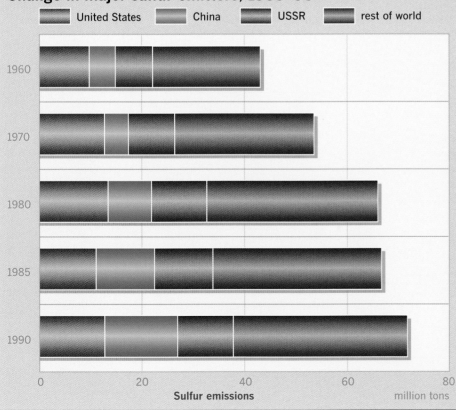

Legend: United States, China, USSR, rest of world

Years: 1960, 1970, 1980, 1985, 1990

Sulfur emissions — million tons (0, 20, 40, 60, 80)

Key words

acid rain
climate change
flue

The history of sulfur

- The burning of hard coal, brown coal, and oil generates sulfur emissions.
- Sulfur emissions are an important constituent of acid rain and a contributor to global climate change.
- In 1900, the largest coal producing country was Great Britain, followed by the United States, then Germany.
- By 1960, the three major coal producing countries were China, the United States, and the USSR.
- By 1990, China predominated in coal production with an output of 1.1 gigatons per year.
- In 1990, the United States, the USSR, and China were the main sulfur emitters, producing approximately 50 percent of the world's total.

Stabilizing emissions

- Although the CIS (former USSR) and the United States appear to have stabilized their sulfur emissions in the last 20 years, recent increases in global emissions have been linked to the rapid industrialization of China.
- Switching from high to low sulfur coals has reduced sulfur emissions in some cases.

Cleaning up emissions

- In a few countries, such as Germany, flue gas desulfurization (FGD) has made an important contribution to emission reductions.
- This is an industrial process in which gases containing sulfur are released and scrubbed from fossil fuel or from exhaust gases.
- The removal of sulfur from fuels is difficult and expensive; but the sulfur formed in combustion can often be removed easily by washing with an alkaline liquid.

© Diagram Visual Information Ltd.

The acid rain problem

- The term *acid rain* was first used in 1872, after a link was made between sulfur dioxide emissions from the burning of coal in Manchester, England, to the acidification of nearby rainfall.
- The term is now used to describe all forms of pollution associated with the burning of fossil fuels.
- Snow, sleet, and mist, collectively known as *wet deposition*; and gases, dusts, and smog, collectively known as *dry deposition*, are now included in the definition of acid rain.
- Acid rain is measured using a scale called *pH*: the lower a substance's pH, the more acidic it is.

Effects of acid rain

- In the 1980s, acid rain was identified as a major international environmental problem mainly affecting the over-populated and heavily industrialized areas of Europe and North America.
- Acid deposition pollution can travel hundreds of miles across national boundaries and state lines.
- Mountainous regions suffer most from acid deposition because the often thin mountain soils cannot neutralize the acid.
- Lakes and rivers far from industrial centers in parts of Scandinavia and Scotland have become acidified, with considerable fish stock depletion.
- An area known as the black triangle, bordering Germany, the Czech Republic, and Poland has been the scene of the most intense fallout.
- Acid rain has also been the major cause of tree death, a particular problem in Eastern Europe.

Acid rain: the global picture

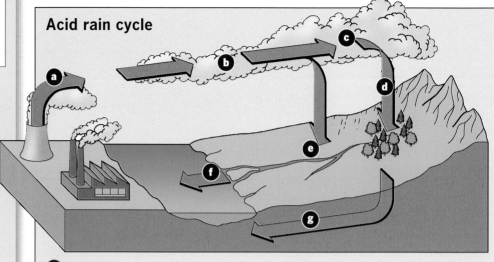

Acid rain cycle

a Acid rain is produced by the release of sulfur dioxide (SO_2) and nitrogen oxides (NO_x) into the atmosphere from factories and power stations.

b Gases combine with water to make sulfuric and nitric acids.

c Acidic clouds can travel for long distances from the source.

d Acid rain and snow fall on trees, killing them.

e Acid rain runs into rivers, killing fish and other organisms.

f Acidified water runs into lakes, killing fish.

g Acidified water leaches nutrients and heavy metals out of soil. These wash into lakes, polluting them.

Acid rain levels and extent of forest damage in Europe

Proportion of forest damaged

- high (more than 25%)
- moderate (15–25%)
- light (below 15%)

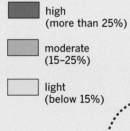

a Great Britain
b Sweden
c Netherlands
d Belgium
e Germany
f Luxembourg
g France
h Switzerland
i Poland
j Czech Republic
k Slovakia
l Austria
m Hungary

Acid rain: eastern USA

Key words

acid rain
pollution

Effects of acid rain
Critical acidity for North American fish in lakes and streams

Yellow perch

Brook trout

Lake trout

Smallmouth bass

Rainbow trout

Common shiner

7.0   6.5   6.0   5.5   5.0   4.5   4.0
pH

- pH is a measure of acidity. The lower the pH, the more acidic the water.
- Fish species have different abilities to withstand excess acidity.
- The dark fish show favorable pH ranges; the light fish are placed in less favorable ranges.
- Absent symbols indicate that the fish cannot survive in the acidity shown.

The Acid Rain Program, 1995

- These maps represent snapshots of wet sulfate deposition over time.
- Following the 1995 implementation of the Acid Rain Program, total sulfate deposition fell in a dramatic and unprecedented reduction of up to 25 percent over a large area of the eastern United States.
- The greatest reductions occurred in the northeastern states, where many of the most acid-sensitive ecosystems are located.

Sulfate deposition

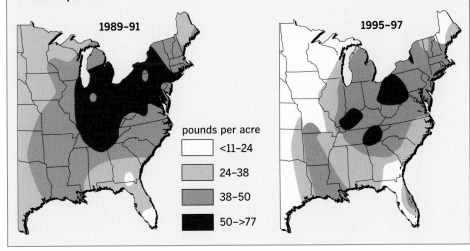

1989–91   1995–97

pounds per acre
- <11–24
- 24–38
- 38–50
- 50–>77

Effects of acid rain

- Acid rain has been widespread across North America for decades, leading to the acidification of lakes and streams, causing human respiratory problems, thinning forests, and corroding monuments and buildings.
- Acid rain can diminish the ability of lakes and streams to sustain fish and other aquatic species.
- In some sensitive lakes and streams, acidification has severely depleted even the hardiest species, such as the brook trout.
- As pH approaches 5.0, major changes in the makeup of plankton communities occur, less desirable species of mosses and plankton may begin to invade, and the progressive loss of some fish populations is likely.
- Below pH of 5.0, the water is largely devoid of fish and the bottom becomes covered with non-decayed material.
- Studies in Canada and the United States indicate that there is a link between this pollution and respiratory problems in sensitive populations, such as children and asthmatics.
- It has been estimated that around 50 percent of the sulphate deposited in Canada comes from sources in the United States.

The Acid Rain Program
- The overall goal of the Acid Rain Program is to achieve significant environmental and public health benefits through reductions in emissions of sulfur dioxide and nitrogen oxides.
- To achieve this goal, the program employs both traditional and innovative approaches for controlling air pollution.
- The program also encourages pollution prevention and energy efficiency.

Key words

chlorofluoro-	greenhouse
carbons (CFCs)	effect
fossil fuel	greenhouse gas
global warming	

Causes and effects

- The *greenhouse effect* is caused by an accumulation of certain types of gases in the upper atmosphere.
- Theses gases include carbon dioxide, methane, chlorofluorocarbons (CFCs) and water vapor.
- Infrared radiation in the Sun's rays bounces back off Earth into space.
- Greenhouse gases act as a barrier to the infrared radiation and reflect some of it back down onto Earth.

Consequences

- The infrared radiation becomes trapped between the layer of greenhouse gases and Earth's surface, bouncing back and forth.
- The radiation is absorbed by the planet and its atmosphere and contributes to the phenomenon known as global warming.

Carbon dioxide

- The burning of organic and fossil fuels produces large amounts of carbon dioxide.
- Wood, coal, oil, and petroleum-based fuels produce CO_2 when they combust.

Methane gas

- Methane gas is a product of the decomposition of organic material.
- It is also produced within the guts of herbivorous livestock and by rotting vegetation.

CFCs

- CFCs were used until recently as coolants in refrigerators and propellants in aerosols. They readily escape into the atmosphere.

Water vapor

- Water vapor is produced by water evaporating into the atmosphere.
- Rivers, lakes, oceans, and plants all generate vast amounts of water vapor.

The greenhouse effect

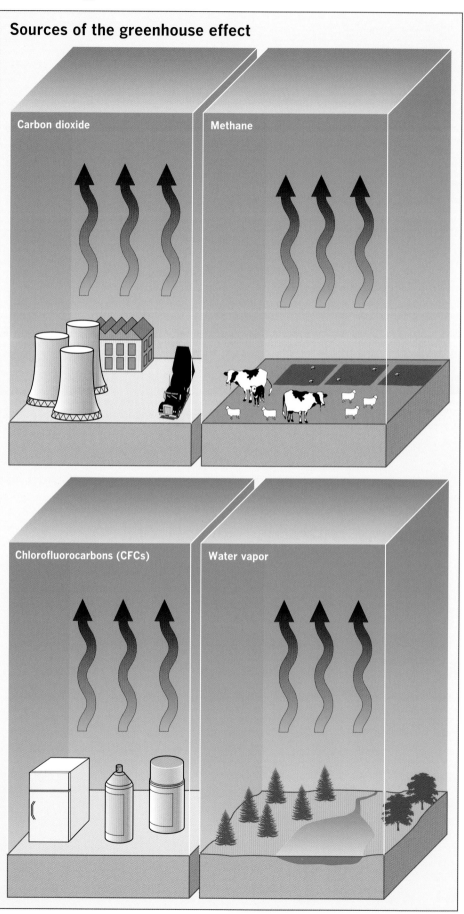

Sources of the greenhouse effect

Carbon dioxide

Methane

Chlorofluorocarbons (CFCs)

Water vapor

Greenhouse gas estimates

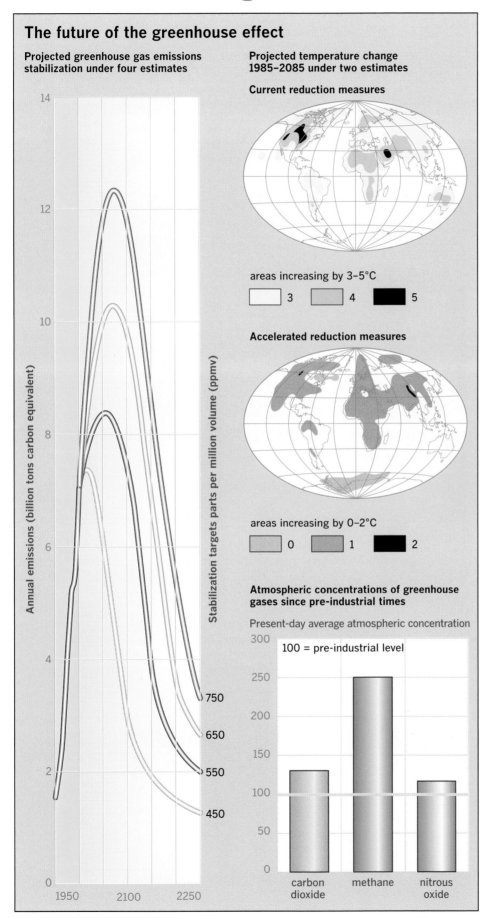

The future of the greenhouse effect

Projected greenhouse gas emissions stabilization under four estimates

Annual emissions (billion tons carbon equivalent)

Stabilization targets parts per million volume (ppmv)

750
650
550
450

1950   2100   2250

Projected temperature change 1985–2085 under two estimates

Current reduction measures

areas increasing by 3–5°C

3   4   5

Accelerated reduction measures

areas increasing by 0–2°C

0   1   2

Atmospheric concentrations of greenhouse gases since pre-industrial times

Present-day average atmospheric concentration

100 = pre-industrial level

300
250
200
150
100
50
0

carbon dioxide   methane   nitrous oxide

Key words

Environmental   Industrial
Protection   Revolution
Agency (EPA)   Kyoto protocol
fossil fuel
greenhouse gas

Natural greenhouse effect

- Greenhouse gases create a natural greenhouse effect that keeps the surface of Earth about 33°C warmer than it otherwise would be.
- Since the beginning of the Industrial Revolution around 1750, concentrations of the long-lived greenhouse gases in the atmosphere have risen as a result of human activities: primarily fossil fuel use, land-use change, and agriculture.
- Concentrations of CO_2, the main greenhouse gas, are currently increasing by about 0.5 percent per year; CH_4 by about one percent; and N_2O also by about 0.5 percent.
- Overall total U.S. emissions have risen by 13 percent from 1990 to 2003.
- According to the Environmental Protection Agency (EPA), total U.S. greenhouse gas emissions are projected to increase by 43 percent between 2000 and 2020.

Efforts at reduction

- More than a decade ago, most countries joined the United Nations Framework Convention on Climate Change.
- In 1997 some governments agreed to the Kyoto Protocol, which came into force on February 16, 2005.
- The Kyoto Protocol set legally-binding targets for 39 countries, giving each country a target amount of greenhouse gases that may be emitted between 2008–12.
- Each country must ensure that its emissions do not exceed this amount.
- The amounts assigned for individual countries add up to a total cut in greenhouse gas emissions of at least five percent from 1990 levels in the commitment period.
- However, scientists believe that it will be virtually impossible to restore the atmosphere to its pre-industrial levels of CO_2.

© Diagram Visual Information Ltd.

Key words

fossil fuel
global warming
greenhouse gas

Global warming

● Global warming refers to an expected rise in the global average temperature due to the continued emission of greenhouse gases, produced by industry and agriculture, which trap heat in the atmosphere.

● According to scientists, Earth's surface temperature has risen by about one degree Fahrenheit (0.6°C) in the past century and warming has accelerated during the past two decades.

● Evidence shows that most of the warming over the last 50 years is attributable to human activities.

Causes of global warming

● Human activities have altered the chemical composition of the atmosphere through the build-up of greenhouse gases, primarily carbon dioxide, methane, and nitrous oxide.

Greenhouse gases

● Carbon dioxide, the most important human-made greenhouse gas, is released primarily by the burning of fossil fuels such as coal, oil, and natural gas.

● Concentrations of greenhouse gases have risen considerably over the past 50 years and are still increasing, despite worldwide attempts to reduce emissions.

● Increasing concentrations of greenhouse gases are likely to accelerate the rate of global warming.

Effects of global warming

● Changing patterns of precipitation frequency and intensity, changes in soil moisture, and a rise of the global sea level are expected to be accompanied by higher temperatures.

Global warming: sources

Global temperature change, 1890–2000

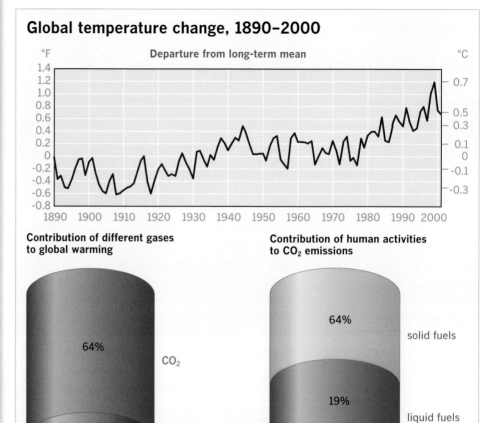

Contribution of different gases to global warming
Contribution of human activities to CO₂ emissions

Contributions to global warming by region, 1990–99

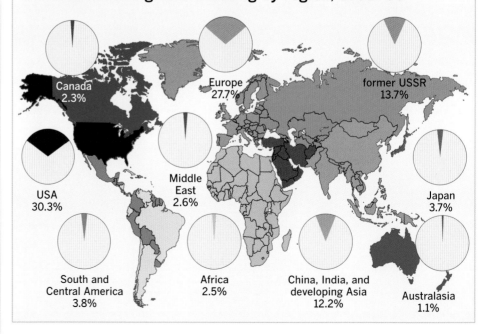

Global warming: effects

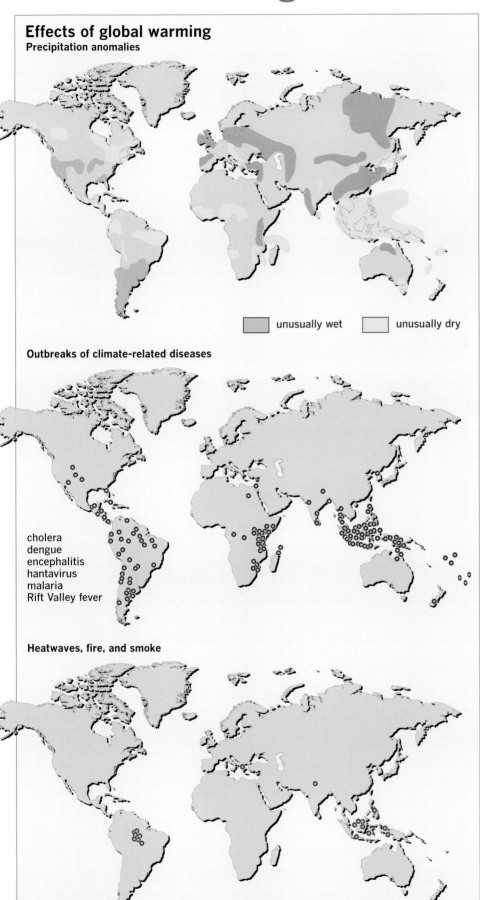

Effects of global warming
Precipitation anomalies

■ unusually wet ■ unusually dry

Outbreaks of climate-related diseases

cholera
dengue
encephalitis
hantavirus
malaria
Rift Valley fever

Heatwaves, fire, and smoke

Key words

biodiversity
climate change
global warming
greenhouse gas

Temperature rises

● Increasing concentrations of greenhouse gases are likely to accelerate the rate of climate change.

● Global mean surface temperatures have increased 0.5–1.0°F (0.3–0.6°C) since the late nineteenth century.

● The twentieth century's ten warmest years all occurred in the final 15 years of the century and, of these, 1998 was the warmest year on record.

● According to the Intergovernmental Panel on Climate Change (IPCC), the average global surface temperature could rise 1–4.5°F (0.6–2.5°C) through the next fifty years, and 2.2–10°F (1.4–5.8°C) through the next century.

Impact of global warming

● Associated environmental effects of global warming include biodiversity loss, sea level rise, increased drought, spread of disease, and a shift in weather patterns with an increase in extreme weather events.

● Evaporation will increase as the climate warms, and this will increase average global precipitation.

● Soil moisture is likely to decline in many regions, resulting in the prediction of falling crop yields in much of Africa and India and a loss of forest size in the Amazon.

● Snow cover in the Northern Hemisphere and floating ice in the Arctic Ocean will continue to decrease.

● Sea levels will rise as glaciers and ice sheets melt, flooding coastal cities and countries.

Predicting the future

● Scientists are trying to project what the exact impact will be throughout the twenty-first century.

● Prediction is difficult, especially at a local level, because computer models used to forecast global climate change are ill-equipped to simulate how things may change on smaller scales.

Key words

global warming
Gulf stream

Rising seas

- With the increase of Earth's temperature due to global warming, the resulting warmer temperatures are expected to raise the sea level by expanding ocean water, melting mountain glaciers, and melting parts of the Greenland Ice Sheet.
- Measurements suggest that sea level has already risen worldwide by 6–8 inches (15–20 cm) in the last century.
- The IPCC estimates that sea level will rise 3.5–35 inches (9–88 cm) by the year 2100.

Impact of rising sea level

- For every inch (cm) the sea rises, around three feet (1 m) of coastal land is lost to the sea.
- Sea level rise will significantly increase the flood risk to coastal populations.
- In Bangladesh approximately 17 million people live less than three feet (1 m) above sea level.
- The southern Mediterranean, Africa, southern Asia, and Southeast Asia are the regions most vulnerable to the impact of flooding.
- Human health will be at risk, and moving large numbers of people away from flooded regions will increase the risk of diseases spreading.
- There is likely to be a reduction in the quantity and quality of freshwater, further affecting human health.
- Important biological communities are likely to be lost because some species will not be able to adapt quickly enough to the changes in salinity or loss of ice cover.
- Climate models also suggest that rising sea levels will cause a shift in the Gulf Stream, which provides Europe with its mild climate.

Coasts at risk from sea level rise

High risk areas

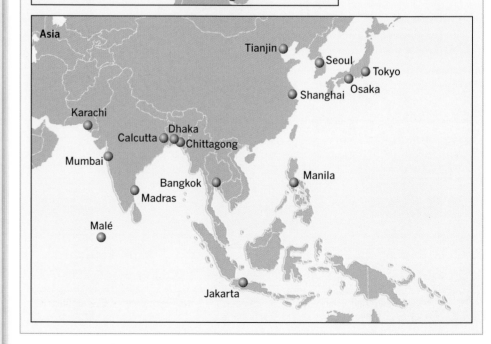

The Americas

New York

New Orleans

Miami

Nassau

Guayaquil

Rio de Janeiro

São Paulo

Buenos Aires

Africa

Alexandria

Dakar

Freetown

Monrovia

Lagos

Abidjan   Accra

Libreville

_____ coasts that are highly vulnerable to sea level rise

● cities that are highly vulnerable to sea-level rise

Asia

Tianjin

Seoul

Tokyo

Shanghai   Osaka

Karachi

Dhaka

Calcutta   Chittagong

Mumbai

Bangkok   Manila

Madras

Malé

Jakarta

Sea level rise estimates

Populations directly affected by flooding
Annual numbers in different regions under three different estimates

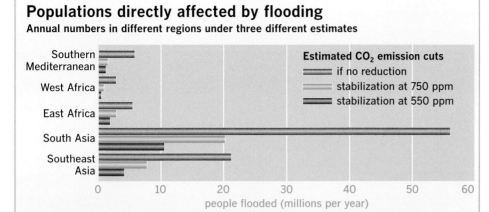

Estimated CO$_2$ emission cuts
- if no reduction
- stabilization at 750 ppm
- stabilization at 550 ppm

Regions: Southern Mediterranean, West Africa, East Africa, South Asia, Southeast Asia

x-axis: people flooded (millions per year) — 0, 10, 20, 30, 40, 50, 60

No reduction in CO$_2$ emissions

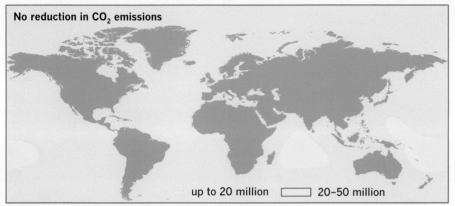

- up to 20 million
- 20–50 million

The estimated number of people flooded each year in the 2080s, if there is no reduction of CO$_2$ emissions.

Stabilized emissions

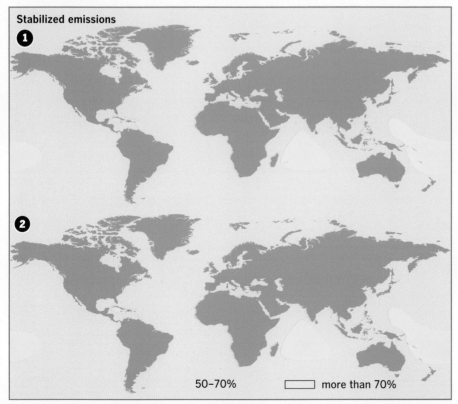

①

②

- 50–70%
- more than 70%

The percentage reduction in numbers of people flooded under emissions of CO$_2$ stabilized at (**1**) 750 parts per million (ppm) and (**2**) 550 ppm.

Key words

Environmental Protection Agency (EPA)

Future rise

- The flood risk to coastal populations will significantly increase if sea levels rise.
- According to a report by the EPA, global warming is most likely to raise sea levels six inches (.15 m) by the year 2050 and 13 inches (.34 m) by the year 2100.
- There is also a ten percent chance that climate change will contribute 12 inches (.3 m) by 2050 and 25.6 inches (.65 m) by 2100.
- Along the coast of New York, which is representative of the U.S. East Coast, the sea level is likely to rise ten inches (.26 m) by 2050 and 21.7 inches (.55 m) by 2100.

Developing world

- The areas worst affected by a rise in sea levels will be the developing nations in South and Southeast Asia.
- Scientists estimate that a 39-inch (100 cm) sea level rise would affect six million people in Egypt with 12–15 percent of agricultural land lost, 13 million in Bangladesh with 16 percent of national rice production lost, and 72 million in China.
- By the 2080s the annual number of people flooded could be 34 million under the 750 parts per million (ppm) CO$_2$ estimate, and 19 million under the 550 ppm estimate.

Reducing the impact

- Various studies have been prepared to show the possible impact of reducing emission levels.
- The EPA predicts that if global emissions are stabilized by the year 2050 the rate of sea level rise will be reduced by 28 percent by 2100.
- If emissions were stabilized by the year 2025 then the rate of sea level rise would be reduced by half.

Key words

ecosystem
infrastructure

United States Gulf Coast

- Scientists predict that the sea level along the Gulf Coast is likely to rise by 15–40 inches (38–101 cm) by 2100.
- The Gulf Coast region has a flat topography, and with only a few inches of sea level rise the coastline would be moved considerably inland.
- This threatens towns, community infrastructure, port facilities, and ecosystems.
- Coastal wetlands help to retain and purify water, stabilize sediments, and protect coastal areas from storm surges. These natural services are valued at millions of dollars and would be lost if wetlands shrink or deteriorate in quality.
- If these barrier islands and wetlands are lost, storm waves could reach further inland during major storms.

New Orleans

- In 2005, Hurricane Katrina caused catastrophic damage to the Gulf Coast region, particularly to New Orleans, and highlighted its vulnerability to storms and floods.
- The hurricane caused large loss of life and it is expected that the region will take years to rebuild and recover at great expense.

Egyptian Nile Delta

- Rising sea levels would destroy weak parts of the Nile Delta sand belt that is essential for the protection of lagoons and low-lying reclaimed lands.
- The economic effect would be very serious as one third of Egypt's fish catches are made in these lagoons.
- Rising sea levels would change the water quality and affect freshwater fish.
- Agricultural land would be lost.
- A 3.3-foot (1 m) rise would affect a population of 6.1 million and 1,740 square miles (4,507 km²) of cropland.

Risk in close-up: the Gulf Coast and the Nile Delta

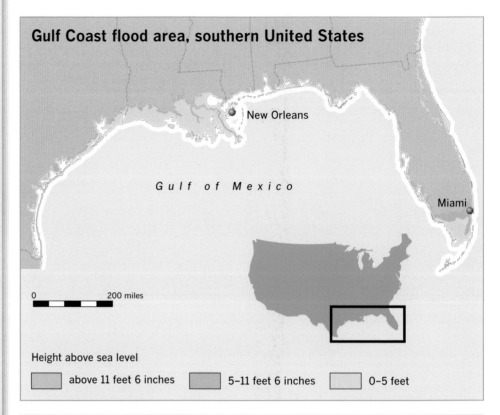

Gulf Coast flood area, southern United States

0   200 miles

Height above sea level

above 11 feet 6 inches   5–11 feet 6 inches   0–5 feet

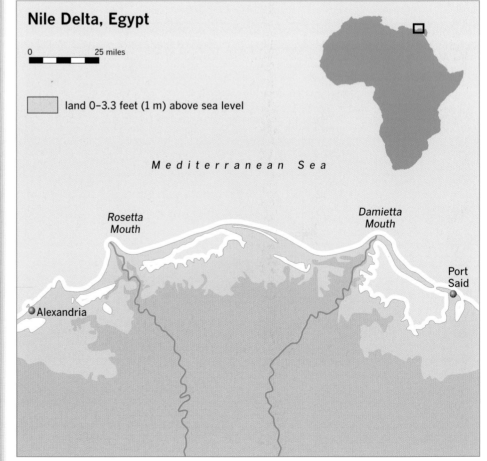

Nile Delta, Egypt

0   25 miles

land 0–3.3 feet (1 m) above sea level

Mediterranean Sea

Risk in close-up: Bangladesh and the Netherlands

Key words

tropical cyclone

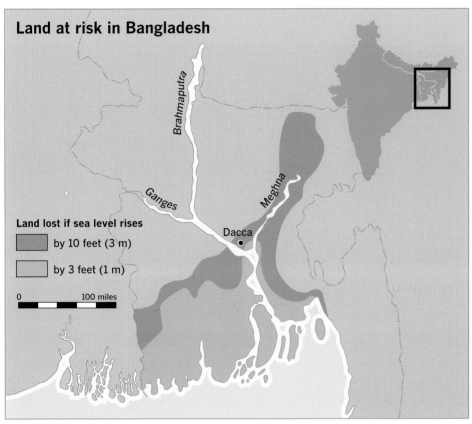

Land at risk in Bangladesh

Brahmaputra

Ganges

Meghna

Dacca

Land lost if sea level rises

by 10 feet (3 m)

by 3 feet (1 m)

0   100 miles

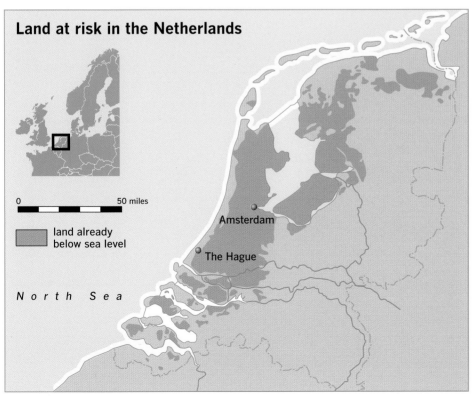

Land at risk in the Netherlands

0   50 miles

Amsterdam

The Hague

North Sea

land already
below sea level

Bangladesh

- Bangladesh, one of the world's poorest nations, is heavily populated and is also the country most vulnerable to sea level rise.
- Large areas are situated just below sea level, in the estuary of three large rivers, and are often seriously affected by flooding.
- Bangladesh has very little flood protection, such as the coastal dikes in the Netherlands, so an increase in tropical cyclones and monsoon rains would become more damaging.
- Scientists predict that if sea levels rise by three feet (1 m), with no implementation of flood protection measures, one fifth of Bangladesh would disappear under water.
- Due to the high population density, the number of people affected would be extremely high, and 10–15 million people will lose their homes.
- A ten-foot (3 m) rise in sea levels would completely inundate the capital, Dacca.

The Netherlands

- The Netherlands has low-lying coasts and will be seriously affected by any rise in sea levels.
- A quarter of the country, including the capital Amsterdam, lies below sea level and is protected from the sea by coastal dikes, which were first begun in 500 BCE.
- The protection afforded by the coastal dikes has reduced the area of land under threat from rising sea levels to less than one percent.
- In the future the Netherlands will experience the effects of rising sea levels, but by enhancing the existing systems, the country should remain safe.
- The government is allocating 1.27 billion euros (more than $1 billion) up to 2020 to enhance the existing flood defenses.

Key words

*chlorofluoro-
  carbons (CFCs)*
Dobson unit
ozone
ozone layer

Holes in the ozone layer

Natural ozone

● Ozone (O_3) plays a vital role in the stratosphere, the region of the atmosphere 6–30 miles (10–48 km) above Earth's surface, by absorbing ultraviolet radiation from the Sun that is harmful to humans.

Holes in the ozone layer

● The ozone layer at the poles, has been severely depleted over the last 20 years, especially over Antarctica.

● The special meteorological conditions in Antarctica allow chlorofluoro-carbons (CFCs) to be more effective there in depleting ozone than anywhere else on Earth.

● The winter temperatures in the Arctic stratosphere are not as persistently low for extended periods as over Antarctica, which results in less ozone depletion in the Arctic.

● Over the years, the ozone hole has increased rapidly and is now as large as the Antarctic continent.

● The 2000 ozone hole reached its greatest extent in early September at almost 11 million square miles (28.4 million km²) and was the largest ever recorded.

Measuring the ozone layer

● A research group from the British Antarctic Survey first noticed the loss of ozone in the lower stratosphere over Antarctica in the 1970s.

● Ozone layer thickness is expressed in terms of Dobson units, which measure what its physical thickness would be if compressed in Earth's atmosphere.

The Antarctic ozone layer hole
Ozone holes in Antarctic spring (September 7th–October 13th), 1980–2005

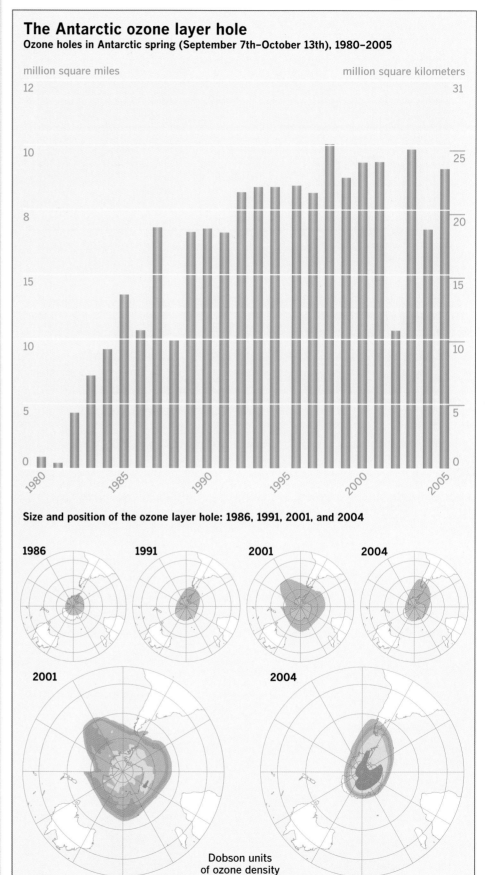

Size and position of the ozone layer hole: 1986, 1991, 2001, and 2004

Dobson units
of ozone density

100   125   150   175   200   225

Causes of ozone depletion

Key words

chlorofluoro-
   carbons (CFCs)
Montreal
   protocol
ozone

Progress of CFCs to ozone layer

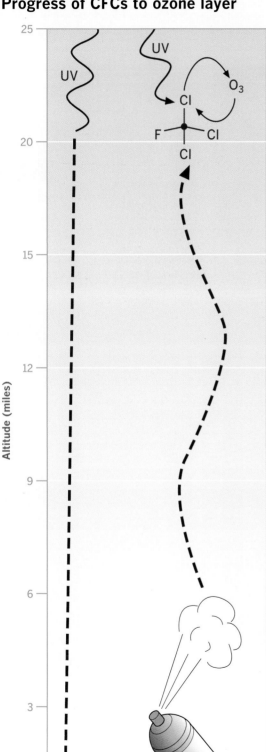

Chlorine reacts chemically with ozone and reduces it.

CFCs break up only in the stratosphere.

A thinner ozone layer passes more ultraviolet (UV) radiation.

CFCs are released by humans.

More ultraviolet radiation reaches the surface of Earth.

Threat to the ozone layer

- Stratospheric ozone is threatened by some of the human-made gases that have been released into the atmosphere, especially chlorofluoro-carbons (CFCs).
- CFCs were produced from the 1940s to the 1970s to be used as refrigerants, electrical cleaners, propellants in aerosols, and the constituents of insulation products.
- CFCs mix in the atmosphere all over the world and survive until, after one to two years, they reach the stratosphere and are broken down into their separate elements (chlorine, fluorine, and carbon) by ultraviolet radiation.
- The chlorine atoms that are released by ultraviolet radiation react chemically with ozone and break it down.
- In the process of reacting with ozone, yet more chlorine is produced, which continues to react with the ozone in the stratosphere, in a process that progressively reduces the ozone until the chlorine is removed from the stratosphere by other processes.

Limiting the damage

- The first global agreement to restrict CFCs came with the signing of the Montreal Protocol in 1987, which aimed to reduce them by half by the year 2000.
- Production of the main CFCs was to be halted by the signatories by the end of 1995.
- The World Meteorological Organization anticipated that these limitations would lead to a recovery of the ozone layer by 2050.
- However, recent investigations suggest the problem is perhaps on a much larger and longer-term scale.

Key words

epidemic
food chain
global warming
ozone layer

Human health

- Although the ozone layer blocks most of the harmful ultraviolet (UV) radiation received from the Sun, small amounts do reach Earth's surface.
- UV radiation is absorbed mainly in the skin and in the outer layers of the eye, and does not penetrate any deeper into the human body.
- The greatest threat to human health from increased UV exposure is an increase in the incidence of the skin cancer melanoma.
- The incidence of skin cancer in the United States has reached epidemic proportions, and one in five Americans will develop skin cancer.

Marine environment

- A consequence of ozone depletion for the marine environment is the likely reduction in the numbers of phytoplankton: the photosynthesizing organisms in the sea that form the base of the marine food chain and absorb CO_2 from the atmosphere, thereby helping to stave off global warming.
- UV also causes direct damage to young fish, shrimp and crab larvae, and other small animals.
- Further up the food chain, this means a reduction in fish stocks, marine animals, and seabirds.

Agriculture and plant life

- Crop yields will suffer because exposure to high concentrations of UV radiation has been shown to stunt the growth and leaf development of most plant varieties.
- UV-sensitive plants can also be more susceptible to pests and disease.

Material degradation

- Many plastics suffer when exposed to UV radiation because photochemical reactions make some plastics brittle, thus shortening their useful lives.

Consequences of ozone depletion

Skin cancer in humans

Levels of risk of skin cancer caused by ozone depletion under different restriction estimates

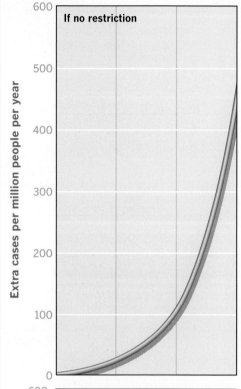

If no restriction

1987 Montreal restrictions

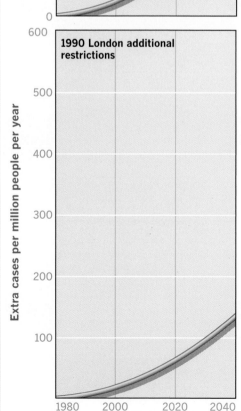

1990 London additional restrictions

1992 Copenhagen and 1997 Montreal amendments

Extra cases per million people per year

Nature under threat

Key words

biodiversity
ecosystem
fossil fuel
habitat

Biodiversity

Estimated number of described (known) species

Kingdom	Described species
Animals: invertebrates	1,272,000
Plants	270,000
Protists (algae, protozoa, etc.)	80,000
Fungi	72,000
Animals: vertebrates	52,000
Bacteria	4,000
Total described species	1,750,000
Possible total (including unknown species)	14,000,000

animals:
invertebrates

72.7%

plants **15.4%**

protists **4.6%**

fungi **4.1%**

animals: vertebrates **3.0%**

bacteria **0.2%**

Nature under threat

- Human activities are increasingly threatening *biodiversity* on Earth.
- While it may never be possible to conserve all remaining natural habitats, it is important to achieve a global conservation strategy with all ecosystem types represented.

Threats to biodiversity

- The main cause of biodiversity loss is human population growth combined with unsustainable patterns of consumption, increasing production of waste and pollutants, urban development, international conflict, and continuing inequalities in the distribution of wealth and resources.
- Throughout history, species have always become extinct in small numbers, but the current rate of extinction is much higher than this background rate.
- Nitrogen deposition—caused by the burning of fossil fuels and excessive fertilizer use—and oil spills have had a major impact on biodiversity.
- The consumption of natural resources such as wild animals for food and forests for wood has reached unsustainable levels and is very damaging to biodiversity.

Trade in endangered species

- International trade in products derived from wildlife is now thought to be worth around $6 billion annually.
- The *Convention on International Trade in Endangered Species* (*CITES*) came into force in 1975, and 167 countries have now signed the treaty.
- International tourists often unintentionally purchase goods made from CITES-listed species.
- Greater awareness by tourists would avoid encouraging to a trade that can threaten a species' survival.

Global 200 "Blueprint for a Living Planet"

- The World Wildlife Fund (WWF) has provided a global ranking of more than 200 of Earth's biologically most outstanding terrestrial, freshwater, and marine habitats.
- The ranking covers all major habitat types from Arctic tundra to tropical reefs, from mangroves to deserts, and include species from every major habitat type.
- Almost half these ecoregions are critically endangered by the direct effects of human activities.

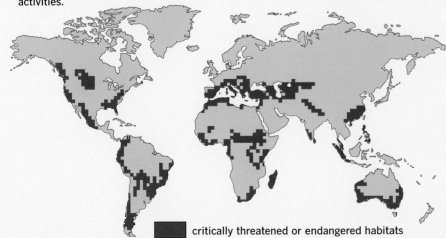

critically threatened or endangered habitats

© Diagram Visual Information Ltd.

Key words

biodiversity

Measuring biodiversity loss

- It is important to measure the rate of biodiversity loss and the possible causes of decline to be able to design and implement effective conservation strategies.
- The *World Conservation Union* or *IUCN*, records the status of world biodiversity in the "Red List" of threatened species.
- This report gives details of the numbers of threatened species in each animal and plant group and categorizes them according to the severity of their status.
- The categories are: extinct; extinct in the wild; critically endangered; endangered; vulnerable; near threatened; least concern; data deficient; and not evaluated.
- Quantitative criteria have been developed for the critically endangered, endangered, and vulnerable categories. Species in each of these groups are thought to share a similar chance of extinction, and the categories are collectively termed "threatened."

Increase in threatened species

- The number of threatened species has been increasing in all groups over recent years.
- Amphibians have shown the largest increase in numbers of threatened species, rising from 124 in 1996–98 to 1,856 in 2004.
- However, it is sometimes difficult to monitor some groups of animals and plants because so little is known about them.
- In many animal and plant groups, especially invertebrates, species are still being discovered.
- Biodiversity loss is best understood for the better-known groups, such as birds and mammals.

Threatened species

Numbers of threatened species by group, 2004

	Described species	Species evaluated	Critically endangered	Endangered	Vulnerable	Total threatened	Percentage described species threatened	Percentage evaluated species threatened
Plants	287,655	11,824	1,490	2,239	4,592	8,321	2.81	70
Birds	9,917	9,917	179	345	689	1,213	12	12
Mammals	5,416	4,853	162	352	587	1,101	20	23
Amphibians	5,743	5,743	427	761	668	1,856	32	32
Reptiles	8,163	499	64	79	161	304	4	61
Fish	28,500	1,721	171	160	469	800	3	46
Insects	950,000	771	47	120	392	559	0.06	73
Crustaceans	40,000	498	56	79	294	429	1	86
Mollusks	70,000	2,163	265	221	488	974	1	45

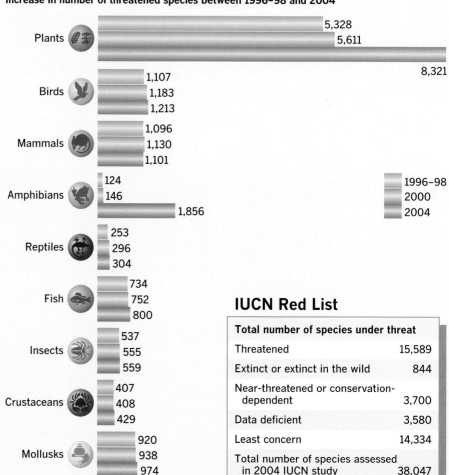

Increase in number of threatened species between 1996–98 and 2004

Plants: 5,328 / 5,611 / 8,321
Birds: 1,107 / 1,183 / 1,213
Mammals: 1,096 / 1,130 / 1,101
Amphibians: 124 / 146 / 1,856
Reptiles: 253 / 296 / 304
Fish: 734 / 752 / 800
Insects: 537 / 555 / 559
Crustaceans: 407 / 408 / 429
Mollusks: 920 / 938 / 974

Legend: 1996–98 / 2000 / 2004

IUCN Red List

Total number of species under threat	
Threatened	15,589
Extinct or extinct in the wild	844
Near-threatened or conservation-dependent	3,700
Data deficient	3,580
Least concern	14,334
Total number of species assessed in 2004 IUCN study	38,047

Extinctions

Species extinction by type

Mollusks

303

Birds

133

Plants

110

Fish

93

Mammals

77

Insects

60

Amphibians

35

Reptiles

22

Crustaceans

8

 = 5 species

NATURE UNDER THREAT

Recording extinctions

- When the last individual of a species dies, the species is said to have become extinct.
- *Extinction* represents the permanent and irreversible loss of a unique evolutionary form and its genetic material.
- By recording extinctions, it is possible to understand why they are happening better. It also assists the identification of species that are most at risk.

Causes of extinction

- Humans have become one of the main causes of extinctions worldwide.
- The direct causes of extinctions are often hard to identify, but invasive alien species, habitat loss, and over-exploitation are all thought to be major contributory factors.
- Birds are among the most studied of animal groups in the world and invasive species have been recorded as responsible for at least 65 extinctions.
- Predation by introduced animals such as rats, cats, and dogs, coupled with habitat destruction and the introduction of diseases has caused many of the extinctions in birds.

Background extinction

- Extinctions have always featured in evolution. They usually happen slowly due to natural events, though many catastrophic or mass extinctions have also occurred.
- The background extinction rate is estimated to be about one species per decade.
- The current extinction rate is between two and three orders of magnitude higher than this background rate.
- Some scientists believe that we are now seeing the beginning of a new mass extinction.

© Diagram Visual Information Ltd.

Key words

extinction

Rare plant species

- The 2004 IUCN Red List includes assessments for 11,824 species of plants and of these, 8,321 are listed as being threatened with extinction.
- However, the real figure is thought to be much higher because sufficient data on many of the plant species is simply not available.
- The numbers of threatened plant species will continue to increase in the future as habitat destruction, pollution, and over-collection of specimens continue to rise.

Star cactus

- The star cactus (*Astrophytum asterias*) is a small, dome shaped, spineless cactus that was once found throughout Texas and Mexico.
- It produces yellow and orange flowers and a berrylike fruit covered with hairs.
- Due to over-collection and habitat loss it has become extinct in Mexico and now exists only in one location in Starr County, Texas.

Pondberry

- The pondberry (*Lindera melissifolia*) is a deciduous shrub from 3–6 feet (1–2 m) tall that was once found across the United States.
- It grows on wet soils and in shallow ponds but has suffered greatly due to habitat loss from the drainage of land for conversion to agriculture.
- Isolated populations are now known only in Georgia.
- As populations become ever more isolated from each other, the chances of pollination decrease.

World's rarest plants

Plants at risk of extinction

Arizona agave (*Agave arizonica*)	United States
Ash meadows milk-vetch (*Astragalus phoenix*)	United States
Bankouale palm (*Wissmania carinensis*)	Somalia, Yemen, Djibouti
Bois de fer (*Vateria seychellarum*)	Seychelles
Bois de prune blanc (*Drypetes caustica*)	Réunion, Indian Ocean
Dall's pittosporum (*Pittosporum dallii*)	New Zealand
Dotalu palm (*Loxococcus rupicola*)	Sri Lanka
Egyptian papyrus (*Cyperus papyrus hadidii*)	Egypt
Fibrosa she oak (*Casuarina fibrosa*)	Australia
Fragrant prickly-apple cactus (*Cereus eriophorus*)	United States
Furbish lousewort (*Pedicularis furbishiae*)	United States
Gigasiphon (*Gigasiphon macrosiphon*)	East Africa
Ginkgo (*Ginkgo biloba*)	China
Green pitcher plant (*Sarracenia oreophila*)	United States
Horseshoe fern (*Marattia salicina*)	Australia
Javan phalaenopsis orchid (*Phalaenopsis javanica*)	Indonesia
Large-flowered fiddleneck (*Amsinckia grandiflora*)	United States
Leafless acacia (*Acacia aphyela*)	Australia
Lord Howe Island passionfruit (*Passiflora herbertiana insulae-howei*)	Pacific
Louisiana quillwort (*Isoetes louisianensis*)	United States
Madeira net-leaf orchid (*Goodyera macrophylla*)	Madeira
Mauritius ebony (*Diospyros angulata*)	Mauritius
Mellblom's spider orchid (*Calenia hastata*)	Australia
Okeechobee gourd (*Cucurbita okeechobeensis*)	United States
Pondberry (*Lindera melissifolia*)	United States
San Clemente Island Indian paintbrush (*Castilleja grisea*)	United States
Schimper's toxocarpus (*Toxocarpus schimperianus*)	Seychelles
Silver gum (*Eucalyptus crenulata*)	Australia
Star cactus (*Astrophytum asterias*)	United States, Mexico
Sunshine diuris orchid (*Diuris fragrantissima*)	Australia
Tennessee purple coneflower (*Echinacea tennesseensis*)	United States
Tree cactus (*Cereus robinii*)	United States
Virginia round-leaf birch (*Betula uber*)	United States
West Himalayan elm (*Ulmus wallichiana*)	India
Western lily (*Lilium occidentale*)	United States
White gum (*Eucalyptus argophloia*)	Australia
Yellow sobralia orchid (*Sobralia xantholeuca*)	Mexico, Guatemala
Zhoushan hornbeam (*Carpinus putoensis*)	China

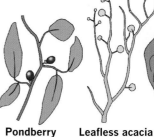

Ginkgo   Okeechobee gourd   Star cactus   Pondberry   Leafless acacia   Gigasiphon

World's rarest land mammals

Key words

extinction

World's rarest land mammals and their present habitat

● = 10 individuals

Vancouver Island marmot (Canada); at least 24

Seychelles sheath-tailed bat; 50–100

Northern hairy-nosed wombat (Australia); 65

Javan rhino (Indonesia); fewer than 60

Hispid hare (Assam rabbit; India, Nepal); 110

Tamaraw (dwarf water buffalo; Philippines); estimated 30–200

Dwarf blue sheep (Sichuan, China); approximately 200

Tonkin snub-nosed monkey (Vietnam); about 200

Yellow-tailed woolly monkey (northern Peru); fewer than 250

Kouprey (Cambodian forest ox; Laos, Cambodia, Thailand, Vietnam); fewer than 250

Malabar large spotted civet (southwest India) fewer than 250 mature individuals

Philippine spotted deer (Panay and Negros islands); a few hundred

Saola (Vu quang ox; Vietnam, Laos); estimated at several hundred

Sumatran rhino (Indonesia); estimated 250–300

Hirola (Hunter's hartebeest; Kenya, Somalia); fewer than 300

African wild ass (Eritrea, Ethiopia, Somalia); possibly only a few hundred

Addax (Niger, Chad, Mauritania); a few hundred

Black-faced lion tamarin (Brazil); as few as 400

Ethiopian wolf; at least 442

Arabian oryx (Oman, Saudi Arabia); 886

Iberian lynx (Portugal, Spain); about 135

Muriqui (woolly spider monkey; Brazil); 700–1,000

Hairy-eared dwarf lemur (Madagascar); fewer than 1,000

Riverine rabbit (Karoo, South Africa); fewer than 250 mature individuals

Giant panda (western China); approximately 1,600

Golden lion tamarin (Brazil); more than 1,000

Golden-rumped lion tamarin (Brazil); about 1,000

Greater bamboo lemur (Madagascar); about 1,000

Human impact
- Many mammal species from around the world are facing the threat of extinction due to overhunting, habitat loss, and other human interventions.
- Many of these critically endangered mammals have avoided complete extinction only through the efforts of conservation organizations.

The giant panda
- The giant panda *(Ailuropoda melanoleuca)* lives in China, in mixed temperate and broadleaf forests, and has been the focus of conservation efforts for decades.
- Pandas, which are the symbol of the World Wildlife Fund (WWF), are classified as bears but have adapted to a purely vegetarian diet and depend almost entirely on bamboo as a food source.
- As China became more populated the panda was hunted and their habitat became increasingly fragmented.
- By 2005, the Chinese government established more than 50 panda reserves, protecting around 45 percent of the remaining giant panda habitat.
- As a result of conservation efforts, in 2004 there were an estimated 1,600 individuals remaining in the wild.

The Javan rhino
- The Javan rhino *(Rhinoceros sondaicus)* is one of the rarest large mammal species in the world.
- Experts believe it is on the verge of extinction, with fewer than 60 individuals surviving in the wild, and none in captivity.
- The two subspecies, which live in Indonesia and Vietnam, are under increasing human population pressure and are often hunted.
- Even with the best conservation efforts, with so few animals left alive, the future of the species is uncertain.

© Diagram Visual Information Ltd.

Key words

cull

The American bison

- The range of the bison (or buffalo, *Bison bison*) in North America once extended south to Mexico and east to the Atlantic.
- Huge herds were found on the Great Plains and it is thought that the original bison population was between 35 and 70 million.

Slaughter

- Great Plains Native Americans relied on bison for meat and hides, killing them in sustainable numbers.
- Commercialized and subsistence hunting by European settlers caused a huge decline in the bison population.
- By the early 1800s bison had disappeared east of the Mississippi.
- The expansion of the American frontier west signaled the onset of a systematic reduction of the Great Plains herds by 1830.
- Bison hunting became the chief industry of the Plains, with organized groups killing upwards of 250 individuals per day.
- Culling of bison was further justified as removal of the food supply of the Native American population.
- The Plains herds had all been wiped out by 1893, except for about 300 animals.

Preservation work

- In 1894 Congress enacted a law to protect bison, and in 1902 a captive herd of 41 animals was placed under government protection in Yellowstone National Park.
- Today there are around 4,000 animals in the park.
- Elsewhere, bison herds have been re-established with total numbers estimated at 250,000.
- However, the herds have low genetic diversity because of the severe depopulation of the nineteenth century.

Overhunting: North American bison

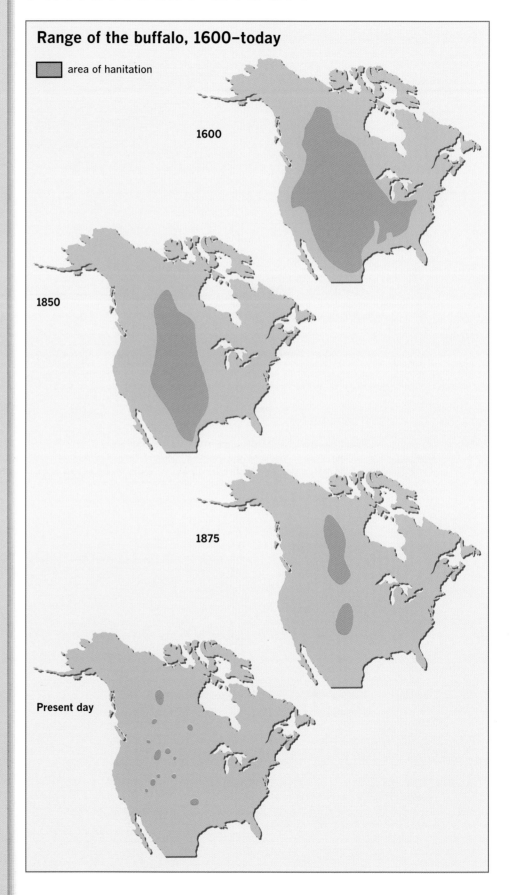

Range of the buffalo, 1600–today

area of hanitation

1600

1850

1875

Present day

Overhunting: baleen and toothed whales

Key words

baleen
baleen whale

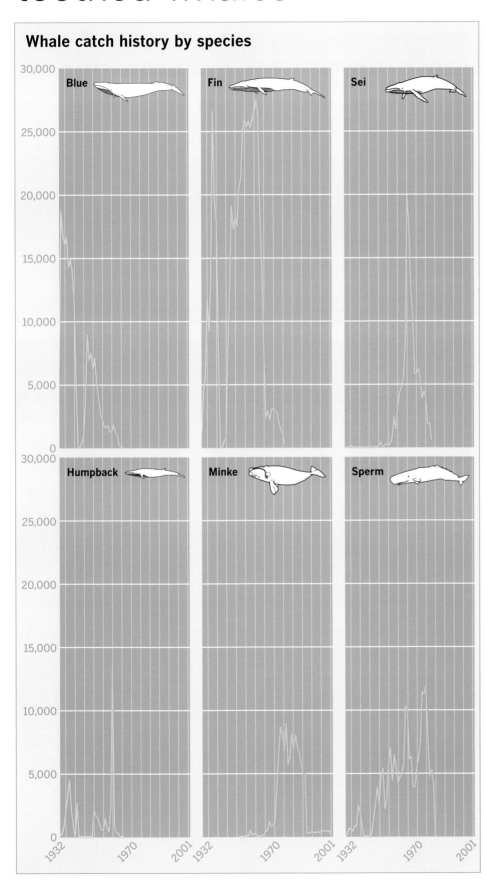

Whale catch history by species

Blue

Fin

Sei

Humpback

Minke

Sperm

Why they were hunted

- Baleen whales are the largest of the whales. They feed on plankton and krill: tiny sea creatures that they strain by the million through sievelike plates in their mouth.
- These whales were originally the most hunted because of their large size.
- They were harvested for their meat, baleen, blubber, and bone.
- The baleen plates from whales were used in the manufacture of women's clothing, fishing rods, and umbrellas from "whale bone."
- Sperm whales are toothed whales that were hunted for spermaceti, a waxy substance they secrete in a special part of their heads.
- Spermaceti was used to make cosmetics and candles.

The blue whale

- The largest of the baleen whales, and the largest animal ever to have existed on Earth, is the blue whale which may reach more than 85 feet (26 m) in length and weigh more than 90 tons.
- The blue whale has been overhunted for some 200 years. The International Whaling Commission estimated there to be between 400 and 1,400 blue whales left in the Southern Hemisphere in 2000.

Uncertain future

- Six species of baleen whale are listed for protection under the United States Endangered Species Act of 1973: the blue, bowhead, fin, humpback, right, and sei whales.
- Although whale hunting has now all but halted, the numbers in some populations are so low that there is great concern for their long-term survival.
- Scientists still do not understand enough about whales to predict if they will ever recover their numbers from massive overhunting.

© Diagram Visual Information Ltd.

Key words

biomass
El Niño

The anchoveta

- One of the most productive fishing areas in the world is a 90,000-square mile area (233,000 km²) off the coast of Peru.
- The coastal upwelling in this region forces nutrient-rich cool water to the surface.
- Phytoplankton thrive on the nutrients and in turn are fed upon by a variety of creatures, including anchoveta.
- Anchoveta are small fish that grow up to eight inches (20 cm) long and swim in huge schools near the surface.
- This huge biomass of fish is an important food source for many creatures, including predatory fish, birds, and mammals.

History of anchoveta fishing

- This enormous natural resource began to be exploited after World War II, and factories were opened to process the fish into fishmeal.
- Equipment used to catch and process the fish was mostly purchased from California where a similar fishery had recently collapsed.
- More efficient and larger fishing vessels led to larger and larger catches in Peru.

Sustainable fishing

- It soon became clear that the fishery could not support such large catches.
- The Peruvian government is now trying to ensure that the anchoveta is fished sustainably, but the industry's capacity is still much greater than the recommended sustainable harvest.

El Niño

- During El Niño years the currents change direction, causing a disappearance of the nutrient-rich upwelling and a collapse in the anchoveta population, which adds further pressure to the industry.

Overfishing: Peruvian anchoveta

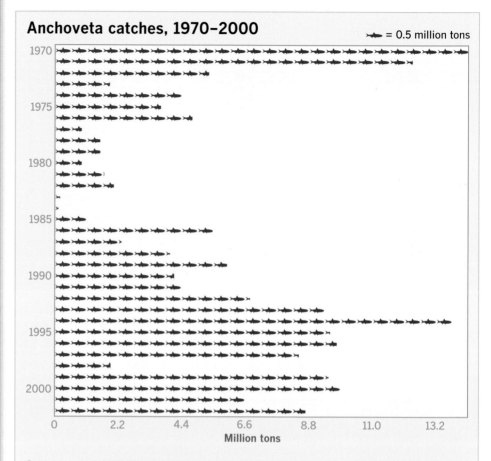

Anchoveta catches, 1970–2000

= 0.5 million tons

Million tons
(x-axis: 0, 2.2, 4.4, 6.6, 8.8, 11.0, 13.2)
(y-axis years: 1970, 1975, 1980, 1985, 1990, 1995, 2000)

Ocean current circulation and the upwelling areas off California and Peru

Normal years

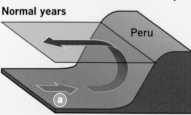

In normal years, cool, nutrient-rich water (**a**) rising off the coast of South America is warmed, and flows westward toward Australia, providing food for anchoveta off the coast of Peru.

El Niño years

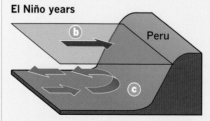

In El Niño years (which occur about 14 times every century) warmer water (**b**) flows toward South America, stopping the rise of the cooler (**c**), nutrient-rich water off the Peruvian coast and reducing the anchoveta population.

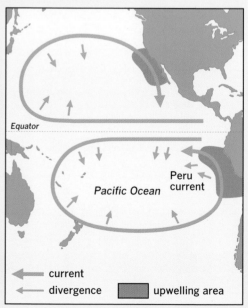

Equator

Pacific Ocean

Peru current

← current
← divergence
■ upwelling area

Overfishing: North Sea herring and Atlantic cod

Key words

ecosystem
fishery
overfishing

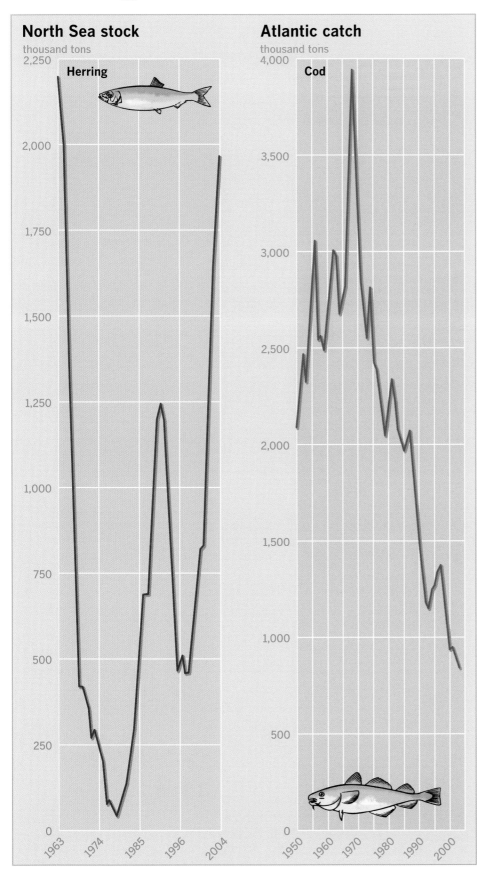

North Sea stock

thousand tons

Herring

Atlantic catch

thousand tons

Cod

The North Sea fisheries
- The North Sea is a shallow sea, kept free of ice by warm ocean currents.
- Overfishing in the North Sea now threatens the entire marine ecosystem.
- Since the 1990s all commercial fish species, including cod, hake, herring, haddock, mackerel, plaice, saithe, and whiting have dropped to dangerously low levels and are at risk of stock collapse.

Cod
- For 450 years, cod were fished sustainably until new fishing techniques and refrigeration led to overfishing.
- Total catches fell off sharply from record levels set in the late 1960s, as deep sea factory trawlers decimated the stocks.
- Between 1962 and 1977, North Atlantic cod declined 82 percent due to relentless overfishing.
- Northern cod were on the verge of extinction as a commercial species when Canada extended its jurisdiction to the 200-mile limit in 1977.
- This reduced the catches for a while, but Canada expanded its fleet and overfishing began again.

Herring
- Overfishing in the 1960s and 1970s reduced the total catch of herring from more than 4.4 million tons in 1966 to 992,000 tons in 1979.
- However, catches have increased somewhat in recent years as stocks have recovered.

© Diagram Visual Information Ltd.

Key words

habitat
extinction

The trade in ivory

- For centuries, elephant ivory has been an important trading commodity, especially in the Far East.
- Legal and illegal movements of ivory totalled 770 tons (75,000 pairs of tusks) during the 1970s.
- A combination of habitat loss and high levels of poaching threatened the African elephant with extinction.

Declining numbers

- The African elephant *(Loxodonta africana)* population declined from about 1.3 million in 1979 to 625,000 ten years later.
- Global concern for elephant conservation resulted in the Convention on International Trade in Endangered Species (CITES) declaring a total ban on ivory trade in 1989.

Increasing demand for ivory

- World demand for ivory remained high, and ivory prices escalated from $50 per pound in 1975 to as much as $500 per pound during the ban period.
- Poaching intensity increased with the use of sophisticated automatic weapons, and some poachers were killing up to 200 elephants a day.
- The CITES ban was only partially effective and poaching continued uncontrolled in some countries.

A better future

- Today, the African elephant is classified as endangered by the IUCN.
- Although poaching continues, the overall population has remained stable.
- However, up to 80 percent of the species range is believed to lie outside protected areas and the future for this animal is far from certain.

Poaching case study: African elephants

Decrease in elephant numbers, 1979–2002

= 50,000

1979

1,300,000

1989

625,000

2002

405,067

African elephant ranges, 2001

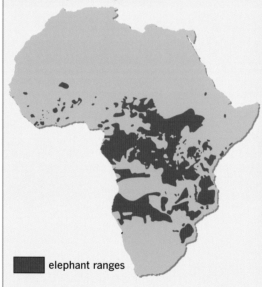

■ elephant ranges

- By 2001, Botswana, Namibia, South Africa, and Zimbabwe all showed increases in their elephant populations, some to such an extent that elephants were beginning to cause serious habitat damage. A conflict became apparent between the interests of conservationists and the needs of those living and farming in the elephant-populated areas of those countries.
- The excess elephants resulting from the ban on poaching had to be culled, increasing the tonnage of ivory stockpiles in each country.
- CITES later allowed these countries to enter into an experimental, limited trade in ivory with Japan.
- Revenue generated from ivory sales supports community development and improved elephant conservation and management.

African elephant regional populations, 2002

West Africa

5,458

Central Africa

= 10,000

16,450

East Africa

117,716

South Africa

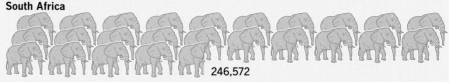

246,572

Poaching case study: Asian tigers

Key words

habitat

Range of surviving Asian tiger

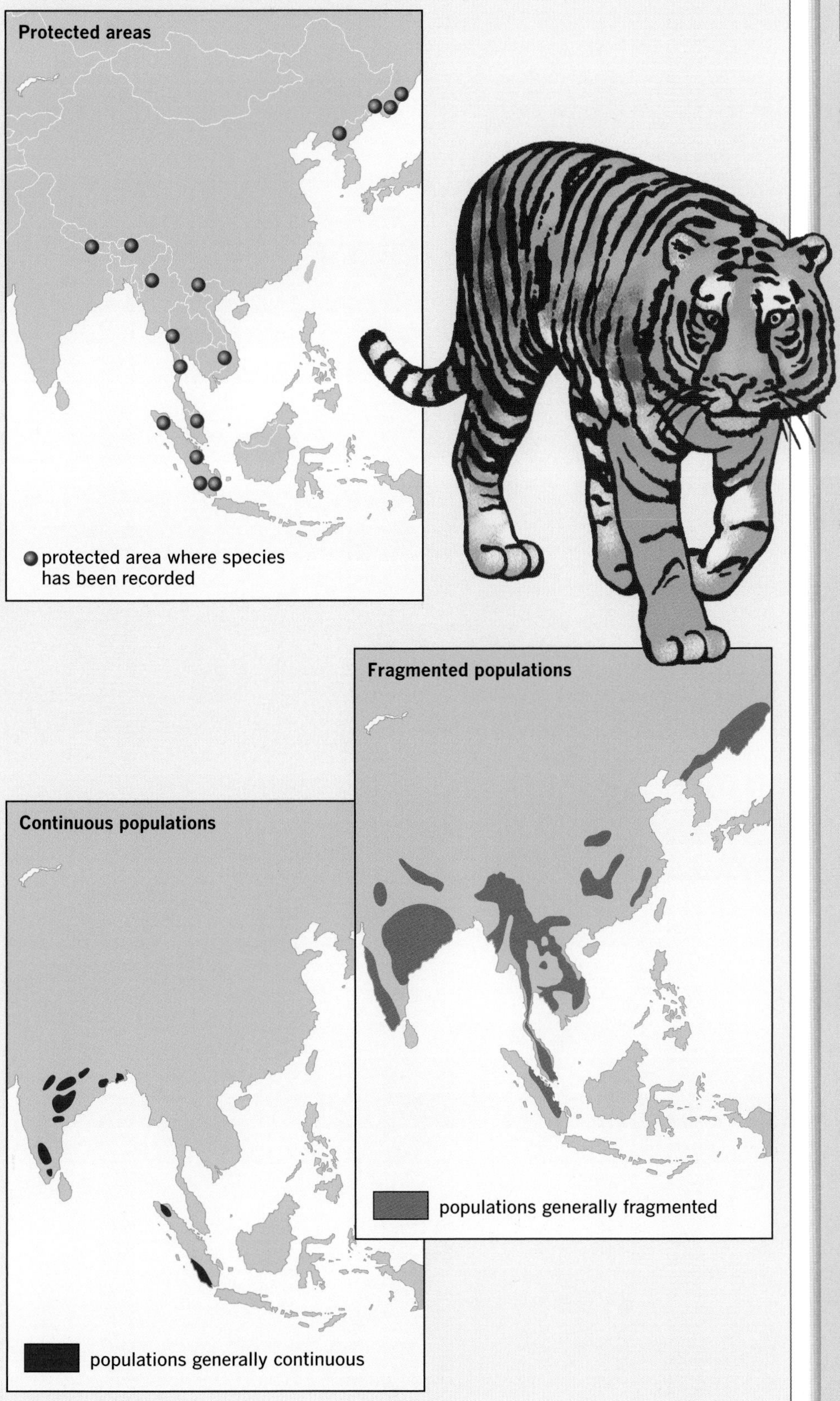

Protected areas

● protected area where species has been recorded

Fragmented populations

populations generally fragmented

Continuous populations

populations generally continuous

Tiger parts and medicine

● Use of the body parts of tigers has been an element of traditional Chinese medicinal practice for centuries.
● Taiwanese pharmacies use skulls and bones, and the penis is often used as an aphrodisiac; skins and heads also find buyers from around the world.

Increase in poaching

● The value of tiger body parts has greatly increased and bones may sell for more than $500 per pound.
● Illegal poaching is now the only way tiger parts can be supplied to consumer markets.
● Far Eastern traditional medicine manufacturers are now targeting India's tiger populations, as tiger numbers are depleted elsewhere in Asia.
● Anti-poaching patrols are often ill-equipped to tackle the problem.

Population crash

● Tiger numbers have fallen dramatically throughout its Asian range—by 95 percent in 100 years.
● Habitat loss, hunting, and poaching have all led to the decline of tigers.
● Three sub-species—the Amur, Sumatran, and South China tigers—are classed as critically endangered.
● Two other subspecies, the Indian or Bengal tiger and the Indo-Chinese tiger, are classified as endangered.

India and Project Tiger

● India contains 60 percent of the world's tigers; it was still legal to hunt them as recently as 1970.
● In 1973, Project Tiger was started with the aim of ensuring the maintenance of a viable population of tigers in India for their scientific, economic, aesthetic, cultural, and ecological values.

Key words

extinction

Hunted for their horns

- The demand for rhinoceros horn as an aphrodisiac or for making ornaments such as dagger handles has caused the most rapid decline ever known in a group of large land mammals.
- The world's rhino populations have fallen by 90 percent since 1970.

Status of the rhino

- Concerted conservation measures taken in South Africa have brought the white rhino back from the verge of extinction.
- There are 11,330 white rhinos in the wild and it is now the only species that is not endangered.
- The two-horned African black rhino suffered a very dramatic decline from 100,000 animals in 1960 to 3,610 surviving today.
- There are approximately 60 Javan rhinos surviving in the wild. They are found only in one park in Indonesia, with some additional animals in Vietnam.
- Fewer than 300 Sumatran rhinos survive in small forested areas of Malaysia and Indonesia.
- Efforts to save the Indian rhino have resulted in a small increase in numbers to 2,500 individuals, but heavy poaching continues.

Conservation measures

- The plight of the rhino has produced innovative conservation measures.
- Black rhinos in Zimbabwe and Namibia have been systematically caught and de-horned to discourage poachers.
- The principle market for rhino horn is traditional eastern medicine.
- To combat this, pharmaceutical substitutes are being prepared for suppliers as an alternative to powdered horns.

Poaching case study: rhinoceros horns

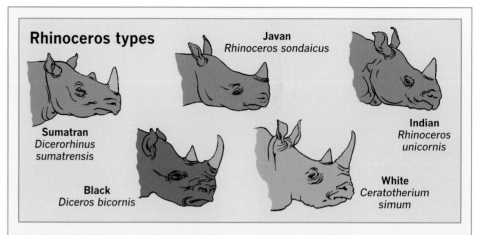

Rhinoceros types

Javan
Rhinoceros sondaicus

Sumatran
Dicerorhinus sumatrensis

Indian
Rhinoceros unicornis

Black
Diceros bicornis

White
Ceratotherium simum

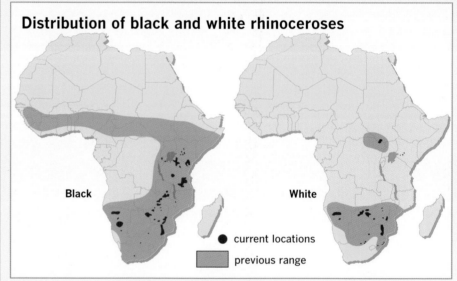

Distribution of black and white rhinoceroses

Black

White

● current locations

▬ previous range

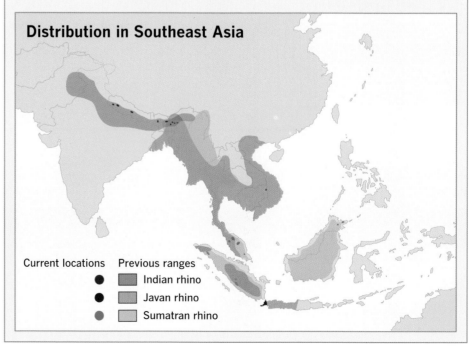

Distribution in Southeast Asia

Current locations   Previous ranges

● ▬ Indian rhino

● ▬ Javan rhino

● ▬ Sumatran rhino

Threatened species: North America and the Caribbean

Key words

biodiversity
endemic species

Species at risk

	Mammals	Birds	Reptiles	Amphibians	Fish	Mollusks	Other invertebrates	Plants	Total
Caribbean Islands									
Anguilla	0	0	4	0	11	0	0	3	18
Antigua and Barbuda	0	2	5	0	11	0	0	4	22
Aruba	1	1	3	0	12	0	1	0	18
Bahamas	5	10	6	0	15	0	1	5	42
Barbados	0	3	4	0	11	0	0	2	20
Bermuda	2	3	2	0	11	0	25	4	47
Cayman Islands	0	3	3	0	10	1	0	2	19
Cuba	11	18	7	47	23	0	3	163	272
Dominica	1	4	4	2	11	0	0	11	33
Dominican Republic	5	16	10	31	10	0	2	30	104
Grenada	1	2	4	1	12	0	0	3	23
Guadeloupe	5	2	5	2	11	1	0	7	33
Haiti	4	15	9	46	12	0	2	28	116
Jamaica	5	12	8	17	12	0	5	208	267
Martinique	0	3	5	1	11	1	0	8	29
Montserrat	1	2	3	1	11	0	0	3	21
Netherlands Antilles	3	4	6	0	13	0	0	2	28
Puerto Rico	2	12	8	13	9	0	1	52	97
St Kitts and Nevis	1	2	3	0	11	0	0	2	19
St Lucia	2	5	6	0	10	0	0	6	29
St Vincent and Grenadines	2	2	4	1	11	0	0	4	24
Trinidad and Tobago	1	2	5	9	15	0	0	1	33
Turks and Caicos Islands	0	3	5	0	10	0	0	2	20
Virgin Islands, British	0	2	6	2	10	0	0	10	30
Virgin Islands, USA	1	5	5	1	10	0	0	9	31
North America									
Canada	16	19	2	1	24	1	10	1	74
Mexico	72	57	21	190	106	5	36	261	748
St Pierre and Miquelon	0	1	0	0	1	0	0	0	2
United States	40	71	27	50	154	261	300	240	1,143

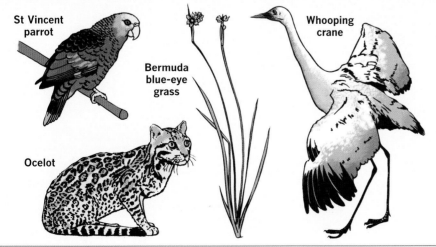

St Vincent parrot

Bermuda blue-eye grass

Whooping crane

Ocelot

The Caribbean

- The Caribbean archipelago consists of three main groups of islands: the Bahamas, the Lesser Antilles, and the Greater Antilles.
- Collectively they are a biodiversity hotspot and contain many endemic species.

St Vincent parrot

- The St Vincent parrot (*Amazona guildingii*) is found only on the Caribbean island of St Vincent, and was first listed as endangered in 1970.
- The main causes for its dramatic decline was trade, hunting, and bad weather conditions such as hurricanes.
- Numbers hit an all-time low in the 1980s after a volcanic eruption and a hurricane hit the island.
- Today, the entire population on St Vincent numbers about 800 individuals and it has been reclassified as vulnerable.

North America

- North America covers a vast area and certain parts are very rich in species.
- Pressures from an expanding population and pollution cause many species to be threatened.
- However, there is legislation in place to protect these threatened species.

The whooping crane

- The whooping crane (*Grus americana*), at approximately five feet (1.5 m) tall, is the tallest bird in the United States.
- The population dropped from 1,500 individuals in the late nineteenth century to just 16 by the 1940s.
- Extinction was narrowly avoided, and a slow and slight recovery has increased numbers to more than 200 individuals living in the wild today, but the whooping crane is still classified as endangered.

South and Central America

- South and Central America contain many important biodiversity hotspots, including the Amazon rainforest, the largest forest on Earth.
- Many species in the Amazon and other large areas of forest have yet to be described, and the rapid destruction of these habitats is causing many species to become threatened.

Amphibians in trouble

- The amphibians have suffered a particularly rapid decline in recent years.
- The Global Amphibian Assessment (GAA) was set up to assess all 5,743 species of amphibian in the world.
- One third of the world's species were found to be threatened, and most of these inhabit South and Central America.
- The countries with the largest number of threatened species are Colombia (208), and Ecuador (163).
- Alongside habitat loss and other human pressures it is thought that a newly recognized fungal disease is causing massive amphibian mortality.

The giant otter

- The giant otter (*Pteronura brasiliensis*), the largest otter species in the world, lives throughout the rivers and waterways of South America.
- It can reach six feet (1.8 m) from nose to tail and is prized for its thick, dense fur.
- The giant otter is classed as endangered. It is estimated that there are only between 1,000 and 5,000 individuals left in the wild.
- It is thought that a slow reproduction rate, low population densities, a natural curiosity, and prized fur have led to a rapid reduction in numbers even with low levels of hunting.

Threatened species: South and Central America, Antarctica

Species at risk

	Mammals	Birds	Reptiles	Amphibians	Fish	Mollusks	Other invertebrates	Plants	Total
South and Central America									
Belize	5	3	4	6	18	0	1	30	67
Costa Rica	13	18	8	60	13	0	9	110	231
El Salvador	2	3	5	8	5	0	1	25	49
Guatemala	7	10	10	74	14	2	6	85	208
Honduras	10	6	10	53	14	0	2	111	206
Nicaragua	6	8	8	10	17	2	0	39	90
Panama	17	20	7	52	17	0	2	195	310
South America									
Argentina	32	55	5	30	12	0	10	42	186
Bolivia	26	30	2	21	0	0	1	70	150
Brazil	74	120	22	24	42	21	13	381	697
Chile	22	32	0	20	9	0	0	40	123
Colombia	39	86	15	208	23	0	0	222	593
Ecuador	34	69	10	163	12	48	0	1,815	2,151
Falkland Islands (Malvinas)	4	16	0	0	1	0	0	5	26
French Guiana	10	0	7	3	13	0	0	16	49
Guyana	13	3	6	6	13	0	1	23	65
Paraguay	11	27	2	0	0	0	0	10	50
Peru	46	94	6	78	8	0	2	274	508
Suriname	12	0	6	2	12	0	0	27	59
Uruguay	6	24	3	4	11	0	1	1	50
Venezuela	26	25	13	68	19	0	1	67	219
Antarctica									
Antarctica	0	8	0	0	0	0	0	0	8
Bouvet Island	0	1	0	0	0	0	0	0	1
French Southern Territories	2	14	0	0	1	0	0	0	17
Heard Island and McDonald Islands	0	12	0	0	0	0	0	0	12
South Georgia and the South Sandwich Islands	1	11	0	0	0	0	0	0	12

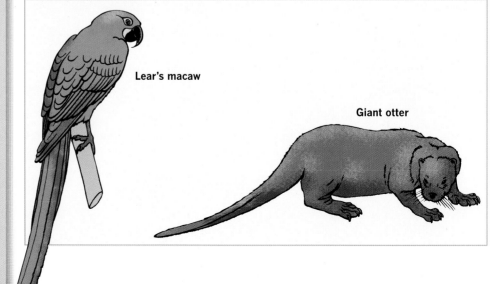

Lear's macaw

Giant otter

Threatened species: Europe

Key words

habitat
ecosystem
endemic species

Species at risk

Europe	Mammals	Birds	Reptiles	Amphibians	Fish	Mollusks	Other invertebrates	Plants	Total
Albania	1	9	4	2	17	0	4	0	37
Andorra	1	0	0	0	0	1	3	0	5
Austria	5	8	0	0	7	22	22	3	67
Belgium	9	10	0	0	6	4	7	0	36
Bosnia and Herzegovina	8	8	1	1	11	0	10	1	40
Bulgaria	12	11	2	0	10	0	9	0	44
Croatia	7	9	1	2	27	0	11	0	57
Czech Republic	6	9	0	0	7	2	17	4	45
Denmark	4	10	0	0	7	1	10	3	35
Estonia	4	3	0	0	1	0	4	0	12
Faroe Islands	4	0	0	0	7	0	0	0	11
Finland	3	10	0	0	1	1	9	1	25
France	16	15	3	3	16	34	31	2	120
Germany	9	14	0	0	12	9	22	12	78
Gibraltar	1	5	0	0	10	2	0	0	18
Greece	11	14	6	4	27	1	10	2	75
Greenland	7	0	0	0	4	0	0	1	12
Hungary	7	9	1	0	8	1	24	1	51
Iceland	7	0	0	0	8	0	0	0	15
Ireland	4	8	0	0	6	1	2	1	22
Italy	12	15	4	5	17	16	42	3	114
Latvia	4	8	0	0	3	0	8	0	23
Liechtenstein	2	1	0	0	0	0	5	0	8
Lithuania	5	4	0	0	3	0	5	0	17
Luxembourg	3	3	0	0	0	2	2	0	10
Macedonia, Former Yugoslav Republic of	9	9	2	0	4	0	5	0	29
Malta	1	10	0	0	11	3	0	0	25
Monaco	0	0	0	0	9	0	0	0	9
Netherlands	9	11	0	0	7	1	6	0	34
Norway	9	6	0	0	7	1	8	2	33
Poland	12	12	0	0	3	1	14	4	46
Portugal	15	15	1	0	20	67	15	15	148
Romania	15	13	2	0	10	0	22	1	63
Serbia and Montenegro	10	10	1	1	20	0	19	1	62
Slovakia	7	11	1	0	8	6	13	2	48
Slovenia	7	7	0	2	16	0	42	0	74
Spain	20	20	8	4	24	27	36	14	153
Svalbard and Jan Mayen	5	2	0	0	2	0	0	0	9
Sweden	5	9	0	0	6	1	12	3	36
Switzerland	4	8	0	1	4	0	30	2	49
United Kingdom	10	10	0	0	12	2	8	13	55

Iberian lynx

Wild gladiolus

Europe

- Europe covers a large land area and has supported human populations since prehistoric times.
- As a result, many of the unique habitats and species that once existed there have become extinct. Ever expanding populations and habitat loss has also led to many species becoming endangered.
- However, throughout much of Europe there is strict wildlife legislation, which now protects many threatened animals and their habitats.

Mediterranean hotspot

- The Mediterranean ecosystem in Europe has a very high number of endemic plant species.
- Of the 22,500 species of plants found here, 11,700 (52 percent) exist nowhere else.
- This makes the region very important for conservation, particularly since it has many threatened species.

The Iberian lynx

- The Iberian lynx (*Lynx pardinus*) is listed as critically endangered by the IUCN and is the rarest cat species in the world.
- Historically it lived throughout Spain and Portugal, but now exists only in scattered populations, most of which do not have long-term viability.
- Lynx populations rapidly declined in the last quarter of the twentieth century from around 1,500 animals in the late 1970s to only 135 by 2004.
- This decline is thought to be mainly due to the loss of its main prey, the rabbit, which was wiped out by myxamitosis.
- Hunting, habitat loss, and human encroachment have also been responsible for the lynx's decline.

Key words

biodiversity
deforestation
habitat
pollution

Asia and biodiversity

- Asia covers a vast area that includes many different habitat types and a staggering array of biodiversity.
- In many countries there is illegal logging, hunting, and habitat conversion underway at a rapid pace.
- Many species are consequently under threat.

Indonesia

- Indonesia is one of the most biologically diverse countries in the world.
- However, growth-oriented development policies are placing mounting pressure on natural resources.
- The result has been a huge reduction in suitable habitats for endangered species.
- Indonesia now has 146 threatened mammal species, far more than any other country in the world.
- It also has 121 threatened bird species, a figure matched only by Brazil.
- Pollution, deforestation, erosion, and corruption in the government are only adding to the problems.
- Other countries in Asia, such as China, India, Malaysia, and Sri Lanka, all have large numbers of threatened species that require conservation.

The last tiger stronghold

- The Sundarbans area of India and Bangladesh is the world's largest mangrove forest.
- It is home to the largest remaining population of wild tigers.
- Recent estimates put the number of tigers on the Bangladesh side at 500, with around 250 on the Indian side.
- The Sundarbans is protected as a World Heritage Site, but more than six million people live in and around the forests, and it is hard to limit their environmental impact.

Threatened species: Asia

Species at risk

	Mammals	Birds	Reptiles	Amphibians	Fish	Mollusks	Other invertebrates	Plants	Total
East Asia									
China	80	82	31	86	47	1	3	443	773
Hong Kong	1	20	1	3	7	1	0	6	39
Japan	37	53	11	20	27	25	20	12	205
Korea, DPR (North)	12	22	0	1	5	0	1	3	44
Korea, Republic of (South)	12	34	0	1	7	0	1	0	55
Macao	0	2	0	0	3	0	0	0	5
Mongolia	13	22	0	0	1	0	3	0	39
Taiwan	11	29	8	8	23	0	0	78	157
North Asia									
Belarus	6	4	0	0	0	0	8	0	18
Moldova	4	8	1	0	9	0	5	0	27
Russian Federation	43	47	6	0	18	1	29	7	151
Ukraine	14	13	2	0	11	0	14	1	55
South and Southeast Asia									
Bangladesh	22	23	20	0	8	0	0	12	85
Bhutan	21	18	0	1	0	0	1	7	48
British Indian Ocean Territory	0	0	2	0	4	0	0	1	7
Brunei (Darussalam)	11	25	4	3	6	0	0	99	148
Cambodia	23	24	10	3	12	0	0	31	103
Disputed Territory	0	0	0	0	1	0	0	0	1
India	85	79	25	66	28	2	21	246	552
Indonesia	146	121	28	33	91	3	28	383	833
Laos	30	21	11	4	6	0	0	19	91
Malaysia	50	40	21	45	34	17	2	683	892
Maldives	0	2	2	0	8	0	0	0	12
Myanmar	39	41	20	0	7	1	1	38	147
Nepal	29	31	6	3	0	0	1	7	77
Philippines	50	70	8	48	49	3	16	212	456
Singapore	3	10	4	0	13	0	1	54	85
Sri Lanka	21	16	8	44	23	0	2	280	394
Thailand	36	42	19	3	36	1	0	84	221
Timor-Leste	0	7	1	0	3	0	0	0	11
Vietnam	41	41	24	15	23	0	0	145	289
West and Central Asia									
Afghanistan	12	17	1	1	0	0	1	1	33
Armenia	9	12	5	0	1	0	7	1	35
Azerbaijan	11	11	5	0	5	0	6	0	38
Bahrain	1	7	4	0	6	0	0	0	18
Cyprus	3	11	3	0	7	0	0	1	25
Georgia	11	8	7	1	6	0	10	0	43
Iran	21	18	8	4	14	0	3	1	69
Iraq	9	18	2	1	3	0	2	0	35
Israel	13	18	4	0	12	5	5	0	57
Jordan	7	14	1	0	5	0	3	0	30
Kazakhstan	15	23	2	1	7	0	4	1	53
Kuwait	1	12	1	0	6	0	0	0	20
Kyrgyzstan	6	4	2	0	0	0	3	1	16
Lebanon	5	10	1	0	9	0	1	0	26
Oman	12	14	4	0	18	0	1	6	55
Pakistan	17	30	9	0	14	0	0	2	72
Palestinian Territories	0	4	0	0	0	0	0	0	4
Qatar	0	7	1	0	4	0	0	0	12
Saudi Arabia	9	17	2	0	9	0	1	3	41
Syria	3	11	3	0	9	0	3	0	29
Tajikistan	7	9	1	0	3	0	2	2	24
Turkey	15	14	12	5	30	0	13	3	92
Turkmenistan	12	13	2	0	8	0	5	0	40
United Arab Emirates	5	11	1	0	6	0	0	0	23
Uzbekistan	7	16	2	0	4	0	1	1	31
Yemen	6	14	2	1	11	2	0	159	195

Threatened species: Africa

© Diagram Visual Information Ltd.

Species at risk

	Mammals	Birds	Reptiles	Amphibians	Fish	Mollusks	Other invertebrates	Plants	Total
North Africa									
Algeria	12	11	2	1	10	0	12	2	50
Egypt	6	17	6	0	14	0	1	2	46
Libya	5	7	3	0	9	0	0	1	25
Morocco	12	13	2	2	11	0	8	2	50
Tunisia	10	9	3	0	9	0	5	0	36
Western Sahara	4	3	0	0	11	0	1	0	19
Sub-Saharan Africa									
Angola	11	20	4	0	9	5	1	26	76
Benin	6	2	1	0	8	0	0	14	31
Botswana	6	9	0	0	0	0	0	0	15
Burkina Faso	6	2	1	0	0	0	0	2	11
Burundi	7	9	0	6	0	1	3	2	28
Cameroon	42	18	1	50	35	1	3	334	484
Cape Verde	3	4	0	0	14	0	0	2	23
Central African Republic	11	3	1	0	0	0	0	15	30
Chad	12	5	1	0	0	1	0	2	21
Comoros	2	10	2	0	4	0	4	5	27
Congo	14	4	1	0	10	1	0	35	65
Congo, DR	29	30	2	13	10	14	8	65	171
Côte d'Ivoire	23	11	2	14	11	1	0	105	167
Djibouti	4	6	0	0	9	0	0	2	21
Equatorial Guinea	17	6	2	5	8	0	2	61	101
Eritrea	9	7	6	0	9	0	0	3	34
Ethiopia	35	20	1	9	0	3	3	22	93
Gabon	11	5	1	2	12	0	1	107	139
Gambia	3	2	1	0	11	0	0	4	21
Ghana	15	8	2	10	8	0	0	117	160
Guinea	18	10	1	5	8	0	3	22	67
Guinea-Bissau	5	1	1	0	10	0	1	4	22
Kenya	33	28	5	4	29	16	11	103	229
Lesotho	3	7	0	0	1	0	1	1	13
Liberia	20	11	2	4	8	1	2	46	94
Madagascar	49	34	18	55	66	24	8	276	530
Malawi	7	13	0	5	0	9	2	14	50
Mali	12	5	1	0	1	0	0	6	25
Mauritania	7	5	2	0	11	0	1	0	26
Mauritius	3	13	5	0	7	27	5	87	147
Mayotte	0	3	2	0	1	0	1	0	7
Mozambique	12	23	5	3	21	4	1	46	115
Namibia	10	18	4	1	11	1	0	24	69
Niger	10	2	0	0	0	0	1	2	15
Nigeria	25	9	2	13	12	0	1	170	232
Réunion	3	8	2	0	5	14	2	14	48
Rwanda	13	9	0	8	0	0	4	3	37
Saint Helena	1	20	1	0	10	0	2	26	60
São Tomé and Principe	3	10	1	3	7	1	1	35	61
Senegal	11	5	6	0	18	0	0	7	47
Seychelles	3	13	3	6	10	2	2	45	84
Sierra Leone	12	10	3	2	8	0	4	47	86
Somalia	15	13	2	0	16	1	0	17	64
South Africa	29	36	20	21	49	18	109	75	357
Sudan	16	10	2	0	8	0	2	17	55
Swaziland	6	6	0	0	0	0	0	11	23
Tanzania	34	37	5	40	28	17	16	239	416
Togo	7	2	2	3	8	0	0	10	32
Uganda	29	15	0	6	27	10	9	38	134
Zambia	11	12	0	1	0	4	3	8	39
Zimbabwe	8	10	0	6	0	0	2	17	43

Sub-Saharan Africa

- South of the Sahara, Africa contains a variety of habitats including savannah, rainforests, and important coastal environments.
- Many species of animal and plant exist in Africa, including the largest mammals found on land.
- Animals such as elephant, buffalo, giraffe, and wildebeest (gnu) all require large areas to live in and often travel great distances across national borders.
- Many species of animal and plant are threatened by habitat loss caused by fast growing populations and illegal hunting.
- Poaching in many countries has been very difficult to stop because of the vast areas involved, the limited resources, and lack of infrastructure.
- Some species have been driven to the brink of extinction by illegal hunting.
- All problems in Africa are confounded further by widespread poverty.

The highland gorilla

- The highland gorilla (*Gorilla gorilla*) lives in remote areas of Rwanda, the Democratic Republic of the Congo, and Uganda.
- They are classed as critically endangered and now number only 350 individuals in the wild.
- Illegal hunting and trapping for meat and trophies have been the main causes of its decline.
- Dedicated conservation groups provide the highland gorilla with round-the-clock protection in the hope that it will survive.

Key words

endemic species
habitat

Oceania

- Oceania consists of the many Pacific island states plus Australia, New Zealand, and Papua New Guinea.
- As in the Caribbean, there are many endemic species on the small isolated islands that are often threatened with extinction.
- Australia, New Zealand, and Papua New Guinea all contain many unique species, and due to habitat loss and human population pressures many of these are also threatened.
- Australia has the largest number of threatened species in the region at 621, including 63 mammal species and 60 bird species.

The kagu

- The kagu (Rhynochetos jubatus) is a bird endemic to New Caledonia, where it is found in a variety of habitats from scrub to forests.
- This species is classified as endangered on the basis of its very small, fragmented populations with very restricted extents.
- The current total population is estimated at 654 individuals.

Corroboree frog

- The corroboree frog (Pseudophryne corroboree) is found only in a very small area of snowgum woodlands and sphagnum bogs in Kosciuszko National Park in New South Wales, Australia.
- Corroboree is the aboriginal word for a gathering or meeting; these frogs used to gather in large numbers to mate.
- Today, only a few hundred corroboree frogs remain in three populations and the species is listed as endangered.

Threatened species: Oceania

Species at risk

Oceania	Mammals	Birds	Reptiles	Amphibians	Fish	Mollusks	Other invertebrates	Plants	Total
American Samoa	3	9	2	0	4	5	0	1	24
Australia	63	60	38	47	74	176	107	56	621
Christmas Island	0	5	3	0	4	0	0	1	13
Cocos (Keeling) Islands	0	1	1	0	3	0	0	0	5
Cook Islands	1	15	2	0	4	0	0	1	23
Fiji	5	13	6	1	8	2	0	66	101
French Polynesia	3	33	1	0	9	29	0	47	122
Guam	2	6	2	0	6	5	0	3	24
Kiribati	0	5	1	0	4	1	0	0	11
Marshall Islands	1	2	2	0	7	1	0	0	13
Micronesia	6	8	2	0	6	4	0	4	30
Nauru	0	2	0	0	3	0	0	0	5
New Caledonia	6	16	2	0	10	10	1	217	262
New Zealand	8	74	12	4	16	5	9	21	149
Niue	0	8	1	0	3	0	0	0	12
Norfolk Island	0	17	2	0	2	12	0	1	34
Northern Mariana Islands	2	13	2	0	5	2	0	4	28
Palau	3	2	2	0	6	5	0	3	21
Papua New Guinea	58	33	9	10	31	2	10	142	295
Pitcairn	0	11	1	0	3	5	0	7	27
Samoa	3	7	1	0	4	1	0	2	18
Solomon Islands	20	21	4	2	5	2	4	16	74
Tokelau	0	1	2	0	3	0	0	0	6
Tonga	2	3	2	0	4	2	0	3	16
Tuvalu	0	1	1	0	5	1	0	0	8
United States Minor Outlying Islands	0	9	1	0	5	0	0	0	15
Vanuatu	5	7	2	0	5	0	0	10	29
Wallis and Futuna Islands	0	9	0	0	3	0	0	1	13

Kagu

Corroboree frog

Biodiversity hotspots

Hotspots

1. Atlantic forest
2. California floristic province
3. Cape floristic region
4. Caribbean islands
5. Caucasus
6. Cerrado
7. Chilean winter rainfall-Valdivian forests
8. Coastal forests of Eastern Africa
9. East Melanesian islands
10. Eastern Afromontane
11. Guinean forests of West Africa
12. Himalaya
13. Horn of Africa
14. Indo-Burma
15. Irano-Anatolian
16. Japan
17. Madagascar and Indian Ocean islands
18. Madrean pine-oak woodlands
19. Maputaland-Pondoland-Albany
20. Mediterranean basin
21. Mesoamerica
22. Mountains of central Asia
23. Mountains of southwest China
24. New Caledonia
25. New Zealand
26. Philippines
27. Polynesia and Micronesia
28. Southwest Australia
29. Succulant Karoo
30. Sundaland
31. Tropical Andes
32. Tumbes-Chocó-Magdalena
33. Wallacea
34. Western Ghats and Sri Lanka

© Diagram Visual Information Ltd.

Key words

biodiversity
diversity hotspot
habitat

Hotspots explained

- *Diversity hotspots* are areas supporting a rich assortment of endemic species of plants and animals that are faced with exceptionally high levels of habitat loss.
- A recent investigation identified 34 areas containing the most threatened reservoirs of plant and animal life worldwide.
- These 34 hotspots cover just 2.3 percent of Earth's surface yet support an estimated 42 percent of terrestrial vertebrates and 50 percent of all vascular plants that are found nowhere else.
- British ecologist Norman Myers conceived the "hotspots" concept in 1988 as a way of pinpointing key areas of global conservation concern requiring high levels of funding.

The oceans

- The oceans, which cover 71 percent of Earth's surface, are areas of particularly high biodiversity.
- More than 9,000 species of fish are exploited for food and provide the primary source of animal protein for large numbers of coastal communities throughout the world.

Pressures

- In the Asia-Pacific region, severe population pressures and industrialization have created a high demand for land and natural resources.
- Logging, land clearance, and associated forest fires have devastated areas of high biodiversity in Indonesia.
- Logging, road building, mining, and oil exploration threaten some of the world's most biologically and culturally diverse areas in the tropical Andes of South America.

© Diagram Visual Information Ltd.

Key words

biodiversity
diversity hotspot
global warming

Reef hotspots

● Coral reefs are important marine habitats that support a great diversity of species.
● The top ten coral reef hotspots account for 34 percent of restricted-range coral reef species.
● Eight of them are close to a biodiversity hotspot.
● Activities destroying habitats in the biodiversity hotspot areas also contribute to coral reef destruction.

Reefs under threat

● More than 60 percent of the world's reefs are threatened by human activities.
● Reef degradation and destruction in these hotspots will deprive some of the world's poorest people of an important source of nutrition and livelihood.
● In the Philippines, coastal populations obtain more than 70 percent of their protein from seafood.
● The leading causes of reef destruction, along with intense fishing and climate change, are sediments, nutrients, and other pollutants from farming, logging, and development.
● Global warming is also already believed to be responsible for destroying or severely degrading 25 percent of the world's coral reefs.
● About six percent of the world's land is in protected parks and reserves but at sea, less than 0.5 percent is afforded any legal protection at all.

Bleaching

● When corals are damaged by nutrients and pollutants in the water they are said to be "bleached."
● This is when the symbiotic organisms inside the coral die.
● Bleached corals turn pale and eventually entire reefs may die.

Coral reef hotspots

Top ten coral reef hotspots

1. Philippines
2. Gulf of Guinea
3. Sunda Islands
4. Southern Mascarene Islands
5. Eastern South Africa
6. Northern Indian Ocean
7. Southern Japan, Taiwan, and southern China
8. Cape Verde Islands
9. Western Caribbean
10. Red Sea and Gulf of Aden

Areas with high concentrations of species

Hawaiian Islands

Gulf of California

St Helena and Ascension Islands

Western Australia

New Caledonia

Great Barrier Reef

Lord Howe Island

Protected areas worldwide

Key words

biodiversity
biosphere

Countries with more than 15 percent of total land area protected, 2003

IUCN protected area categories

Ia Strict Nature Reserve: protected area managed mainly for science

Ib Wilderness Area: protected area managed mainly for wilderness protection

II National Park: protected area managed mainly for ecosystem conservation and recreation

III Natural Monument: protected area managed for conservation of specific natural features

IV Habitat/Species Management Area: protected area managed mainly for conservation through management intervention

V Protected Landscape/Seascape: protected area managed mainly for landscape/seascape conservation and recreation

VI Managed Resource Protected Areas: protected area managed mainly for the sustainable use of natural ecosystems

Ten largest protected areas

Site name	Size in square miles (km²)	IUCN category	Designation
Northeast Greenland	375,300 (972,000)	II	National Park
Ar-Rub'al-Khali, Saudi Arabia	247,100 (640,000)	VI	Wildlife Management Area
Great Barrier Reef, Australia	133,000 (344,360)	VI	Marine Park
Northwestern Hawaiian Islands	131,800 (341,362)	VI	Coral Reef Ecosystem Reserve
Qiangtang, China	115,000 (298,000)	V	Nature Reserve
Macquarie Island, Australia	62,600 (162,060)	IV	Marine Park
Sanjiangyuan, China	58,800 (152,300)	V	Nature Reserve
Northern wildlife zone, Saudi Arabia	39,000 (100,875)	VI	Wildlife Management Area
Ngaanyatjarra Lands, Australia	37,900 (98,129)	VI	Indigenous Protected Area
Alto Orinoco-Casiquiare, Venezuela	32,400 (84,000)	VI	Biosphere Reserve

Globally protected areas

- The United Nations published a list of protected areas throughout the world in 2003.
- The report details 102 protected areas covering 7.03 million square miles (18.2 km²).
- The IUCN defines a protected area as "an area of land and/or sea especially dedicated to the protection and maintenance of biological diversity, and of national and associated cultural resources, and managed through legal and other effective means."

IUCN categories

- Protected area designations used by different countries are often not comparable due to differences in local legislations.
- More than 1,000 different terms are currently in use around the world.
- It was necessary to create a single international system for designating protected areas that everyone could understand.
- The IUCN categories were created and based on management objectives. They range from category Ia—strict nature reserves mainly for scientific study; to category VI—nature reserves that can be used as sustainably managed resources.
- Not all protected areas have assigned IUCN categories.
- More than 34,000 protected areas covering 1.39 million square miles (3.6 million km²) are without IUCN categories and so represent a significant proportion of the global conservation area.
- To date, however, only 67 percent of protected sites or 81 percent of the protected land area has been assigned an IUCN category.

Key words

biodiversity
biosphere
ecosystem

The biosphere project

- *Biosphere reserves* are areas of terrestrial or coastal ecosystems, internationally recognized under the Man and the Biosphere (MAB) Program of the United Nations Educational, Scientific and Cultural Organization (UNESCO).
- They are created to promote the conservation and sustainable use of biodiversity.
- They are nominated by governments and are testing grounds for new and innovative management techniques of land and water conservation and biodiversity.

Appointing a biosphere

- To be designated a biosphere reserve, an area must first fulfill three criteria:
- It must have a conservation function that adds to species, genetic variation, and ecosystems.
- It must have a developmental function that helps to promote sustainable human and economic development.
- The area must have a logistic function by supporting research and the sharing of information relating to global conservation and development.
- Biosphere reserves are not covered by any international conventions, but must meet the above criteria to qualify.
- Together, all the biospheres form a worldwide network that shares information and skills.

Biosphere zones

- The reserves are created using a number of zones including a buffer zone, a transition zone, and a core area that is the only zone offered legal protection.
- It is important that these zones are managed correctly and that the needs of any local and indigenous people are respected.

International biosphere reserves

Biosphere reserves

North America

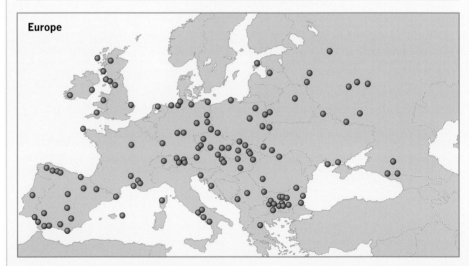

Europe

Zoning in a biosphere reserve

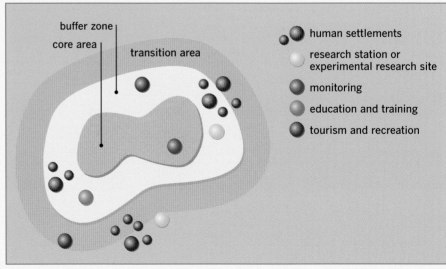

buffer zone
core area
transition area

human settlements
research station or experimental research site
monitoring
education and training
tourism and recreation

World Heritage Natural Sites

Key words

cetacean
endemic species
speciation

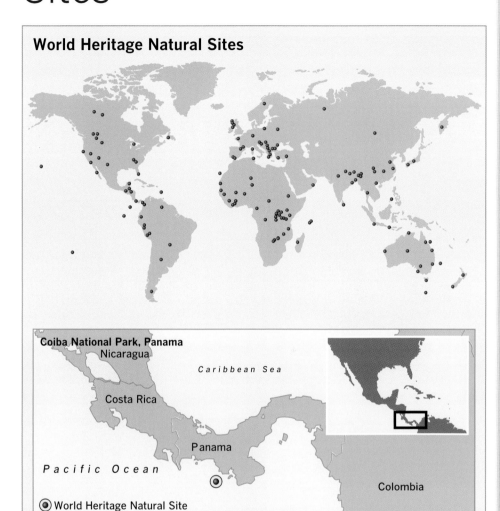

World Heritage Natural Sites

Coiba National Park, Panama

Nicaragua

Caribbean Sea

Costa Rica

Panama

Pacific Ocean

Colombia

◉ World Heritage Natural Site

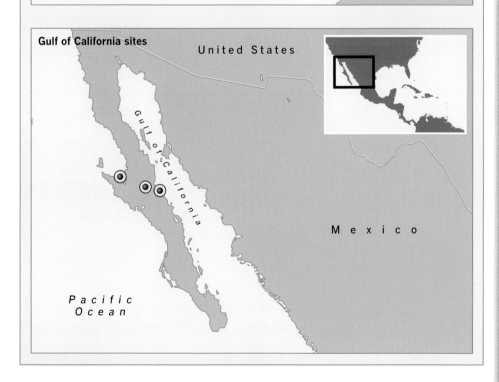

Gulf of California sites

United States

Gulf of California

Mexico

Pacific Ocean

Natural and cultural heritage

- *World Heritage Sites* are defined under the *World Heritage Convention*, which came into force in 1975 and has been signed by 180 countries.
- UNESCO sought to encourage the identification, protection, and preservation of natural and cultural sites throughout the world that are considered to be of outstanding value to humanity.
- When a World Heritage Site is appointed it then belongs to all people of the world irrespective of the territory on which it is located.
- The World Heritage list currently contains 812 properties of which 628 are cultural, 160 natural, and 24 mixed, across 137 countries worldwide.

Coiba National Park, Panama

- Coiba is a national park off the southwest coast of Panama. It became a World Heritage Natural Site in 2005.
- The protected site consists of Coiba island, 38 smaller islands, and the surrounding marine areas.
- The park contains important tropical moist forests that are home to many endemic species of mammals, birds, and plants.

Gulf of California

- An area in the Gulf of California, northeastern Mexico, comprising 244 islands, islets, and coastal areas was designated as a World Heritage Natural Site in 2005.
- The Gulf of California and the surrounding islands have long been used to study speciation, and almost all major oceanographic processes are present here.
- The site also contains 39 percent of the world's total species of marine mammals and 33 percent of the world's marine cetaceans.

© Diagram Visual Information Ltd.

Key words

ecosystem
habitat

Ramsar Convention

- The *Convention on Wetlands of International Importance* was signed in Ramsar, Iran in 1971 and came into force in December 1975.
- Known as the *Ramsar Convention*, this agreement provides a framework for international cooperation for the conservation of wetland habitats and is the only global environmental treaty that deals with a particular ecosystem.
- The mission of the Ramsar Convention is "the conservation and wise use of all wetlands through local, regional, and national actions and international cooperation, as a contribution toward achieving sustainable development throughout the world."
- Convention signatories are committed to designating at least one wetland that meets the criteria for the list.
- Currently more than 1,400 wetlands from 146 countries are included in the list.

The importance of wetlands

- Wetlands are defined as areas of marsh, fen, peat land, or water, with water that is static or flowing, fresh, brackish, or salt—including areas of marine waters, the depth of which at low tide does not exceed 19 feet (5.8 m).
- Wetlands provide many important ecological services, such as water filtration, and can act as natural buffer zones for human settlements.
- They also provide a habitat for many species of plant and animal and constitute a resource of economic, scientific, and recreational value.

Wetlands of international importance

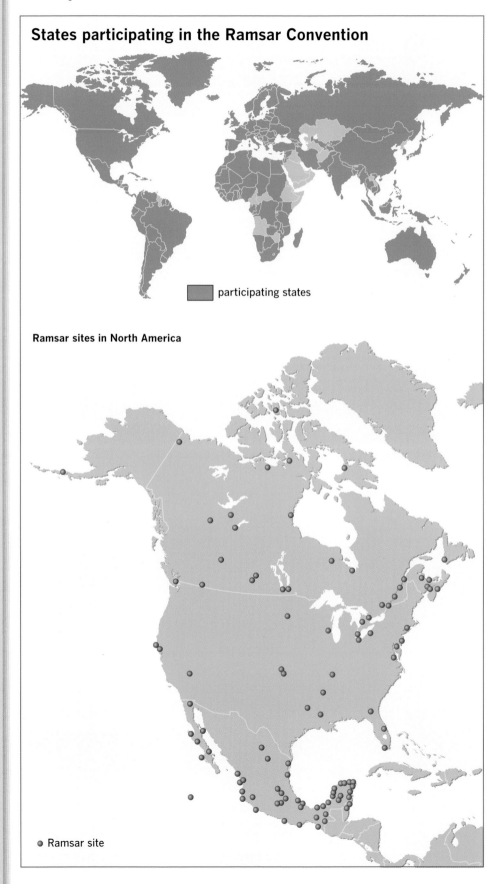

States participating in the Ramsar Convention

□ participating states

Ramsar sites in North America

● Ramsar site

Environmental disasters

Environmental disasters in modern society

nuclear power

The industrial processes and activities of modern societies often give rise to environmental disasters.

toxic discharges

hazardous wastes

oil spillages

Shrinkage of the Aral Sea

The maps chart the shape and size of the Aral Sea from 1960. Most of the shrinkage has occurred with the increasing industrialization of local agriculture since 1985.

1960

1985

Aral Sea

Syr Darya

Kazakhstan

Turkmenistan

Uzbekistan

Kyrgyzstan

Tajikistan

Amu Darya

Caspian Sea

1989   **1993**   **1997**   **2010**

Key words

irrigation
toxic

Environmental disasters

- The environmental effects of human carelessness in the disposal of toxic substances have sometimes been disastrous and the cause of many deaths.
- The disposal of volatile substances such as chlorine, toluene, and propane gas, and even their transport, are hazardous undertakings that can have disastrous outcomes.
- Unrefined oil, if released at sea creates a thick viscous film that is extremely difficult to remove.
- If they become coated with oil, sea creatures, especially birds, often die in large numbers.
- Many of the huge range of chemicals now produced are highly toxic, yet they are commonly released into rivers and seas with little thought for their effects on either wildlife or humans.
- Nuclear power and fuel, once hailed as the answer to cheap trouble-free electricity have, through a series of terrible accidents, come to be regarded as very high risk options for power generation.
- However, environmental disasters do not only result from the release of chemicals or toxic substances.

The shrinking Aral Sea

- The Aral Sea is an enclosed lake in the central part of the Turanian Plain, Central Asia, fed by the Amu Darya and Syr Darya, two of the largest rivers in the region.
- Originally the fourth-largest lake in the world, the Aral Sea has now shrunk to eighth-largest.
- This has been caused almost entirely by the diversion of its feeder rivers for irrigation purposes, with the surrounding irrigated land having increased from 7.4 million acres (3 million ha) to more than 20 million acres (8 million ha) today.

Key words

oil spill

Number and frequency

- In the United States alone, 14,000 oil spills are reported to the Environment Protection Agency each year, the vast majority of which involve small amounts of oil.
- Large spills of more than 700 tons from tankers are rare and their frequency has decreased significantly in the last 30 years.
- Although few in number, these large spills can have devastating consequences for the environment.
- Large spills account for a high percentage of the total oil spilled and in the ten-year period 1990–99 one percent of incidents were responsible for 75 percent of the total oil spilled.

Quantity spilled

- Over the past 30 years, the total amount of oil spilled per year has varied widely from 670,000 tons in 1979 to 9,918 tons in 1995.
- Around 85 percent of spills are classed as small (less than seven tons).
- The worst year for oil spills was 1979 when, of the 670,000 tons spilled, 316,000 tons was from a single accident, the *Atlantic Empress* collision near Tobago in the Caribbean.

Causes of oil spills

- Most tanker spills happen during routine operations in ports, or at oil terminals while oil is being loaded or unloaded, or the ship is being refueled.
- Most of the large spills are caused by collisions or groundings and 20 percent of these accidents result in discharges of more than 700 tons.
- Natural oil seeps and human activity on the land also contribute to the total amount of oil spilt.

Oil spills

Oil spills greater than 700 tons

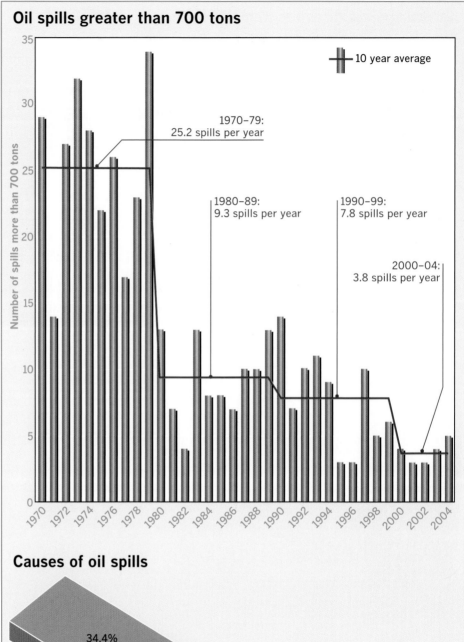

10 year average

1970–79:
25.2 spills per year

1980–89:
9.3 spills per year

1990–99:
7.8 spills per year

2000–04:
3.8 spills per year

Number of spills more than 700 tons

Causes of oil spills

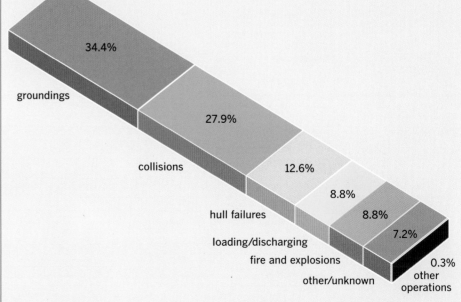

34.4% groundings

27.9% collisions

12.6% hull failures

8.8% loading/discharging

8.8% fire and explosions

7.2% other/unknown

0.3% other operations

The world's worst oil tanker spills

Key words

oil spill

The worst oil tanker spills resulting in coastal pollution

Rank	Ship	Year	Location	Oil lost (tons)
1	Atlantic Empress	1979	off Tobago, West Indies	316,000
2	Castillo de Bellver	1983	off Saldanha Bay, South Africa	277,000
3	Amoco Cadiz	1978	off Brittany, France	246,000
4	Haven	1991	Genoa, Italy	160,000
5	Torrey Canyon	1967	Scilly Isles, United Kingdom	131,000
6	Urquiola	1976	La Coruña, Spain	110,000
7	Independenta	1979	Bosphorus, Turkey	105,000
8	Jakob Maersk	1975	Oporto, Portugal	97,000
9	Braer	1993	Shetland Islands, United Kingdom	94,000
10	Aegean Sea	1992	La Coruña, Spain	82,000
11	Exxon Valdez	1989	Prince William Sound, Alaska	41,000
12	The Prestige	2002	off Galicia, northwestern Spain	15,000

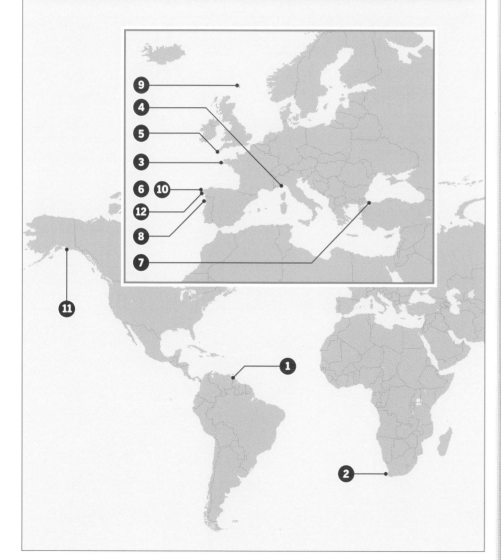

Damaging oil spills

- The most damaging oil spillages are not necessarily the largest.
- When oil is spilled close to environmentally sensitive areas such as natural coastlines and marine reserves, it can cause widespread damage.
- The *Exxon Valdez* oil spill in 1989 is very well known because of the extensive damage to the Alaskan coastline that resulted, yet it is only ranked as the 35th biggest oil spill of all time.
- Large spills out at sea attract relatively little publicity because quite often they do not cause damage on the scale of spills near coastlines.
- The *ABT Summer*, for example, spilled 280,000 tons of oil 700 nautical miles off the coast of Angola in 1991.
- The coastline was not immediately polluted so the accident escaped widespread media attention.

Spills caused by war

- Occasionally, oil fields and refineries have been set ablaze and tanker terminals discharged into the sea deliberately during conflict or war.
- The most extreme and destructive example of this tactic was in 1991 during the first Gulf War when the Iraqi leader Saddam Hussein ordered the destruction of Kuwait's extensive oil fields and the release of oil into the Gulf.
- However, due to the dangerous situation it is very difficult to estimate the amount of oil burned or spilled into the environment during warfare.
- It is estimated that the quantity of oil released into the Gulf in 1991 was between 0.5 and 11 million barrels, which is equivalent to about 32 tanker spills on the scale of the *Exxon Valdez*.

Kuwaiti oil field fires, 1991

Key words

oil spill

Deliberate oil spill

- The biggest oil spill to date occurred during the 1991 Gulf War when the Iraqi Army occupying Kuwait began destroying tankers, oil terminals, and oil wells in late January 1991.
- Approximately one million barrels of oil spilled onto the land and about eight million barrels of oil spilled directly into the Persian Gulf, forming a 600 square mile oil slick.
- Four hundred miles of the western shoreline of the Gulf was polluted with oil and between 15,000 and 30,000 birds were killed.
- An estimated third of the total amount of oil released evaporated.

Air pollution

- About 74 million tons of oil was burned, which produced about 2.3 million tons of soot and 2.2 million tons of sulfur.
- The smoke from the burning oil created darkness during daylight hours and the World Health Organization (WHO) estimated that death rates in Kuwait rose by ten percent over the following year because of associated breathing difficulties and skin problems.

Massive cleanup operation

- Recovery operations using skimmers, vacuum trucks, and booms (chains of floating timbers) recovered 1,400,000 barrels of oil from the Gulf.
- The water intakes of desalinization plants, industry, and power plants were protected by booms and skimming operations.
- Sensitive natural areas were also boomed to reduce oil contamination.

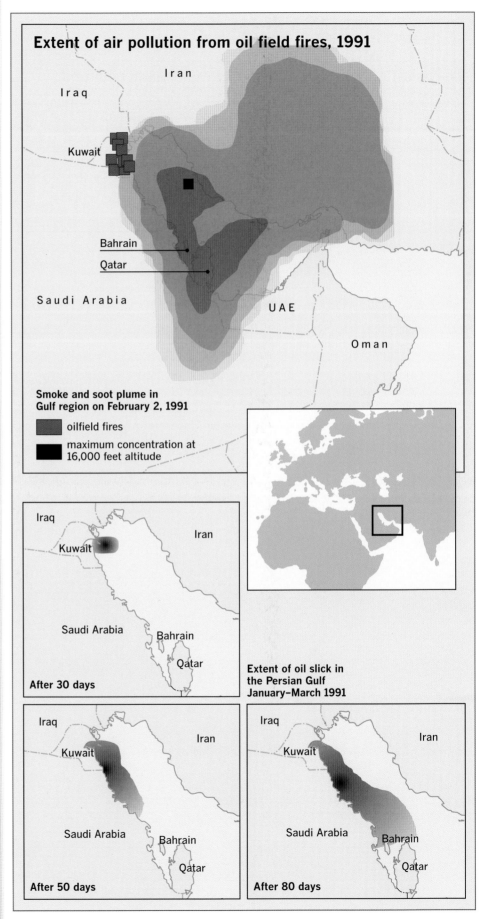

Extent of air pollution from oil field fires, 1991

Iran
Iraq
Kuwait
Bahrain
Qatar
Saudi Arabia
UAE
Oman

Smoke and soot plume in Gulf region on February 2, 1991

- oilfield fires
- maximum concentration at 16,000 feet altitude

Iraq
Kuwait
Iran
Saudi Arabia
Bahrain
Qatar

After 30 days

Extent of oil slick in the Persian Gulf January–March 1991

Iraq
Kuwait
Iran
Saudi Arabia
Bahrain
Qatar

After 50 days

Iraq
Kuwait
Iran
Saudi Arabia
Bahrain
Qatar

After 80 days

Nuclear disaster 1: Three Mile Island, USA, 1979

Key words

nuclear disaster
nuclear reactor
radiation

How a pressurized water reactor (PWR) works

A pressurized water reactor (PWR) generates heat by promoting nuclear fission in the reactor core. Control rods slow the reaction by absorbing neutrons, so they are withdrawn to allow the reactor to heat up to operating temperature. Water, kept under pressure to prevent it boiling, circulates through the core and carries heat from the reactor to a heat exchanger. The heat exchanger boils separate water in the steam generator. The steam spins a turbine connected to a generator, which produces electricity.

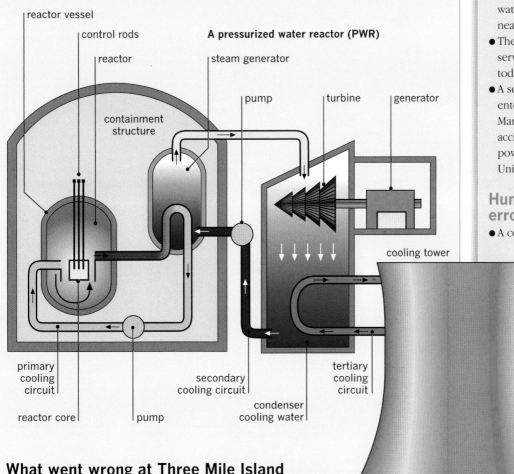

A pressurized water reactor (PWR)

Three Mile Island reactor

- The Three Mile Island pressurized water reactor (PWR) power station is near Harrisburg, Pennsylvania.
- The original *nuclear reactor* entered service in 1974 and is still working today.
- A second reactor, which had just entered service, was destroyed in March 1979. It was the first major accident at a commercial nuclear power plant and the worst in United States history.

Human and mechanical error

- A combination of human error, mechanical failure, and poor control room design led to a loss of coolant involving a partial reactor core meltdown, and the release of radioactivity into the environment.
- Nobody was killed and no adverse health effects caused by radiation have been found in the population around Three Mile Island.
- The average radiation dose to people within ten miles of the plant was eight millirem—about the same as having a chest X-ray.

What went wrong at Three Mile Island

- At 4.00 a.m. on March 28, 1979 a minor malfunction stopped water flowing around the secondary cooling circuit. This allowed the temperature of the water in the primary cooling circuit to rise, increasing its pressure.
- A safety valve opened to relieve the pressure building up in the reactor vessel.
- The reactor "scrammed"—the control rods automatically dropped into the reactor to shut it down.
- The relief valve should then have shut, but became stuck open, allowing more coolant to escape. The operators did not realize this was happening.
- Emergency pumps automatically pushed replacement water into the reactor system, but the operators shut these down, believing that the reactor vessel was already full of coolant.
- As coolant boiled away, the reactor became hotter and the core was partly exposed, damaging the fuel rods and releasing radioactive material, some of which escaped into the environment.
- A chemical reaction in the exposed part of the reactor produced hydrogen, some of which ignited, raising fears of a major explosion.
- It took a month to achieve a safe "cold shutdown," with the reactor cooled by convection of unpumped coolant.

Cleaning up the leak

- The clean up took 12 years and cost an estimated $1 billion.
- The accident caused widespread alarm and dealt a serious blow to public confidence in nuclear energy, leading to a sharp decline in nuclear power construction throughout the 1980s and 1990s.

Key words

nuclear disaster
nuclear reactor
radiation
radioactive
  particles

Worst ever nuclear accident

- The accident at the Chernobyl nuclear power plant in Ukraine (former USSR) on April 26, 1986 was the most serious in the history of nuclear power.
- The accident was the result of a flawed reactor design, operated by inadequately trained personnel with insufficient safety awareness.
- The resulting steam explosion and fire released about five percent of the radioactive reactor core into the atmosphere.
- Most radioactive material was deposited over a wide area around the plant, but a significant amount was carried downwind.
- The fallout contaminated about 58,000 square miles (150,000 km²) of Belarus, the Russian Federation, and Ukraine, with a combined population of about five million people.

Fallout

- Traces of radioactive fallout from Chernobyl have been detected throughout the Northern Hemisphere.
- Thirty power plant employees and firemen were killed within days or weeks, including 28 with acute radiation syndrome.
- Seven hundred cases of thyroid cancer have been linked to radiation exposure resulting from the accident.
- During 1986, about 116,000 people were evacuated from around the reactor and 220,000 people were relocated from the contaminated area.
- A UN report found that there is no firm scientific evidence of significant radiation-related health effects to most of the estimated one million people exposed.
- Psychosocial effects among those affected are, however, emerging as a serious problem, similar to those arising from other major disasters, such as earthquakes, floods, and fires.

Nuclear disaster 2: Chernobyl, Ukraine, 1986

The accident at Chernobyl

Prior to a routine shutdown, the crew at Chernobyl Reactor Number 4 began preparing for a test to find out how long the turbines would spin and supply electricity following a loss of power from the reactor.

They carried out a series of actions, including disabling automatic shutdown mechanisms and withdrawing control rods in contravention of safety protocols.

Similar tests had been carried out at Chernobyl and other plants, despite the fact that these reactors were known to be very unstable at low power.

As the flow of coolant water was reduced, the reactor became hotter. When the operator tried to shut down the unstable reactor, there was a catastrophic power surge. This was a know design problem, resulting from the use of graphite as the moderator in combination with water as the coolant.

The fuel elements ruptured and the explosive force of superheated steam blew the massive steel cover plate off the reactor, releasing fission products to the atmosphere. A second explosion threw out fragments of burning fuel and graphite from the core and allowed air to rush in, causing the graphite moderator to burst into flames. The graphite burned for nine days, causing the main release of radioactivity into the environment.

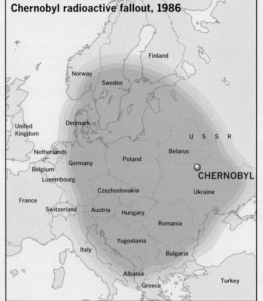

Chernobyl radioactive fallout, 1986

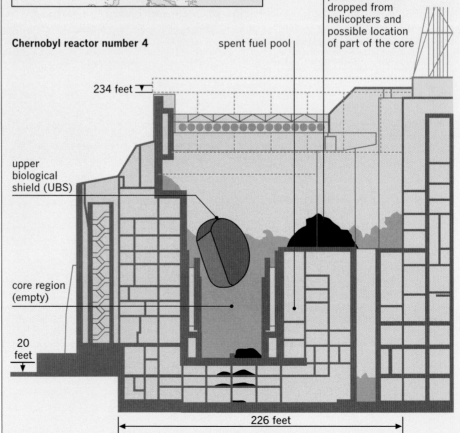

Chernobyl reactor number 4

The Chernobyl aftermath

Key words

nuclear disaster
nuclear reactor
radiation
radioactive
  particles

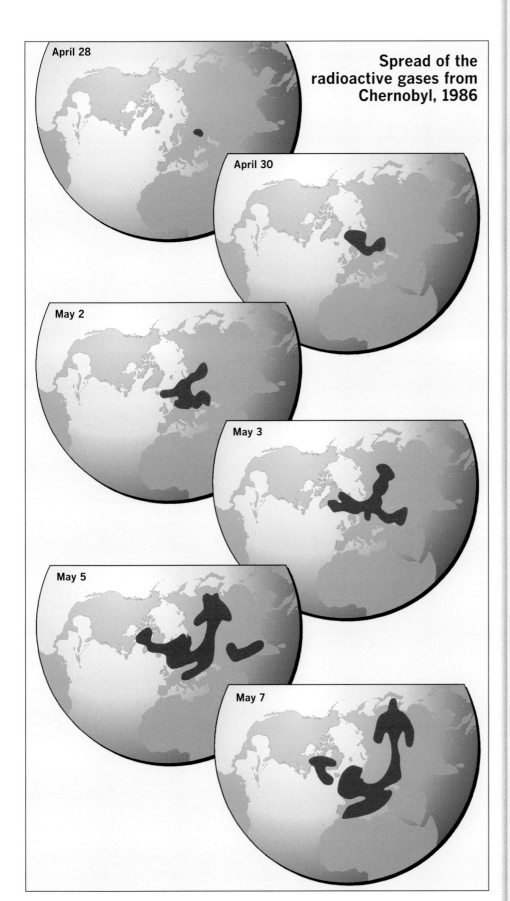

April 28

April 30

May 2

May 3

May 5

May 7

Spread of the radioactive gases from Chernobyl, 1986

Containing the leak

- At least 600 emergency workers fought to contain the fire at Chernobyl, receiving high doses of radiation in the process.
- About 5,500 tons of boron, dolomite, sand, clay, and lead were dropped by helicopter onto the burning core in an attempt to extinguish the blaze and stop the release of radioactive particles.

Cleaning up the accident

- About 600,000 civilian and military personnel took part in recovery operations to decontaminate the area.
- The workers also helped with the construction of a sarcophagus to contain the reactor and a new town for reactor workers.
- The remaining three reactors at Chernobyl resumed operation for several years, though the last one was decommissioned in December 2000.
- The original concrete sarcophagus sealing in the wrecked reactor is unsafe and remedial work will cost at least $715 million.

Spread of Chernobyl gases

- Radioactive material released from the Chernobyl explosion included xenon gas, iodine, caesium, and approximately five percent of any radioactive material remaining in the reactor after the explosion.
- The bulk of the material fell as dust and debris in the immediate vicinity of the reactor.
- Lighter materials were carried by wind over southern Russia.
- Some circulated over northern Europe and the North Atlantic.

© Diagram Visual Information Ltd.

Key words

chlorine gas
toxic

Mississauga chemical release

- Just before midnight on Saturday, November 10, 1979 a 106-car freight train carrying gases and poisonous chemicals was derailed at Mississauga, near Toronto, Canada.
- Canadian Pacific Railway Train 54 was transporting a mixed cargo including propane, chlorine, styrene, toluene, and caustic soda.
- Friction from a faulty wheel bearing 25 miles from Toronto led to overheating, which eventually split the axle.
- The carriage derailed, followed by 23 other carriages, many of which burst into flames.
- Other derailed tanker cars ruptured, releasing a volatile mixture of vapors and flammable liquids
- Within minutes there was a massive explosion creating a fireball rising 5,000 feet (1,524 m) into the air that was visible for more than 60 miles.

Chlorine gas

- Chlorine gas is heavier than air and was used as a chemical weapon during the First World War.
- As soon as it became known that a leaking tanker containing 90 tons of chlorine was lying among unexploded propane tankers with the potential for a major chlorine gas release, an emergency evacuation was ordered—the biggest in Canadian history.
- Out of a total local population of 284,000 people, 218,000 were evacuated.
- A complicated and hazardous operation followed to make the wrecked tankers safe, but it was found that much of the chlorine had been sucked up into the flames of the fire and dispersed harmlessly over Lake Ontario. A disaster on the scale of Bhopal, India had been narrowly avoided.

Chemical release 1: Mississauga, Canada, 1979

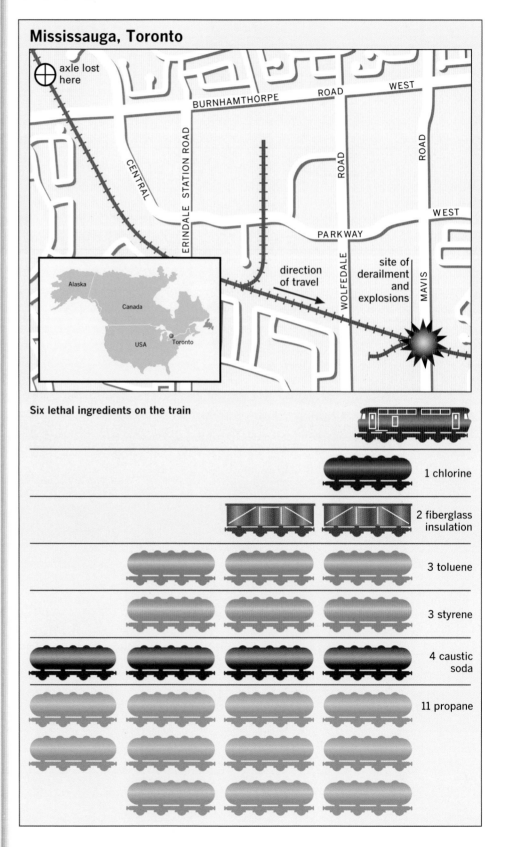

Mississauga, Toronto

axle lost here

BURNHAMTHORPE ROAD WEST

CENTRAL

ERINDALE STATION ROAD

ROAD

ROAD

WEST

PARKWAY

WOLFEDALE

MAVIS

direction of travel

site of derailment and explosions

Alaska

Canada

USA

Toronto

Six lethal ingredients on the train

1 chlorine

2 fiberglass insulation

3 toluene

3 styrene

4 caustic soda

11 propane

Chemical release 2: Bhopal, India, 1984

Key words

pesticide
toxic

Bhopal, Madhya Pradesh, India

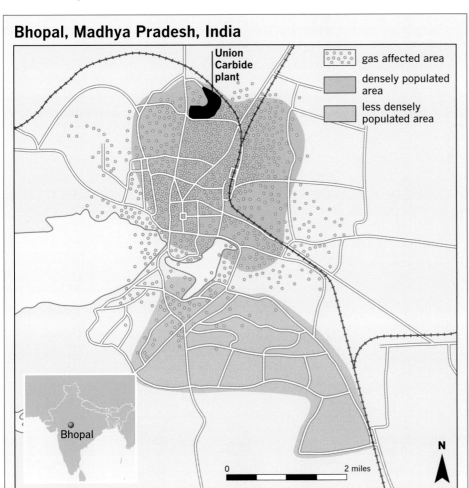

Union Carbide plant

- ∘∘∘ gas affected area
- densely populated area
- less densely populated area

Bhopal

N

0   2 miles

A lethal cocktail

1 Water added to or leaking into methyl isocyanate (MIC) storage tanks causes uncontrolled reaction and explosion, releasing poisonous gas.

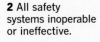

2 All safety systems inoperable or ineffective.

Connection to flare tower disabled for maintenance.

Vent gas scrubber turned off.

Refrigeration plant shut down in June.

Water curtain not high enough to reach gas.

3 Gas cloud rapidly spreads from Union Carbide plant to urban areas.

Gas escapes at night

- At midnight on December 2, 1984, 44 tons of highly poisonous methylsocyanate (MIC) gas escaped from the Union Carbide Corporation pesticide production facility at Bhopal, India.
- The gas, which is heavier than air, stayed close to the ground and was swept downwind five miles over the town.
- MIC is an organic chemical used to produce the insecticide Sevin.
- The chemical is extremely toxic to humans and even brief exposure may cause death or serious health effects, including pulmonary edema and brain damage.
- At least 3,000 people died in the night and at least another 15,000 in the aftermath, with more than 50,000 permanently disabled.

Cause of the leak

- The precise cause of the release is disputed and the official Union Carbide investigation concluded that the plant was sabotaged by a disgruntled employee who added water to a tank of MIC in an attempt to spoil it.
- The addition of water to the tank led to a vigorous reaction that raised the pressure, and gas was released through the relief valve system.
- The leak was first discovered at 11.30 PM but by the time anything was done at 12.15 AM, it was too late.
- Union Carbide, now owned by Dow Chemicals, agreed to an out-of-court settlement with the Indian government of $470 million in 1989.
- A lot of the money never reached the victims' families, with the average compensation payment about $580.

Key words

abundance Term used in ecology to describe plentiful amounts of a particular species or resource.

acidification The process by which geographical areas or ecosystems become more acid.

acid rain Rain acidified by sulfuric, nitric, and other acids.

acute Diseases with a rapid onset and a short though severe course.

Africa The world's second largest continent comprising many of the worlds poorest countries.

agriculture The science of utilizing land to produce crops and raise livestock.

AIDS Acquired immunodeficiency syndrome, a condition that destroys the human immune system.

air pollution Contamination of the air, especially by smoke or gases from vehicles or factories.

alga (pl. **algae**) Any of a large number of plantlike photosynthetic organisms ranging from single-celled creatures to giant kelp in the oceans.

alkaline Term used to describe substances with a pH greater than 7, opposite of acidic.

alkalinization The process by which ecosystems become more alkaline through either natural or human-made processes.

ammonia Nitrogen based chemical (NH_3) used to manufacture fertilizers.

amphibian A vertebrate of the class Amphibia characterized by having an aquatic larval stage with gills and a land-dwelling adult stage with lungs, e.g. frogs.

anaerobic Term used to describe a process or organism that works or lives without the presence of oxygen.

anthropogenic Any impact on the environment that is caused by humans.

antiretroviral drugs Drugs that inhibit the reproduction of retroviruses, used to treat HIV infections.

arable land Land which has been cultivated for farming.

archipelago A large group of islands usually distinctly grouped together.

arsenic Highly poisonous element used extensively in insecticides and weed killers.

artisanal fisheries Highly individualistic labor-intensive local fishing operations.

Asia The world's largest continent comprising many developing countries including the two most populous nations of the world, India and China.

asthma A chronic respiratory disease which usually arises from allergies.

atmosphere All the gaseous mass surrounding Earth comprising many different layers.

bacillus thuringiensis A spore forming bacteria that is naturally toxic to insects and is used as an insecticide.

baculovirus A type of virus that specializes as a pathogen of insects and is used as a biological control agent for the control of pest species.

baleen A horny material from the upper jaws of baleen (filter-feeder) whales that was traditionally used as a structural material in the ribs of fans or as stays in corsets.

baleen whale Any of the usually large whale species in the suborder Mysticeti that feed on krill using baleen plates in their mouth to filter the tiny marine creatures.

bedrock Solid rock usually found beneath other layers that make up Earth's crust.

benthic The area or zone at the bottom of the sea or lake regardless of depth.

bioaccumulation When chemicals are stored and gradually accumulate in the bodies of organisms.

biodiversity The full range of species, genes, and ecosystems in a given geographical location.

biological communities Plant and animal species that live together and interact.

biological control Controlling pests using biological rather than chemical means, usually by the introduction of natural predators.

biomass The total mass or amount of all living things in one particular area.

biosphere The part of Earth and the atmosphere where living organisms exist.

biosphere reserve Internationally designated areas that are managed to combine conservation with the sustainable use of natural resources.

birth control Any voluntary method of controlling the number of children conceived, usually involving contraception.

birth defect A physical or mental abnormality that develops during or at birth.

birthrate The rate of live births against the existing population in human societies.

bleaching Phenomenon by which coral lose their colour and eventually die as a result of pollution or environmental changes.

blubber A thick insulating layer of fat under the skin of large marine mammals such as whales and seals.

British Thermal Unit (btu) One btu is the amount of heat required to raise the temperature of one pound of water by one degree Fahrenheit.

by-catch The part of a fishing catch made up of non-target species that is unwanted or commercially unusable.

cadmium A blue and white soft metallic element (Cd) used in solders, batteries, and nuclear reactor shields.

calcium A silvery metallic element (Ca) found in limestone that is a major component of animal bone.

calorie A unit used for measuring the energy content of foods (kilocalories).

cancer Uncontrolled multiplication of cells in the body; a major cause of deaths in the developed world.

carbohydrate Any of a large group of organic compounds including starch, sugars, and cellulose.

carbon cycle The continuous cycle of carbon through the atmosphere, oceans, and living organisms.

carbon dioxide (CO$_2$) A gas naturally found in air, the carbon of which is fixed by plants during growth.

carbon monoxide (CO) A poisonous, colorless, and odorless gas produced by the incomplete combustion of carbon.

carbon sink A natural environment that absorbs and stores more CO$_2$ from the atmosphere than it releases.

carcinogenic Any cancer-causing agent.

carnivore Any animal that consumes other animals as a source of nutrition.

cash crop A crop that is grown for direct sale and not for animal feed or human subsistence, such as coffee or tobacco.

cereal A grass food crop such as oat, wheat, and corn.

cesium A silvery-white, soft metal element (Cs) that is liquid at room temperature and used in photoelectric cells.

cetacean The whales and dolphins, a group of mostly marine mammals that are characterized by having smooth, hairless skin.

chaco A large, mostly uninhabited lowland plain of South America.

chlorine gas A highly poisonous gas made from chlorine.

chlorofluorocarbons (CFCs) Compounds of chlorine and fluorine known to deplete the ozone layer and act as greenhouse gases.

cholera Bacterial disease of the small intestine with acute symptoms including diarrhea, vomiting, and dehydration.

chronic A long lasting disease or condition where symptoms frequently recur.

climate change The long-term change in the world's weather patterns now thought to be a result of the greenhouse effect.

colonization The act of humans, plants, or animals populating an area.

communicable disease a disease that is transmitted between people.

competition In ecology, when two or more organisms demand the same limited environmental resources, such as food or living space.

compound A substance composed of two or more elements.

computer models Computer programs used to predict events, trends, or actions by using mathematical formulas.

conservation The protection, preservation, restoration, and management of wildlife and natural resources.

contraception The intentional prevention of pregnancy through the use of physical barriers or other means.

copper A metal element (Cu) that is a good conductor of heat and electricity, used for electrical wiring and water pipes, and in the production of alloys.

coral Marine invertebrate organisms that build reefs.

coral reef Rocklike calcium carbonate structures composed of generations of coral polyps.

crop A cultivated plant or agricultural produce, such as legumes, grains, vegetables, or fruit.

crop variety A crop with different characteristics suited to growing in different regions.

crossbreeding The creation of different breeds or varieties by hybridization.

crude oil The base form of oil as it is extracted from the ground and used to make all petroleum products.

cull The controlled reduction of a population of animals by killing some of them.

cultivation When land is prepared to grow crops for the production of food.

dam A physical barrier across a river or other water body to control the flow of water or generate power.

DDD An insecticide similar to DDT with similar properties.

debt burden Term used when a country has a large debt which it finds difficult or impossible to repay.

debt relief A scheme launched in 1996 by the IMF and World Bank to reduce debt.

deciduous Trees that drop their leaves at the end of a growing season.

decomposition The breakdown and decay of organic materials.

deforestation The complete removal of trees from a particular region.

demography The study of characteristics of human populations, such as growth, distribution, and density.

denudation The removal of vegetation and soil, exposing the bare rock underneath.

depletion When resources such as fish stocks become reduced from overfishing or pollution.

desert A barren and desolate geographical area often with low rainfall and extremes of temperature.

desertification The process whereby fertile land becomes desert due to overgrazing or the removal of vegetation.

development assistance Monetary assistance provided from one country to another to help with development.

diarrhea Frequent and excessively watery feces usually associated with a gut condition or disease.

diarrheal diseases Any of a number of diseases that are associated with diarrhea including food poisoning and dysentery.

Dichloro-diphenol-trichloroethane (DDT) A pesticide with dangerous bio-concentration effects; it is banned in many countries.

dieldrin A very toxic chlorinated hydrocarbon compound used as an insecticide.

diversity The biological variation of life in the world.

diversity hotspot A geographical area containing great biological diversity such as a species-rich rainforest.

Dobson unit A unit of measurement of the ozone in Earth's atmosphere, the normal range of which is 300–500 Dobson units.

doubling time The time it takes a population at current growth rates to double in number.

drift net A very large net supported by floats that is carried along in the current.

drought A long period of low or no rainfall that affects the ability to grow crops or obtain freshwater.

eco-service A services provided by natural ecosystems that is of benefit to humanity and would be expensive to reproduce if the ecosystem was destroyed.

ecosystem An ecological community along with its environment, functioning together as a unit.

ecotourism Tourism in areas of ecological or natural interest, usually under the guidance of a wildlife expert.

education The act of learning and acquiring new skills.

electrolyte An ion such as sodium, potassium, and chloride, required for the body to retain water effectively.

element One of the 92 naturally occurring substances that are not combinations of other substances.

El Niño A warming of the ocean surface off the west coast of South America that occurs irregularly every 4–12 years.

emission A substance such as CO_2 discharged into the air from any type of emitter such as a car or factory.

endangered species A species of plant or animal in danger of extinction.

endemic species A species that is native to a particular region and which generally has a restricted distribution, outside of which it does not exist.

environmental impact A term used to describe the effects of a particular action on the environment.

Environmental Impact Assessment A rigorous procedure established to assess the effects of a development on the environment.

environmental persistence The amount of time a chemical or substance will remain in the environment before breaking down.

Environmental Protection Agency (EPA) An independent federal agency set up to coordinate programs that protect the environment and reduce pollution.

epidemic A disease outbreak that spreads quickly and affects many individuals in a particular area.

eradication The total and complete removal of a pest.

erosion Natural weathering processes such as rain, wind, and frost, which cause material to break away from Earth's surface.

Europe The world's second smallest continent west of Asia comprising many developed nations.

eutrophication The over-enrichment of water by nutrients, causing plants to grow excessively and water to deoxygenate with the death of associated organisms.

evaporation The conversion of a substance from liquid to vapor.

exponential growth When growth occurs at an increasingly rapid rate.

extinction When the last remaining individual of a species dies, the species then ceases to exist.

factory trawler Large fishing vessel that remains at sea for months, catching and processing fish.

fallout The descent to the surface of Earth of tiny radioactive particles following a nuclear explosion or nuclear accident.

fallow When an area of farmland is set aside during the growing season to allow it to recover.

family planning The regulation of the number and time interval between children in a family through the use of birth control.

famine A shortage of food usually on a national level often as a result of drought or war.

fecundity The potential or capacity for producing offspring.

female sterilization A surgical procedure in which the fallopian tubes are blocked or cut, preventing the egg from traveling to the uterus for fertilization.

fertility A measure of the ability of a population to bear offspring or the actual birthrate of a population. Also used to describe the suitability of land to grow crops.

fertilizer A substance that make soil more fertile such as manure or synthetic chemicals containing nitrates.

filter-feeding organism An aquatic organism that obtains its food by straining or sieving water.

fishery An area containing at least one commercially viable fish species that supports an industry.

fish stocks A measure or estimate of the abundance of commercial fish in a particular area.

flood protection Physical barriers such as levees, dams, and dykes that protect an area from flooding.

flue A pipe for conveying hot air, gas, or smoke to a chimney.

Food and Agriculture Organization (FAO) The United Nations' agency dedicated to the elimination of world hunger.

food chain A sequence of organisms where each member is preyed upon by the organism one step higher in the chain.

food production indexes A measure of the value of food produced by different countries.

forest fire A large-scale fire in a forested region.

fossil fuel A geologically ancient substance such as coal, oil, or gas that gives off CO_2 when burned as a fuel.

fragmentation When continuous environments are broken down into smaller pieces due to habitat destruction.

frontier forest Large undisturbed and mostly pristine forests thought to be of great environmental value.

fungus Any organism within the kingdom Fungi including the mushrooms, yeasts, molds, and smuts.

Gaia hypothesis A theory that the biosphere acts as a self-sustaining, self-regulating organism.

gaseous pollutants Any substances discharged in gaseous form that are damaging to the environment.

gene A specific location on a chromosome that codes for a particular characteristic such as eye or hair color.

gene bank A facility that stores DNA for species or varieties.

genetically modified (GM) crop A crop that has been genetically altered to enhance its characteristics.

genetic diversity The genetic variation between and within species that helps life persist in the face of epidemic diseases and climatic change.

genetic engineering Inserting genes from one source into another using molecular techniques.

genetic mutation A process that changes the genetic makeup of an organism.

genocide The systematic extermination of an entire group of people.

genome The entire genetic makeup of a particular organism.

germinate Beginning to grow or sprout.

glacier A huge mass of ice that moves very slowly over a landmass.

global economy A measure of the international economy characterized by free trade in goods and services.

global warming An average increase in the temperature of Earth's atmosphere, especially a sustained increase sufficient to cause climate change.

grazing Animals feeding on growing grass.

greenhouse effect A phenomenon whereby Earth's atmosphere traps solar radiation causing the atmospheric temperature to rise.

greenhouse gas A gas such as carbon dioxide or methane that contributes to the greenhouse effect and global warming.

Green Revolution A 1960s program to boost world food supplies using innovative high-yielding hybrid cereals.

Gross Domestic Product (GDP) Total value of all the goods and services produced within a nation.

Gross National Product (GNP) The total value of goods and services produced by a nation.

groundwater Water beneath Earth's surface, usually between soil and solid rock, that supplies springs and wells.

guinea worm A parasitic nematode worm found in Asia.

Gulf stream A warm current of the Northern Atlantic Ocean originating in the Gulf of Mexico.

habitat An environment or area where an organism or ecological community normally lives or occurs.

half-life The time required for a chemical or substance to fall to half its original strength.

healthcare The management of illnesses through the services offered by medical professions.

heart disease An abnormality of the heart or blood vessels supplying the heart.

heavy metal A metallic element with high atomic weight that is generally toxic.

herbicide Subtances toxic to plants used to control weeds.

Human Immunodeficiency Virus (HIV) The virus that eventually causes AIDS.

hunting The catching of animals for consumption.

hydrocarbon An organic compound containing only hydrogen and carbon.

hydroelectric power The generation of electricity using water.

hydrogen An organic compound consisting of only hydrogen and carbon.

illegal logging Cutting down trees for profit without permission.

illiteracy Being unable to read or write.

immigration The movement of people into a country.

incineration The burning of waste.

indicator species A species that indicates the health of the environment.

indigenous people People living and occurring naturally in a region.

industrial effluent The discharge of liquid waste from factories.

industrialized country A state that has shifted its main production from agriculture to industry.

industrial pollution The emission of harmful substances from factories or industry.

Industrial Revolution The mechanization of industrial production that started in eighteenth-century England.

infectious diseases Diseases that can be transmitted between individuals through physical contact, such as HIV, or through the air, such as influenza.

infrastructure Basic facilities in a country or city such as transportation, roads, and schools.

integrated pest management (IPM) The management of pests using chemical, biological, and cultural methods.

intensive farming The exhaustive use of land for farming.

invertebrates All animals without a backbone.

in vitro A procedure conducted in an artificial environment instead of within a living organism.

irrigation Supplying land artificially with water to grow crops.

ivory A hard white substance that forms the tusks of elephants and some other mammals.

Kyoto protocol An international agreement to reduce greenhouse gas emissions.

landfill A method of waste disposal where garbage is buried on land.

land reclamation The act of filling in coastal areas or wetlands to build on.

larva (pl. **larvae**) The immature life stage of some insects.

lead A soft metallic element (Pb) that is used in bullets, paints, and radiation shielding.

levee An embankment designed to stop flooding.

life expectancy The length of time a person or animal is expected to live, usually given in demographic statistics.

liquid pollutant A liquid that is damaging to the environment.

livestock Any animals kept for consumption or dairy produce.

local government Regional authorities making decisions at a local level.

logging The removal of trees and forests for profit.

magnesium Silvery white metallic element (Mg) used in incendiary bombs and flash photography.

malaria An infectious disease caused by the plasmodium parasite and spread by the anopheles mosquito.

malnutrition Health problems directly related to a poor diet.

mammal Any animal in the class Mammalia characterized by having mammary glands and hair.

mangrove forest Forests found growing on tropical coastlines with their roots in seawater.

marine pollution Pollution found in the oceans or around coastlines.

mass extinction The loss of many species over a short period of geologic time.

mealybug Sap-sucking insect pest of the class Orthoptera.

mechanization Replacing equipment with more advanced and automated technology.

meltdown The overheating and subsequent melting of a nuclear reactor core.

mercury Metallic silvery element (Mg), liquid at room temperature, used in thermometers.

metabolism The chemical processes within living cells that are necessary to maintain life.

methane Colorless, odorless, flammable gas that is the main constituent of natural gas.

metropolitan Relating to a city or built-up urban area.

microorganism Any organism of microscopic size.

mining The extraction of raw materials from Earth.

mitigation Lessening the impact of a development on the environment by providing some form of alternative.

monoculture The cultivation of a single crop species.

Montreal protocol A treaty that governs the ozone layer and monitors the production and use of ozone depletants.

mosquito A small flying insect of the Class Diptera responsible for spreading the disease malaria.

municipal waste Domestic garbage from urban areas.

myxamitosis A virus affecting rabbits.

national debt The overall debt owed by a government.

national government The authority that makes decisions at a national level.

natural gas A naturally occurring gas found in porous rocks under Earth's surface.

natural selection The reproduction of animals and plants most suited to a particular environment.

neutralize To alter the pH of a substance toward 7 (neutral), which is neither acidic nor alkaline.

nitrate A chemical used in fertilizers that is harmful to aquatic organisms at high concentrations.

nitrogen A nonmetallic element (N) that makes up over four fifths of the volume of air.

nitrogen oxide Any of several oxides of nitrogen.

noncommunicable condition A disease or condition that cannot be transmitted from one individual to another, such as heart disease or depression.

non-governmental organization (NGO) An organization providing assistance to developing nations that is independent of any national government.

Northern Hemisphere The half of Earth north of the equator.

North Sea A sea that is the location of productive fishing areas and oil fields between the United Kingdom and northern continental Europe.

nuclear disaster Any accident involving the escape of nuclear material.

nuclear reactor A device containing a controlled fission chain reaction to produce energy.

nuclear waste Radioactive waste usually from nuclear power stations.

nutrients Sources of nourishment such as in food.

nutrition The science of food and nourishment.

obesity A medical condition characterized by high levels of body fat.

Oceania The islands of the Pacific Ocean and Australasia.

Official Development Assistance (ODA) Economic aid from the governments of developed countries to developing states.

oil spill A release of oil into the environment that is usually accidental.

opencast mining The extraction of raw materials from open pits.

organic chemical Any chemical with a hydrogen carbon structure.

organic farming Farming without the use of any synthetic fertilizers or pesticides.

organic matter Any compounds containing carbon, usually derived from living organisms.

organochlorine A group of pesticides containing chlorine, including DDT.

osmosis The diffusion of fluid across a membrane from a low solute concentration to a higher solute concentration.

overcrowding A situation in which there are more people or animals in a location than it can support.

overfishing When a body of water has been fished to such an extent that it causes an overall loss of living creatures.

overgrazing When animals graze vegetation excessively, causing damage to the vegetation.

ozone An allotrope of oxygen formed naturally in the ozone layer.

ozone layer A belt of ozone gas in the upper atmosphere that filters ultraviolet radiation.

pampas A huge plain in south-central South America.

parasitic wasp An insect of the class Hymenoptera that lays eggs on or in the bodies of their live prey.

particulate A minute particle of a substance.

pathogen An agent that causes disease in an organism or person.

pension Money paid regularly as a retirement benefit.

per capita For each individual person.

persistent organic pollutants (POPs) Chemical substances that persist in the environment and which are hazardous to human health.

pest Any animal or plant injurious to human interests.

pesticide A type of chemical used to kill pests of all kinds, but most commonly insects.

petabecquerel (PBq) A unit of measurement of radioactive waste or escaped material in the environment.

pH The measure of a substance's acidity or alkalinity.

phosphate An organic compound containing phosphate used in fertilizers.

phosphorus Nonmetallic, explosive element (P) used in incendiary devices.

photosynthesis The production of carbohydrate in plants using carbon dioxide and water with sunlight.

phytoplankton Photosynthetic plankton such as algae.

plowing Making land ready for crop growing using a plow.

pneumonia A bacterial lung disease.

poaching The illegal hunting of protected animals.

pollination The transfer of pollen to the stigma of a flower to complete the reproduction of plants.

pollution Harmful substances or other agents introduced to the environment.

pollution abatement Legislation aimed at the prevention, reduction, and elimination of pollution.

polychlorinated biphenyl (PCB) A toxic environmental pollutant that can accumulate in animal tissue.

polyvinyl chloride (PVC) A widely used hard-wearing plastic.

population The total number of inhabitants in a particular area or of a particular race or class.

population density The number of people living in a particular area.

population growth rate The rate at which a population of plants, animals, or people grows.

potassium A silvery, soft, explosive metallic element (K) used in fertilizers.

potato blight A destructive fungal disease of potatoes.

poverty A state of existence in which human beings lack the means of providing all their basic material needs.

precipitation Any form of water-related weather such as rain and snow.

predation The capture of prey for food.

protein A fundamental component of all living cells including enzymes and antibodies.

public sector A section of the economy providing government services.

public transport A transport system within a country or city that is used by people to travel.

purse seine A large fishing net drawn into the shape of a bag for catching fish shoals.

quarrying The extraction of stone from open pits or quarries.

radiation Energy emitted from radioactive substances.

radioactive particles Particulate radioactive matter.

reclaimed land Land that has been reclaimed from the sea through engineering.

recycling The reuse of materials to save on waste production.

reforestation The replanting of trees and forests.

refugees People who flee a troubled area in search of safety in times of war or political unrest.

renewable energy Energy generated from renewable sources such as wind, sunlight, and waves.

resistance When pests become immune to pesticides through natural selection.

rhizofiltration The removal of toxins from water through plant growth.

rice The starchy grain of a cereal used as a staple food throughout the world.

river blindness A parasitic worm disease spread by blackfly that can cause blindness.

root crop A crop with large roots such as the potato or beet.

rotation system The successive planting of different crops in the same area to control disease and enhance the soil.

ruminant An animal such as a sheep, cow, or goat, with a stomach divided into four parts.

ruminant digestion The specialized way in which ruminants eat by regurgitating partially digested food.

runoff Precipitation, snow, and ice melt, and all other water that flows from the land into the ocean.

rural Related to the countryside.

rural decline The process by which people leave rural communities.

Sahara Desert The largest desert in the world, located in North Africa.

salinity A measure of how much salt a liquid contains.

salinization The accumulation of salt in soil.

sanitation The clean and safe disposal of sewage.

satellite mapping The use of satellite cameras to map large areas of earth.

savannah The large flat grasslands found in the tropics and subtropics.

schistosomiasis A tropical disease common in poorer countries caused by consuming water infected with schistosomes.

seizure A sudden convulsion.

selective breeding The selection of plants or animals used for breeding to develop better varieties or breeds.

sewage Liquid and solid human waste and rainfall carried away in sewers.

sewer A system of pipes for the safe disposal of sewage and rainwater.

sex pheromone A scent released by insects and other animals to attract members of the opposite sex.

shore The area of land adjacent to a body of water that is covered at high tide and submerged at low tide.

skin cancer A malignant tumor or growth in the skin often attributed to exposure to ultraviolet radiation.

slums An urban area or district that is usually heavily populated with inferior housing and squalid living conditions.

smog A mixture of fog and smoke.

social services Services such as welfare and healthcare provided by governments to help improve the general standard of living of the population.

sodium carbonate A crystalline compound produced in large quantities, used in the manufacture of glass and chemicals.

soil degradation The spoiling of soil by regressive processes in which it becomes less fertile.

soil erosion The loss of soil by the action of wind or rain.

spawning ground An area that fish move to in order to spawn (release eggs).

speciation An evolutionary process whereby a biological species is formed from the division of a species into two or more distinct separate species.

statistics The use of numbers to characterize a population.

sterile male technique The sterilization of male insects so that the females will produce infertile eggs.

storm surge A temporary rise in sea level along a coast as a result of storm winds.

stratosphere Layer of the atmosphere in which ozone concentration is at its highest.

sub-Saharan Africa The African continent lying south of the Sahara.

subsistence Existing with a minimum level of resources.

sulfur A yellow non-metallic element (S), used in pharmaceuticals and rubber vulcanization.

sulfur dioxide (SO_2) A toxic colorless gas present in industrial emissions.

sulfuric acid A highly corrosive acid.

sulfur oxide (SO_x) Any of several oxides of sulfur.

sustainable development Social development that meets the needs of people without compromising the needs of future generations by environmental damage.

symbiotic A close association between two or more species.

The Americas North, Central, and South America collectively.

The Earth Summit Popular name for the United Nations Conference on Environment and Development (UNCED) held in Rio de Janeiro in 1992.

tilling Preparation of land for the growing of crops.

tobacco A crop cultivated for its leaves, which are smoked.

toothed whale Any of the whales that have teeth, such as killer whales and dolphins.

topography The land features of a place or region.

topsoil The uppermost layer of soil.

toxic Any chemicals or substances capable of causing injury or death to an organism.

trait Any genetic or physical characteristic such as eye color.

transgenic An organism containing genes from a different species or breed.

transmigration The movement of large numbers of people across political borders.

tributary A stream that flows into larger streams or rivers.

tropical cyclone A storm originating over tropical or subtropical waters.

tropical forest A forest found within the tropics, including rainforests.

trypanosome A microscopic protozoan parasite spread by biting insects, which causes diseases such as sleeping sickness.

tsetse fly A biting fly found in Africa, which is responsible for spreading sleeping sickness.

tuberculosis An infectious, bacterial, and long lasting disease affecting the lungs.

ultraviolet (UV) radiation Radiation within the ultraviolet range.

UNHCR United Nations High Commissioner for Refugees.

urban Relating to a city or town environment.

urbanization The gradual migration of people from rural environments to cities.

vaccine A substance that stimulates the immune system to fight off future infections.

vector An organism such as a mosquito that spreads disease.

vehicle emissions Gases and pollutants emitted from motor vehicles.

volatile substance A substance that is unstable or likely to explode.

waterborne diseases Any diseases which are usually related to the lack of adequate sanitation such as cholera and typhoid.

water pollution Harmful material that damages the quality of water or organisms within it.

weeds Any plants considered undesirable or damaging to human interests.

welfare Financial or other aid provided by the government to its people.

wetland Low-lying areas saturated with water such as swamps or marshes.

WHO The UN's specialized agency for health, the World Health Organization.

wind erosion The movement of sediments and soil by the wind.

Internet resources

There is a lot of useful information on the internet. Information on a particular topic may be available through a search engine such as Google (**http://www.google.com**). Some of the sites that are found in this way may be very useful, others not. Below is a selection of Web sites related to the material covered by this book.

The publisher takes no responsibility for the information contained within these Web sites. All the sites were accessible in April 2006.

British Antarctic Survey
The British Antarctic Survey and its antecedents have been conducting scientific research in Antarctica for almost 60 years.
http://www.antarctica.ac.uk

Earthtrends
An initiative by the World Resources Institute to provide information about environmental, social, and economic trends.
http://earthtrends.wri.org

Environmental Protection Agency (EPA)
The federal agency with the remit "to protect human health and the environment."
http://www.epa.gov

FAOstat
Statistical databases produced by the Food and Agricultural Organization of the United Nations.
http://faostat.fao.org

Fishonline
A resource provided by the Marine Conservation Society enabling consumers to identify fish caught by environmentally-friendly methods only.
http://www.fishonline.org

Food and Agriculture Organization (FAO)
The United Nations organization that "leads international efforts to defeat hunger. Serving both developed and developing countries, FAO acts as a neutral forum where all nations meet as equals to negotiate agreements and debate policy."
http://www.fao.org

Global Warming International Center
Disseminates information on global warming science and policy, serving governments, nongovernmental organizations, and industries.
http://www.globalwarming.net

GreenFacts.org
A Belgian organization that aims to "make complex scientific consensus reports on health and the environment accessible to nonspecialists."
http://www.greenfacts.org

Greenpeace
A leading campaign for the conservation of the planet's resources. One of its priorities is the prevention of human-induced climate change.
http://www.greenpeace.org

International Research Institute for Climate Prediction
Aims to enhance the knowledge, anticipation, and management of the impacts of seasonal climate fluctuations, to improve human welfare and the environment.
http://iri.ldeo.columbia.edu

Open Directory Project: Environment
A comprehensive listing of internet resources in the field of environmental issues.
http://dmoz.org/Science/Environment/

Organization for Economic Co-operation and Development (OECD)
An international organization with 30 member states "sharing a commitment to democratic government and the market economy." An excellent source of economic and other statistics.
http://www.oecd.org

Oxfam International
One of the world's largest and most influential charities, Oxfam "seeks increased worldwide public understanding that economic and social justice are crucial to sustainable development."
http://www.oxfam.org

ReefBase
A comprehensive resource containing information about the extent of the world's coral reefs, the threats they face, and what should be done to protect and manage them.
http://www.reefbase.org

The Ozone Hole

An organization dedicated to "preventing the destruction of the ozone layer, preventing global warming, and the preservation of Earth's environment."

http://www.theozonehole.com

United Nations Children Fund (UNICEF)

"UNICEF is mandated by the United Nations General Assembly to advocate for the protection of children's rights, to help meet their basic needs, and to expand their opportunities to reach their full potential."

http://www.unicef.org

United Nations Educational, Scientific and Cultural Organization (UNESCO)

As part of its remit on the natural sciences, UNESCO has several programs dedicated to assessing and managing Earth's natural resources.

http://www.unesco.org

United Nations Environment Program (UNEP)

A United Nations organization with the mission statement: "To provide leadership and encourage partnership in caring for the environment by inspiring, informing, and enabling nations and peoples to improve their quality of life without compromising that of future generations."

http://www.unep.org

United Nations Framework Convention on Climate Change (UNFCCC)

A forum for the 189 nations that are signatories to the 1994 Convention on Climate Change.

http://unfccc.int

World Bank

A major source of funding for developing nations that has the stated aim of "global poverty reduction and the improvement of living standards."

http://www.worldbank.org

World Conservation Monitoring Center (WCMC)

"The biodiversity assessment and policy implementation arm of the United Nations Environment Program."

http://www.unep-wcmc.org

World Conservation Union (IUCN)

Also known as the International Union for the Conservation of Nature and Natural Resources, the World Conservation Union aims to "influence, encourage, and assist societies throughout the world to conserve the integrity and diversity of nature and to ensure that any use of natural resources is equitable and ecologically sustainable."

http://www.iucn.org

World Food Program (WFP)

The food aid branch of the United Nations with the stated aim of using food aid to "meet emergency needs" and to "support economic and social development."

http://www.wfp.org

World Health Organization (WHO)

The United Nations agency for health: its stated aim is "the attainment by all peoples of the highest possible level of health. Health is defined in WHO's constitution as a state of complete physical, mental, and social well-being and not merely the absence of disease or infirmity."

http://www.who.int/en/

Worldwatch Institute

The Worldwatch Institute has been a leading provider of information about environmental, social, and economic trends since 1975.

http://www.worldwatch.org

World Wildlife Fund (WWF)

The largest privately-funded international conservation organization in the world. The World Wildlife Fund in North America (World Wide Fund for Nature, WWF, in the rest of the world) is "committed to reversing the degradation of our planet's natural environment and to building a future in which human needs are met in harmony with nature."

http://www.worldwildlife.org

Index

Index of subject headings.

a

b

c

d

e

f

g

h

i

k

l